Baltic Capitals

Tallinn · Rīga · Vilnius · Kaliningrad

The Bradt Story

The first Bradt travel guide was written by Hilary and George Bradt in 1974 on a river barge floating down a tributary of the Amazon in Bolivia. From their base in Boston, Massachusetts, they went on to write and publish four other backpacking guides to the Americas and one to Africa.

In the 1980s Hilary continued to develop the Bradt list in England, and also established herself as a travel writer and tour leader. The company's publishing emphasis evolved towards broader-based guides to new destinations – usually the first to be published on those countries – complemented by hiking, rail and wildlife guides.

Since winning *The Sunday Times* Small Publisher of the Year Award in 1997, we have continued to fill the demand for detailed, well-written guides to unusual destinations, while maintaining the company's original ethos: that adventurous travel is more enjoyable if the wishes of the local people are taken into consideration.

Travel guides are by their nature continuously evolving. If you experience anything which you would like to share with us, or if you have any amendments to make to this guide, please write; all your letters are read and passed on to the author. Most importantly, do remember to travel with an open mind and to respect the customs of your hosts – it will add immeasurably to your enjoyment.

Happy travelling!

Hilary Bradt

Hilary Bradt

19 High Street, Chalfont St Peter, Bucks SL9 9QE, England
Tel: 01753 893444 Fax: 01753 892333
Email: info@bradt-travelguides.com
Web: www.bradt-travelguides.com

Baltic Capitals
Tallinn · Rīga · Vilnius · Kaliningrad

contributing editor
Neil Taylor

additional authors
Stephen Baister
Gordon McLachlan
Chris Patrick

Bradt Travel Guides, UK
The Globe Pequot Press Inc, USA

First published in 2001 by Bradt Travel Guides
19 High Street, Chalfont St Peter, Bucks SL9 9QE, England
Published in the USA by The Globe Pequot Press Inc,
246 Goose Lane, PO Box 480, Guilford, Connecticut 06437-0480

British Library Cataloguing in Publication Data
A catalogue record for this book is available from the British Library
ISBN 1 84162 018 1

Library of Congress Cataloging-in-Publication Data
Baltic capitals : Tallinn, Riga, Vilnius, Kaliningrad / contributing editor,
Neil Taylor ;
authors, Stephen Baister, Gordon McLachlan, Chris Patrick.
p. cm.
Includes bibliographical references and index.
ISBN 1-84162-018-1
1. Tallinn (Estonia)—Guidebooks. 2. Rīga (Latvia)—Guidebooks. 3.
Vilnius (Lithuania)—Guidebooks. 4. Kaliningrad (Kaliningradskaēi
oblastź' Russia)—Guidebooks. I. Taylor, Neil. II. Baister, Stephen.
III. McLachlan, Gordon W. IV. Patrick, Chris.
DK503.924.B35 2001
914.7904'86—dc21   00-066278

Photographs *Front cover* Tallinn door (Tricia Hayne), Cosmonaut Memorial,
Kaliningrad (Matt Rudd), Vilnius street scene (Rachel Russell), House of the Cat,
Rīga (Mark Wadlow/Russia & Eastern Images)
Text Stephen Baister and Chris Patrick (SC); Hilary Bradt (HB); Tricia Hayne (TH);
Gordon McLachlan (GM); Matt Rudd (MR); Rachel Russell (RR)
Illustrations Rebecca de Mendonça
Maps Steve Munns, Alan Whitaker

Typeset from the author's disc by Donald Sommerville/Wakewing
Printed and bound in Italy by Legoprint

Authors

Neil Taylor is director of Regent Holidays, a British tour company that has specialised in travel to the Baltic states and Kaliningrad since 1991. He visits the area about four times a year and in 1999 his Bradt guide to Estonia was published. He is on the Board of the Association of Independent Tour Operators (AITO) and writes and broadcasts on general travel trade topics. In 2000, Neil was awarded the Lifetime Achievement Award by the British Guild of Travel Writers.

Stephen Baister studied modern languages at Oxford and London universities and worked as a publisher before becoming a solicitor. While in practice, he represented a number of clients with interests in eastern and central Europe. He was co-author of the *Bradt Guide to East Germany*, published in 1990, and a contributor to *Eastern Europe by Rail* (Bradt Publications 1994). He has a doctorate in East European law from University College London. He is now a Registrar in Bankruptcy in the High Court.

Gordon McLachlan was born in Edinburgh. Following graduation from Edinburgh University, he worked for several years on the sales side of publishing, then assumed a full-time writing career in 1987. His many published books include guides to Germany, Berlin, Poland and Edinburgh, and it was his long professional association with the southern Baltic region which inspired him to add Lithuania to this list. His special interests include music, photography, art and architecture, reading, hiking and gastronomy.

Chris Patrick has a degree in French and German from Oxford University. After graduatiion she lived and worked in Japan and travelled extensively in the Far East. She works now in international research and consultancy and is Director of the Europe Japan Centre. She has assisted a number of organisations from Eastern Europe in doing business in the Far East. She first visited Latvia in 1989 and has returned many times since. She was co-author of the *Bradt Guide to East Germany*, published in 1990, and a contributor to *Eastern Europe by Rail* (Bradt Publications 1994).

Contents

Introduction

The late 1990s saw the term 'short break' take on a totally new dimension in the travel business. Tourists who previously limited their horizons to Paris and Amsterdam were suddenly offered shopping weekends in Minneapolis or a glimpse at the Taj Mahal. The three Baltic capitals soon realised that they could fill a gap between these two extremes. With a flying time of three hours from London or four from Birmingham, Manchester and Glasgow, with the abolition of visas, and with the 'Westernisation' of hotels, each offers a fulfilling three or four days either on their own or as part of a longer visit to two or the three of them. Except perhaps in December and January, the weather is good enough for walking between the major attractions, all of which now cater for the English-speaking visitor.

The time difference is one or two hours from Britain, the airports are close to the city centre and immigration procedures are very quick so a visitor might well reach a hotel in one of the Baltic capitals more quickly than one in Berlin or Rome.

Kaliningrad took longer to realise the potential of catering for short-stay visitors. Only in 1999 were visas issued on arrival at both the land borders and at the airport. Travel was often an obstacle course with little non-Russian material available and in the early 1990s tourists had been treated with suspicion and fear. Neither the shops nor the few open museums could really offer any temptations. Seeing, however, the success of Vilnius to the north and Krakow to the south has been a major stimulus to compete. There is much still to do and older visitors will quickly find some parallels with the Soviet Union but regular visitors point to the month by month changes. There is now a genuine need for a guidebook; five years ago this claim could not have been made.

Parallels with many other parts of Europe will immediately strike the visitor. The towering Gothic steeples in Tallinn, Rīga and Kaliningrad emphasise the importance of the Baltic German community. The domes and colour of the Russian orthodox churches are constant reminders of the two hundred years the Baltic Republics spent in the Russian Empire. The use of mobile phones by all generations is one of many habits picked up by the renewed links to Sweden and Finland. France, Italy and Spain have made their mark in the local restaurants, whilst Britain has concentrated on the pubs. Local footballers, of course, play not only in Europe but for teams all over the world!

Allow time in all four capitals for evening concerts; in the winter the architecture of the buildings will be as much an attraction as the music. Most date from the late 19th century and avoided damage both from bombing and from over-zealous modernisers during the Soviet period. In the summer, music moves to the lakes, to the parks, to the riverside and to the coast. The concert repertoire will mix local music with Western classics and high standards can be guaranteed Allow time too for shopping since local materials and craftsmanship stand out in all the local markets. Wool, linen, copper and amber are all transformed into original gifts. Local photographers, historians and translators have now finally got together to publish excellent souvenirs of each city. With efficient postal services, they can easily be sent home. Above all, take in the changes that have taken place in the last ten to twelve years. There is no longer the need to look on a visit to the Baltics as an adventure. The best compliment that can be paid to them is to regard them as ordinary European capitals.

ACKNOWLEDGEMENTS

In preparing the text on Königsberg, I must give particular thanks to Lorenz Grimoni, Director of the Königsberg Museum in Duisburg. He gave me access to the museum archives which cover all aspects of pre-war life in the city and which house research done by Germans in Kaliningrad since 1990 when they were able to return there. Future generations in particular will be grateful for all the work done in the museum to preserve the memory of what had been an important German city. In Kaliningrad itself, my guide, Olga Danilova, has shared her enthusiasm, realism and knowledge on each of my visits. I owe Olga a great debt, as do most English-speaking visitors. The staff at Baltma Tours always seemed to meet my increasingly complicated requests and must be congratulated on cutting out much of the Soviet visa bureaucracy that still plagues the rest of Russia.

Practical Information

WHEN TO GO

Most tourists to the Baltic states visit in the summer months between late April and early October. July and early August are very busy in the cheaper hotels since this is the German and Scandinavian school holiday period. Temperatures in the summer can reach 25°C/80°F quite regularly, though they often hover around 20°C/70°F. Good weather can never be guaranteed in this area. Clouds can quickly congregate, turning a sunny morning into a dismal afternoon, but the reverse is equally true, too. Day trips should never be undertaken without a coat and strong shoes. Tallinn hardly sees a night around midsummer at June 23 and the days are long in all four countries from May until September. The deluxe and business-class hotels often reduce their prices in July and August to attract tourists at a time when their normal clientele is absent.

More tourists are now seeing the attractions of winter visits to these four cities. Culture flourishes then, temperatures do not drop much below freezing, and queues are non-existent at the major sites. From western Europe winter air fares have now dropped to a level which makes weekend breaks in these cities very popular. January and early February should be avoided because of the short hours of daylight then and the occasional bitter day, but other months should offer a pleasant stay. Christmas is now taken seriously in the Baltics and a well-planned short shopping trip should more than cover the air fare.

TIME ZONES

Before World War II, Estonia and Latvia were two hours ahead of GMT and Lithuania one hour ahead, as was East Prussia. During the Soviet occupation the three Baltic republics and the Kaliningrad region were forced to use Moscow time which is three hours ahead of GMT. Courageous local nationalists during this period would often keep their watches an hour behind Moscow time as an act of defiance to the USSR and of loyalty to the former regime. On regaining independence changing back the time was one of the first acts of the new governments and in the early 90s they all kept in step, to be joined later by Kaliningrad. From 1997, however, they have not always acted in tandem for a variety of reasons. In summer 2000 Kaliningrad adopted summer time two hours ahead of Britain and one hour ahead of Western Europe, but the other three did not, so are now one hour ahead of Britain and have the same time as most of the rest of Europe throughout the year. As these decisions are often taken at relatively short notice, it is important to reconfirm timings of international travel shortly before departure. Tickets may have been issued abroad before a change was announced.

RED TAPE

Estonia, Latvia and Lithuania abolished the Soviet visa system immediately after their independence in 1991. Nationals of all EU countries and the United States do not need visas at all. Australians, Canadians and New Zealanders need one for Latvia. Canadians also need one for Estonia, and New Zealanders for Lithuania. However, for these nationalities a visa for one Baltic state is valid for the other two as well so they never need obtain more than one visa, even if they plan to visit more then one country.

Kaliningrad initially followed Russia by adopting the former Soviet visa system but a fall in the number of tourists forced them to break away from this in 1999. All tourists still need a visa, which is only granted on the basis of pre-booked accommodation, but it is now issued on arrival. This can be at Kaliningrad airport or on the road crossings from Poland and Lithuania. This is easily arranged by travel agents abroad in conjunction with their agents in Kaliningrad. The only exception is for visitors planning to arrive by train. They will have to obtain their visas from Russian embassies abroad, but given the difficulties of this procedure and the state of the international trains that serve Kaliningrad, few visitors are likely to choose this method. Visas are for specific dates and accommodation so must be arranged several weeks in advance. It is not possible to backpack in Kaliningrad or to have an open-dated visa.

Consular help in the Baltics

Australia, Britain and the United States have consulates in each of the three Baltic capitals. The British consulates can provide assistance to nationals of most Commonwealth countries in emergencies and also to nationals of EU countries that do not have their own consulates. Kaliningrad has four consulates representing Belarus, Denmark, Lithuania and Poland. The Danish one, situated in the Scandinavian Airlines office at Sovietsky 1, tel: 55-01-05, handles emergencies for all Western tourists. The German government has expressed interest in opening a consulate in Kaliningrad but Moscow has remained unwilling to allow this. See also pages 26, 62, 123 and 168.

MONEY MATTERS

Each country has its own currency and payment in any other one is impossible. All four are convertible and can be exchanged throughout the three Baltic countries. As banks and exchange bureaux do not usually charge commission, small amounts left over can be re-exchanged without difficulty. In Tallinn, Rīga and Vilnius, banks and exchange bureaux change all major Western currencies. Those at airports are always open for incoming flights but at land borders and at railway and bus stations they tend to close between 20.00 and 08.00, even though many international buses and trains travel through the night. Exchange bureaux in the towns are usually open seven days a week from around 09.00 to 19.00. Most hotels change money, some at any time of day, but rates are always better in exchange bureaux. On day trips out of town, remember to change sufficient money before departure since exchange and credit card facilities may not be available en route. In the Kaliningrad *oblast*, apart from at the land border with Lithuania, it is often only possible to exchange German marks or US dollars into roubles. It is forbidden to make any payments in foreign currency. Thomas Cook at London Gatwick Airport exchanges all four currencies, but it is otherwise difficult to obtain them in advance in western Europe.

Estonia

The Estonian kroon is fixed at a rate of 8 kroon to 1 German mark, so in mid 2000 there were around 25 kroon to the UK pound and 16 to the US dollar. It is therefore also fixed to the euro at a rate of just below 16 kroon to the euro. The lowest note is for 1 kroon and the highest for 500. As a result, many tourists do not use coins at all during their stay, although these exist for 10, 20 and 50 cents and for one kroon.

Latvia

The Latvian lat is tied to a range of Western currencies and is worth around £1.10 or US$1.80. In contrast to Estonia, coins are issued up to 2 lats and notes from 5 lats upwards. As the lat is worth a little more than £1, the money there is very convenient for British tourists to calculate as coins and notes match their British counterparts fairly closely. Coins are issued for 1, 2, 5, 10, 20 and 50 santimi and for 1 and 2 lats, notes for 5, 10, 20 and 50 lats. (Gamblers and money-launderers may also find the 100 and 500 lat notes of use.) Outside Latvia, it is sometimes difficult to exchange coins so these should be re-exchanged before departure, and on the Latvian side of land borders.

Lithuania

The Lithuanian lit is tied to the US dollar at a rate of four lits to one dollar so there are about six to the UK pound. During 2001 it may be tied instead to the euro. There are coins for 5, 10, 20 and 50 cents and for 1, 2, and 5 lits. There are notes for 10, 20, 50 and 100 lits and some still in circulation for 1, 2, and 5 lits but these are gradually being replaced by coins.

Kaliningrad

The Russian rouble has been fairly stable against the US dollar since 1998 and through 2000 the exchange rate was around 27 roubles to the US dollar. With the fall in value of the UK pound and the euro against the dollar in summer 2000, the rouble therefore rose in value against those currencies. Coins are issued for 10, 20 and 50 kopeks and for 1, 2 and 5 roubles. Given the very low prices for most items of interest to tourists, the only notes likely to be of use are those for 10, 20 and 50 roubles, although higher denominations are issued.

Cash machines

These are easily found all over Tallinn but are less common in Riga and Vilnius. Their use is, however, spreading all the time in these three cities. In Kaliningrad they remain rare and the few that exist often do not work.

Credit cards

In Tallinn, Riga and Vilnius the use of cards is as widespread as elsewhere with all major shops, restaurants and hotels taking them. They can be used in hotels in Kaliningrad, but not in shops and only in a few restaurants. They cannot be used at railway or bus stations but, as even long-distance fares are very low, this is not a major problem.

Travellers' cheques

These can usually only be exchanged at banks; hotels and shops are unlikely to accept them. Exchange bureaux at ports can accept them, others usually do not.

COSTS

Whilst hotel costs are similar to those in western Europe, other expenses will be much lower, except at restaurants and clubs clearly geared to affluent foreigners. A bus or train ride of 200km may well cost only £3/US$5, a light lunch £1/US$1.50 and a taxi across town £2/US$3. With low sales taxes, petrol is about half the UK price and a carton of 200 cigarettes costs scarcely more than the price of a packet in Britain. In Kaliningrad, prices are even lower than in the other three cities. Museums do charge admission fees but these are minimal. Locally produced books and maps in English often offer good value. On day trips out, incidental costs will be much lower than in the capitals and on these occasions it is worth looking out for souvenirs since their prices will be geared to local consumers.

Shoppers visiting more than one of the cities will save money by finishing their tour in Kaliningrad, where all the obvious souvenirs are much cheaper than further north. Amber is of course the obvious buy there, together with linen and vodka. Lithuania and Estonia produce tasteful items carved from juniper wood, whereas the best china and glass is sold in Riga.

WHAT TO TAKE

The shops are now so well stocked in all four countries, with prices usually much lower than those in Western Europe, that there is no need to stock up with supplies before departure. Long-gone are the days when travellers took iron rations and a medicine chest to safeguard their survival. An umbrella is essential year-round as clouds can suddenly appear on even the nicest of days. Be prepared similarly for changes in temperature: a sweater may be needed in summer and a spring day can revert to being a winter one. Tough footwear is always essential because of the uneven pavements and the number of sites away from main roads. Relatively formal wear is still the custom for concerts and plays. Westerners attending performances often stand out with their untidy, casual dress.

The foreign-language bookshops in the three Baltic capitals are well supplied with English-language light and serious reading matter but few English (or even German) books are sold in Kaliningrad. Local guides in Kaliningrad are always pleased to receive books in English and many find their way into school and college libraries.

GETTING THERE

Tour operators

Exodus Travels 9 Weir Rd, London SW12 OLT, tel: 020 8673 0859, fax: 020 8673 0779, email: sales@exodustravels.co.uk, web: exodustravels.co.uk. Organise cycling groups to Latvia and Estonia which start in Riga and finish in Tallinn, also general tours covering the three Baltic states. About half the time is spent in the capitals and half in the countryside.

Explore Worldwide 1 Frederick St, Aldershot, Hants GU11 1LQ, tel: 01252 760 100, fax: 01252 760001, email: info@exploreworldwide.com, web: exploreworldwide.com. Operate an extensive general itinerary through the three Baltic states which includes the capital cities.

Martin Randall Travel 10 Barley Mow Passage, Chiswick, London W4 4PH, tel: 020 8742 3355, fax: 020 8742 7766, email: info@martinrandall.co.uk, web: martinrandall.com. Have an extensive programme of group tours to the Baltic states for those interested in art, architecture and music. Guest lecturers accompany every tour. There is a tour each year to the Rīga Opera Festival.

Regent Holidays 15 John St, Bristol BS1 2HR, tel: 0117 921 1711, fax: 0117 925 4866, email: regent@regent-holidays.co.uk, web: regent-holidays.co.uk. The only UK operator to promote Kaliningrad as well as the Baltic states. Group tours cover the four capitals; city breaks are available to each of them and tailor-made individual itineraries can cover any combination of the cities with the surrounding areas. Itineraries can also include Belarus, Finland, Poland and Russia.

Scantours 47 Whitcomb St, Leicester Square, London WC2H 7DH, tel: 020 7839 2927, fax: 020 7839 5891, email: info@scantoursUK.com, web: scantoursuk.com. Offer city breaks, group tours, and individual arrangements to the three Baltic capitals and also combinations with Denmark, Sweden and Finland.

Specialised Tours 4 Copthorne Bank, Copthorne, Crawley, West Sussex RH10 3QX, tel: 01342 712785, fax: 01342 717042, web: www.specialisedtours.com. Arrange short breaks to the three Baltic capitals, a Classical Baltics tour linking the three, and individual arrangements throughout the Baltics.

By air

Most tourists are likely to start and finish their visit this way. SAS Scandinavian Airlines operates to all four cities, and in the case of Tallinn, Rīga and Vilnius, this airline offers several connections a day from Copenhagen and Stockholm which link with most of its services to Europe and America. Their Copenhagen–Kaliningrad flight operates daily except Saturday. SAS also has 'open-jaw' fares which allow travel into, say, Kaliningrad or Vilnius, with a return from Tallinn. Such open-jaw fares are also available using a Baltic airport in one direction and then a Polish or Russian one in another which would make possible an itinerary starting say in Gdańsk and finishing in Rīga. SAS is particularly convenient for travellers from Britain as it serves seven airports – Heathrow, Gatwick, Stansted, Birmingham, Manchester, Glasgow and Edinburgh – so it can offer competitive through-fares to this area from all of them.

There are charter flights from Germany to Kaliningrad in the summer but other flights from Kaliningrad are only to cities in Russia. With the three Baltic capitals, the situation is very different. They are all served by Austrian Airlines, Finnair and LOT Polish Airlines from Vienna, Helsinki and Warsaw respectively. Estonian Air has a daily flight from Tallinn to London Gatwick, except on Saturdays, and twice daily services to Copenhagen and Stockholm. With their code-sharing agreements with SAS Scandinavian Airlines and with Maersk, the Copenhagen and Stockholm flights can often be combined at competitive prices with onward connections. Lithuanian Air has daily flights from Vilnius to London Heathrow and to Amsterdam.

British Airways flies to Rīga from Gatwick and code-shares with Finnair on flights to Tallinn via Helsinki. In 1999 BA flew to Vilnius but this service was withdrawn in spring 2000. It may return in 2001. As BA flies to Gdańsk, Kraków and Warsaw, an open-jaw arrangement can be made to combine a visit to Poland with one to the Baltics, flying via Rīga, Tallinn or Helsinki.

Lithuanian Air and Estonian Air each have a daily flight between Tallinn and Vilnius. Air Baltic, now part of SAS, flies from Rīga to Vilnius and to Tallinn. Fares booked on these sectors individually are very high but discounts are sometimes available when they are booked with other flights on the same carrier. Prices have dropped in recent years for air fares to this area as to many others. Particularly attractive rates are often available from tour operators in conjunction with hotel bookings. In 2000 weekend breaks to Tallinn, Rīga and Vilnius were available from London for around £250 including three nights accommodation, the flight and all taxes.

Rīga Airport has a departure tax of around £17/US$27 whereas Tallinn has no tax and the other two airports a tax of around £7/US$10. Travellers from the UK who stop over in Helsinki on the outbound journey pay only £5 British departure tax whereas those who fly direct to any of the four cities pay the £20 applicable to non-EU destinations.

By train

With the continuing reduction in air fares and the worsening services on international trains, this is unlikely to be a means of transport used by many visitors to reach this area. Customs and immigration procedures can take many hours, usually in the middle of the night. Trains still operate from Kaliningrad to Warsaw and from Tallinn to St Petersburg. There are also trains from Kaliningrad and the Baltic cities to Moscow and Kiev. Belarussian transit visas are now needed for these, as well as the appropriate Russian or Ukrainian visas. In summer 2000 a Russian visa was no longer valid for transit across Belarus.

By bus

Eurolines has an extensive network of services to western Europe from the Baltics and some services to Russia. Eurolines also runs express buses between the Baltic states. These operate several times a day and are the most practical way of land travel between the major cities. They jump the queue at the frontiers so timings are virtually guaranteed. The journey takes around five hours from Rīga to either Vilnius or Tallinn. There is a through service from Vilnius to Tallinn and also routes from Rīga to Kaunas and to Tartu. Reservations can be made abroad through travel agents (see page 4) but tickets are collected from the Eurolines office in the relevant bus station. The fare from Rīga to either Tallinn or Vilnius is around £6/US$9 one-way. English is spoken in all Eurolines offices.

Local companies operate services from Kaliningrad to Nida, Vilnius and Rīga which should be prebooked in view of the visa stipulations. These, too, jump border queues so passengers who may have spent around £5/US$8 for their fare can have the pleasure of overtaking rich businessmen fuming in their Mercedes. There are some similar services to Poland but these are less regular nowadays as local travellers now require visas.

By car

It is virtually impossible to obtain insurance valid for cars brought into the Baltic states and Kaliningrad from the rest of Europe. This stems from the high rate of theft that used to be prevalent in the area and which to some extent continues. Car hire is possible locally but for visitors staying largely in the capital cities is unlikely to be of use. Many of the sites are within walking distance of hotels and others are within easy reach by bus or taxi. For day trips off the beaten track hiring may be worthwhile but as prices for local guides and drivers are very reasonable it is often sensible to consider hiring a car on this basis. Minor roads are not well signposted and local people in the countryside do not usually speak foreign languages.

By ferry
Many tourists like to arrive in Tallinn from Helsinki by ferry. The Seacats introduced by Silja Line in the summer of 2000 reduced journey times to 90 minutes between the capitals and other ferries only take 2–3 hours. Overnight boats operate from Tallinn and Rīga to Stockholm. Several cruise lines visit Kaliningrad, Rīga and Tallinn as part of itineraries around the Baltic Sea.

GETTING AROUND
By air
Air Baltic fly between Tallinn and Rīga, also between Rīga and Vilnius. On both routes there is a morning and an evening flight, timed to suit business travellers going for the day. The one-way fare is around £100 ($150) but discounts are available at weekends and on tickets bought in conjunction with Air Baltic services to western Europe. Estonian Air and Lithuanian Air operate a similar pattern of a morning and evening flight between Tallinn and Vilnius. Fares are a little higher than on the Air Baltic routes, given the longer distance, but again discounts are available when these sectors are booked in conjunction with international services. Many British tourists fly with Lithuanian Air to Vilnius, take the bus via Rīga to Tallinn and then fly back Tallinn-Vilnius-London. There are no flights from Kaliningrad to the Baltic States.

By train
Although train services do operate between all four cities, they are rarely used by tourists since they run overnight and are very slow, taking about eight hours for a journey which takes five hours on the bus. In 1999, a day train was introduced between Tallinn and Rīga which travels via Tartu and through the Sigulda National Park in Latvia. For those with a whole day to spare, it is a scenic journey and the cost is similar to that of the bus. As there are two day trains between Kaliningrad and Vilnius, and the journey takes around six hours, this is the preferable route for visitors wishing to travel directly between the two.

In Kaliningrad trains are a convenient and cheap way to reach the coastal resort of Svetlogorsk, and in Rīga for the same reasons to visit Jurmala. On other journeys, such as from Tallinn to Tartu or from Vilnius to Kaunas, bus services are more frequent and cheaper. Russian is spoken in railway stations throughout the Baltics, but English or German only rarely. Timetables are clearly displayed so to buy a ticket, write down the destination and time of the train, together with the date, if booking ahead.

By bus/trolleybus/tram
The most convenient way to travel between all four cities is by bus. Most services are run by Eurolines and Baltic specialists abroad can prebook these. In the winter, it is often possible to buy a seat on the spot before departure.

The journey time between Tallinn and Rīga and also between Rīga and Vilnius is around five hours. Buses operate about six times a day on both sectors and the one-way fare is around £7/US$10. There is a daily bus from Kaliningrad to Rīga which takes around nine hours and one night bus between Kaliningrad and Vilnius which takes eight hours. The one-way fare on these routes is also around £7/US$10. For those in no rush between Kaliningrad and Vilnius, there are six buses a day between Kaliningrad and Klaipeda which run along the Curonian Spit. These then connect with hourly services between Klaipeda and Vilnius. Allow about ten hours for the whole journey.

Extensive services operate in all four cities and local maps will give details of current routings. In Tallinn, where several competing companies operate, service numbers change quite frequently so it is important to get an up-to-date map. In the other cities, a regular pattern has now been set so few changes are likely in the near future. In Rīga and Vilnius, the airports are served by a good local bus service. This is less regular in Tallinn, but as several hotels have a minibus service and a taxi into town should not cost more than £3/US$5, this does not matter so much. In Kaliningrad the local bus that serves the airport does not pass close to any of the hotels so most tourists are collected by their local travel agent. These agents usually bring the entry visa at the same time.

At the time of writing in summer 2000, tickets bought at kiosks in Tallinn and Vilnius are a little cheaper than those bought on the bus. Visitors staying for several days at hotels in the outskirts should investigate season tickets. Rīga and Tallinn have tourist passes which include free local transport as part of the total package but, as the price of these is rather high, visitors will normally save money by paying fares and admission charges as they go.

Buses link the capitals with all other major cities in their respective countries on a very regular basis. For instance between Tallinn and Tartu, or Vilnius and Kaunas, services operate every half-hour. Timetables are displayed in the bus stations and in most cases the fare is paid directly to the driver.

By taxi

Taxis used to be a nightmare throughout the Baltics but are now properly regulated in all four cities. Within city limits, meter fares apply and this is also the case to and from the airports. Taxis can be easily hailed in the streets and with the lively nightlife for which all four cities are now renowned, they operate almost round the clock. Some of the deluxe hotels operate their own fleets. These are metered; prices tend to be higher but then so is the comfort of the vehicles! Lengthy journeys which would be unthinkable by taxi in western Europe can be undertaken in the Baltics with costs being so much lower.

ACCOMMODATION

A massive programme of hotel renovation took place throughout the area following the demise of the Soviet Union. Apart from in Rīga, where three-star hotels hardly exist, a wide range of hotels is now available and tourists can take for granted a secure clean environment with standard international facilities such as direct dialling from the room and a varied menu in the restaurant. Prices are similar to those in western Europe and vary for familiar reasons, too. Depending on the visitors they expect, some will charge more and some less at weekends. Some offer great discounts to agents abroad as an incentive to book them. Given the range of five-star hotels likely to be available in Rīga and Tallinn by 2001, cheaper rates should be available for July and August in many of them when there is minimal business traffic. Because of the popularity of Tallinn for Finnish tourists, the cheaper hotels there are often fully booked weeks, and even months, in advance so early booking is essential.

In their renovations many hotels are only putting in showers and not baths in the rooms. Tourists who prefer baths should ask their tour operator to stipulate this when making the booking.

EATING AND DRINKING

It is perhaps in restaurants and bars that the transformation from the old days is most apparent in Tallinn, Rīga and Vilnius. *In Your Pocket* and the *City Paper* now list hundreds of choices in each city and what is gratifying is the number that still exist five or six years after opening. Every major cuisine is represented and, with the numbers of restaurants now available, advance booking is often not necessary. It is worth venturing outside the old city areas: the best food is often to be found in modest suburban surroundings. One has to be brutally honest about local food. Whilst there are many perfectly acceptable dishes, few are memorable. However, they should at least be made from fresh ingredients, now that these are available year-round. Thick soups can be recommended in winter as meals in themselves, and pancakes are served with a variety of savoury or sweet fillings. The ranges of coffee, cakes and ice-cream available are one positive legacy of Soviet and German times.

Kaliningrad has made progress recently and there is sufficient choice to cover a stay of a week or so. Prices are so low that it would be invidious to complain about the quality; a wide menu can now be taken for granted but do not yet expect many non-Russian restaurants.

Wine is quite expensive throughout the region and the quality unexciting. It is often better (and much cheaper) to drink local beer. Spirits are good everywhere with a wide local and international choice. Tourists who knew the old USSR will still find it hard to adjust to a small café in the Baltics offering a choice of malt whisky, at prices half those charged in Scotland.

MEDIA AND COMMUNICATIONS
Telephones and post

Public telephones in all four countries are operated by cards which can be bought at local kiosks. Cards are not interchangeable so new ones have to be bought for each country. It is not possible to use credit cards, nor do any phones accept coins. Instructions are usually given in English in the phone booths. The procedure is the same in all four countries: the receiver is lifted, the card inserted and then the number dialled. As the call continues, the reducing value of the card is shown on the screen. Calls to western Europe cost around £0.60/US$1 a minute with reductions in the evenings and at weekends. With competition from mobile phone companies, prices are tending to fall. Prices from hotel rooms are of course higher than this but they are rarely exorbitant. Calls to local mobile phones can cost almost as much as international calls, particularly in Estonia. Calls can be made from all major post offices and, except in Vilnius, they are open all night.

Dialling codes and information specific to the various countries are given in the individual city chapters later in the book.

Post from the three Baltic states is transmitted quickly, reaching western Europe or America within four or five days. From Kaliningrad, post has to travel via Moscow so tends to take at least two weeks. Postage rates in Lithuania are about half those of the other countries. Post offices sell cards at very reasonable rates. Stamps can naturally only be used in their country of origin so do not forget to use them before moving on!

Newspapers and magazines

The *In Your Pocket* series of mini-guides to each of the capitals provides invaluable information for each city, including listings of restaurants, museum opening hours, postage rates and details of public transport. Their irreverent style is a pleasant contrast to the minimal official tourist material that is produced locally. Where appropriate they can be highly critical. For Tallinn, Rīga and Vilnius the guides are produced locally every couple of months, so are always up to date. The Kaliningrad one is produced on an irregular basis from Vilnius so is less reliable. Guides cost the equivalent of £0.60/US$1 and are available at many hotels and kiosks. They are published in full on the website www.inyourpocket.com so this site is worth consulting before departure.

The *Baltic Times* is published weekly in Rīga (in English) and covers contemporary politics in the three Baltic countries. The *Königsberg Express*, published monthly in German in Kaliningrad, fulfils a similar role there. European editions of the main American and British newspapers are available on the morning of publication in Tallinn, Rīga and Vilnius. German papers occasionally reach Kaliningrad. In the winter they are sold in the Kaliningrad Hotel, in the summer also in Svetlogorsk.

The *City Paper*, published in Tallinn bimonthly, in a sense combines the *Baltic Times* and the *In Your Pocket* guides. Each issue costs about £1.30/US$2. It combines useful background articles on politics with thoughtful restaurant reviews and excellent practical information on the three Baltic capitals. It is an excellent introduction to the area and earlier issues are covered on its website www.balticsworldwide.com.

Television

All hotels used regularly by foreign tourists now have satellite television, offering at least one English-language channel. Many offer both American and British channels, realising that most visitors have a clear preference for one or the other.

HEALTH

No inoculations are required for visits to this area and hygiene standards in hotels and restaurants are high. Tap water should not be drunk in Kaliningrad but is safe in the Baltic states. Local hospitals can be trusted to deal with any emergency; long gone are the days when foreigners flew to Helsinki or Stockholm for any minor ailment. Sometimes treatment is free but foreigners are now normally charged a small sum to cover costs.

CRIME

This is much less of a problem than in most European capitals, although pickpockets are a threat in Tallinn and Riga old towns where the maze of small streets makes for an easy get-away. There have recently been attacks on rich foreigners in Tallinn leaving clubs late at night. Car theft is common throughout the area and cars should always be left overnight in a guarded hotel parking lot.

Passports and air tickets can fairly safely be left in hotel rooms, locked in cases. Otherwise usual sensible precautions apply. Do not take out large sums of cash when walking around the main tourist areas. What might be a modest sum to a Western tourist can be a month's pay for a local youngster so it is not surprising that some will succumb to temptation when offered the chance.

Tallinn

Neil Taylor

Whether approached by air, land or sea, Tallinn is immediately identifiable as a capital that looks west rather than east. The departure board at the airport lists London, Copenhagen and Stockholm but rarely St Petersburg. The boats that fill the harbour, be they massive ferries or small yachts, head for Finland and Sweden, not Russia. The traffic jams that are beginning to block the main streets are caused by Volkswagens, Land Rovers and Saabs, not by Ladas. Links with the west are celebrated, those with Russia are commemorated. In May 1998, Tallinn celebrated its 750th anniversary since on May 15 1248 it adopted Lübeck Town Law, which united most members of the Hanseatic League. A month later, as on every June 14, flags were lowered in memory of those deported to the Soviet Union on June 14 1941.

Immediately after independence Western goods started pouring into the shops, and Russian ones are now very hard to find. There is a similar reluctance to buy from any of the other former Soviet Republics. Travel agents offer the same tempting prices for holidays in Turkey, Greece and Italy that are available in western Europe, but nobody is interested in St Petersburg or the Crimea. Architecturally, with the exception of the Alexander Nevsky Cathedral, it is the Germans, Swedes and Danes who have left their imposing mark on the churches and fortifications of the Old Town. Tallinn was always ready to defend itself but in the end never did so. The nearest it came to a major battle was at the conclusion of the Northern War in 1710 but plague had reduced the population from 10,000 to 2,000 so the Swedes offered little resistance to the army of Peter the Great. It has suffered many occupations but, apart from a Soviet bombing raid in 1944, the city has not been physically harmed as no battles were ever fought there.

The division in Tallinn between what is now the Old Town on the hill (Toompea) and the newer town around the port has survived political administrations of every hue. It has divided God from Mammon, Tsarist and Soviet governors from their reluctant Estonian subjects, and now the Estonian parliament from successful bankers, merchants and manufacturers who thrive on whatever coalition happens to be in power. Tallinn has no Capitol Hill or Whitehall. The parliament building is one of the most modest in the Old Town, dwarfed by the town walls and surrounding churches. When fully restored, the Old Town will be an outstanding permanent monument to Gothic and baroque architecture, and a suitable backcloth to formal political and religious activity. Outside its formidable wall, contemporary Tallinn will change rapidly according to the demands of the new business ethos.

HISTORY

Written records on Tallinn date only from the 12th century although it is clear that a small port existed well before then. In 1219 the Danes occupied Tallinn and much of what is now northern Estonia on the pretext of spreading Christianity. The name Tallinn dates from this time and in Estonian actually means 'Danish city'. Although this name was chosen to suggest only temporary occupation, it has been maintained. The first German merchants settled in 1228 and they were to maintain their economic domination until 1919, even during the long periods of Swedish and Tsarist rule. When for instance the Swedes surrendered to the Russians in 1710, the capitulation documents confirmed that German would remain the official language of commerce. Reval, the German name for Tallinn, is sometimes seen in English publications; it probably comes from *Revala*, the old Estonian name for the surrounding area. A more colourful explanation is that it comes from the two German words *Reh* and *Fall*, meaning the falling of the deer as they attempt to escape the Danish occupation.

Peter the Great visited Tallinn on 11 different occasions, so crucial was the city as an ice-free port to his empire. He instigated the permanent expansion of Tallinn beyond the city walls by building Kadriog Palace; the previous history of constant warfare in the vicinity of the town had led to all buildings being makeshift wooden houses which could easily be burnt as a preliminary defence to the city. Tallinn was then to enjoy 200 years of peace and increasing prosperity. Architecturally, though, the Old Town has always remained the centre of Tallinn and its main attraction. Gert Walter, a Baltic German who settled in East Germany and could therefore return to Tallinn during the Soviet period, describes the Old Town as having half a per cent of the surface area of Tallinn but giving it its entire magic.

The completion of the railway link with St Petersburg in 1870 turned Tallinn into a major city. The port was enlarged to handle the increasing volume of goods that could now be brought there and factories were established to take advantage of the larger markets. Fortunately they could adapt quickly in the 1920s to selling westwards rather than eastwards; a similar process took place in the early 1990s, though with more difficulty. Between 1945 and 1990 the city doubled in size and its population is now half a million, about a third of the total population of Estonia.

PRACTICAL INFORMATION
Communications

The *Baltic Times*, published weekly on a Thursday is the best English-language source of news for the three Baltic Republics. It also lists exhibitions and concerts. *Tallinn In Your Pocket* published every two months in invaluable for its independent, and therefore irreverant reviews on restaurants, museums and other sites. *The City Paper*, also published every two months, covers the three Baltic capitals together, in a similar way to *Tallinn In Your Pocket* but with the addition of political articles. European editions of British and American newspapers are on sale in Tallinn at the larger hotels on the day of publication.

Telephones

To reach Tallinn by phone from abroad, dial the Estonia country code 372, the Tallinn city code of 6 and then the six-digit number. Many Estonians now have . mobile phones which are operated by a number of different companies. They each have a separate access code which is dialled after the 372 and which replaces the city code of 6. To reach phones abroad from Tallinn, dial 800 and then the relevant country code. Public phone boxes only take phone cards which can be bought at kiosks. They do not take cash or credit cards. Calls can also be made from post offices.

Post

The Central Post Office is at Narva mnt 1, opposite the Viru Hotel. It has relatively short opening hours, 08.00–20.00 Monday–Friday and 08.00–18.00 on Saturday. It is closed on Sunday. It sells postcards, exchanges money and provides telephone services. Tourists often use the post office at the top of the Old Town at Lossi Plats 4 beside the Alexander Nevsky Cathedral but this is only open 09.00–17.00 Monday–Friday.

Internet

All major hotels have a business centre offering a full range of services including internet access but the charges are high – usually around 100EEK (£4/US$6) per half hour. Terminals are free of charge, but therefore often in use, at the airport and at the National Library. Kaubamaja, the department store at the back of the Viru Hotel, charges 40EEK (£1.75/US$3) an hour, and they are open seven days a week, Monday-Friday 10.00–21.00, Saturday 10.00–20.00 and Sunday 10.00–18.00.

Tours

For tourists who arrive without having pre-booked any excursions, the Tourist Office on Town Hall Square at Raekoja Plats 10 can advise on local operators with regular programmes.

Tourist information

The two 'bibles' for any English-speaking visitor are *The City Paper* and *Tallinn In Your Pocket*, both of which are published six times a year. *The City Paper* covers Rīga and Vilnius as well. It mixes cerebral but amusing articles on the local political scene with reminiscences on earlier times and detailed current listings. *Tallinn In Your Pocket* has extremely detailed listings on everything in Tallinn and each edition has a supplement on another Estonian town. It is particularly helpful for opening hours and current transport information. Both publications should be available at hotel kiosks and at the airport on arrival. Their irreverence is a welcome contrast to other more turgidly written local guidebooks. Serious Baltic tour operators abroad stock these publications and both have websites (see page 193).

For general current affairs information the *Baltic Times* is a weekly political newspaper covering the three countries. The fierce and bitter parliamentary debates it summarises contrast with the seeming stability of the world outside.

Tallinn Tourist Board has a shop front office on Town Hall Square (Raekoja Plats 10) which sells a good range of books, maps and cards. They always have up-to-date editions of *Tallinn In Your Pocket* and *The City Paper.* There is also a large reference folder with timetables for ferries to Finland, buses out of Tallinn and local railways. There is a similar office in the ticket hall by the harbour. This office, like all other tourist offices around Estonia, has a website (see page 193). Visiting these sites before departure will save a lot of time on arrival.

Public holidays

Independence Day	February 24
Midsummer	June 23–24
Restoration of Independence Day	August 20

The Tallinn Card

This was introduced by the local tourist board in June 1998. For 195EEK for one day or 270EEK for two days it offers a free sightseeing tour, free admission to most museums, a free copy of *Tallinn in Your Pocket* and free use of the public transport system. There is no reduction in price on Mondays and Tuesdays when many museums are closed. For those who want to take the sightseeing tour and visit a large number of museums, it may be worthwhile to buy it, but for many tourists it will still be cheaper to pay separately for any admission and bus fare. The prices were still the same in 2000 so, with increasing bus fares and admission fees, it may become more relevant for tourists if the current rates are held still longer.

Banks and money

The Estonian currency is the kroon, abreviated as EEK. It is tied to the German mark at a rate of 1DM = 8EEK so 15.60EEK is equivalent to one euro. In 1999 and 2000, British and American visitors have been able to take advantage of favourable exchange rates to the pound and dollar, given the fall in the value of the euro. In October 2000 the pound bought 26EEK and the dollar 18EEK. Exchange booths are open seven days a week in Tallinn, banks normal office hours. Banks usually offer slightly better exchange rates and they handle travellers' cheques which exchange bureaux do not. The Sampo Bank on the Town Hall Square normally gives good rates for most Western currencies. They also have a branch outside the customs hall on the arrival side of the airport. Cash machines are available throughout the town. Kroon can be obtained abroad, at the Thomas Cook office at Gatwick, in Helsinki, and in the neighbouring Baltic states. Neither banks nor exchange bureaux usually charge any commission so quite small amounts of currency can be exchanged at the land border, harbour, or airport on departure.

Transport

Tallinn Airport

The airport is only 3–4km from the town centre. It was built for the Moscow Olympics in 1980 (sailing events were held in the Baltic) and has adapted well to the demands of Western travellers since independence. A local bus service operates to the town centre every quarter of an hour with the final stop behind the Viru Hotel. This costs 10EEK if tickets are bought from kiosks before boarding the bus. Tickets bought from the driver cost 15EEK. The Central,

Mercure, Olympic, Park and Viru Hotels operate a shuttle bus that meets each flight and the cost is 20EEK with tickets being bought from the driver. During the day taxis are easily available. They are all metered and cost about 100EEK into town. Passengers arriving on late evening flights should pre-book a transfer through their travel agent as few taxis operate then and the bus service usually finishes around 22.30. The local bus from the airport passes the main bus station (*Autobussijaam*), which is useful for those wanting to continue journeys beyond Tallinn. Local buses, transfer coaches and taxis must be paid for in local currency.

There is an **exchange bureau** air-side and also one land-side in the arrivals area. The land-side one offers much better rates for incoming travellers. For travellers arriving from Britain on an Estonian Air flight from Gatwick, the Thomas Cook exchange bureau at Gatwick handles Estonian kroon. There is a cashpoint in the arrivals area. There is no tourist information office or hotel booking agency at the airport. American and British tourists plagued by high airport taxes at home will be relieved to hear that Tallinn airport has none. Flights schedules are available on the website: www.tallinn-airport.ee.

Taxis

Taxis are all metered and start at around 20EEK. Journeys within town should not cost more than 50EEK. As taxis are reasonably priced and always metered, they can be considered for long journeys. For instance, one to Lahemaa National Park, about 100km from Tallinn, is unlikely to cost more than 750EEK.

Local buses

Many tourists to Tallinn never take either a bus or a taxi during their stay as the Old Town is very close to most of the hotels and the steep narrow roads conveniently restrict traffic to walkers. Such visitors, however, miss everything which is cheaply and easily accessible by bus outside the Old Town. There are competing bus companies so exact routes and numbers change from time to time but services are frequent and the public transport map *Tallinn Uhistranspõrdi Kaart* is reprinted sufficiently often to be up to date. In summer 2000 the flat fare was 10EEK for tickets bought from kiosks or 15EEK for tickets bought on the bus. Passes are available for stays of four days or longer. (See also *Tallinn Card* page 16) Good services operate to Pirita and Rocca Al Mare and also to the cheaper suburban hotels such as the Dzingel and Susi.

Bus tour

Currently bus route 7 is the equivalent of New York's M4 or the 38 in London as the route to take instead of an organised sightseeing tour. It starts in the affluent suburb of Nomme, then passes through the now declining 1930s commercial quarter before skirting the Old Town. It then passes the Estonian Theatre, parts of the city wall, Viru Gate, and the main post office before reaching the new commercial quarter where glass and steel are replacing concrete and brick as the main construction materials.

Car hire

This is not advisable within Tallinn. Distances are so short and parking so difficult that public transport and taxis are the sensible way to travel around.

Leaving Tallinn

The long-distance bus station (*Autobussijaam*) is on Lastekodu, off the Tartu Road which leads to the airport. The enquiry number is 643 2857 but do not expect English to be spoken. There are no printed timetables but all services are listed on a large departure board. It gives arrival times and also buses for the return journey. Write down the destination, date and time to present at the booking office since few staff speak English. As a bus or taxi takes only a few minutes from the town centre, it is advisable to go a day ahead to book a specific bus and to check timings. Whilst in the winter and mid-week it may often be easy to catch a bus without pre-booking, around the holiday periods and on less frequent services it is essential. Remember to book on an express for the longer journeys. Prices are very cheap – £5/US$8 to Saaremaa and Hiiumaa islands (including the ferry), Narva or Voru, or £3/US$5 to the nearer towns of Pärnu or Tartu. At least every two hours en route, stops of ten minutes are made which allow time for a cigarette, use of the toilets and purchase of refreshments. Smoking is not allowed on buses.

On most routes, the first bus leaves around 06.00 and the last one around 21.00. To **Tartu**, they operate every half-hour, and the journey takes 2 hours. To **Narva** (3 hours) the service is hourly. Buses go every two hours to **Pärnu** and **Viljandi** and the journey time in both cases is around two hours. Buses to **Kuressaare**, the capital of Saaremaa, operate six times a day and a space on the ferry is always guaranteed. Every town in Estonia, plus many villages such as those in Lahemaa National Park, has a bus service from Tallinn, so it is not usually necessary to change en route.

Accommodation

Although Tallinn now has more than 50 hotels, it is so popular for tourists that in the summer of 2000, they were all completely full on many occasions. Pre-booking is therefore advisable. Specialist agents outside Estonia often have access to allocations at lower rates than are available directly from the hotels. Several new hotels opened in 1999 and 2000 and in most cases they quickly achieved high occupancy rates. From February 2001 there will be a new Radisson Hotel with over 250 rooms, situated behind the Kaubamaja Department Store at Ravala Puiestee 3, tel: 669 0000, fax: 669 0001. Other hotels are planned for the financial quarter near the harbour.

The recommendations that follow are obviously rather arbitrary and omission of a hotel should be taken as resulting from lack of space rather than necessarily as a criticism. It can be assumed that, in all cases, rooms in these hotels have private facilities, the hotel accepts credit cards, and it has a restaurant and bar. Many hotels have saunas which guests can use free of charge. Baths are rare in Estonian hotels, even in four-star establishments, so should be specifically requested. In luxury hotels, expect to pay around £100/US$150 a night, in first class £70/US$110 and in tourist class £30–50/US$50–80. The more expensive hotels sometimes reduce prices at weekends and in July, the local holiday season, whereas the cheaper hotels usually increase them then. Prices always include buffet breakfast.

Luxury

Parkconsul Puhavaimu 13/15, tel: 699-7700, fax: 699-7777, email: pctallinn@consul-hotels.com, web: www.consul-hotels.com.

For the time being, this hotel is in a class on its own, though envious competitors must soon try to emulate it. A townhouse owned by many successful Baltic Germans over the years has been converted into Tallinn's first truly luxurious hotel. At present it has just 27 rooms so still maintains the air of a gracious private residence. There is a small conference centre, but it seems incongruous. The hotel is a setting for constant but unostentatious indulgence, for cigars rather than cigarettes, for champagne rather than wine. The restaurant, like all the best ones in Tallinn, is in a cellar and has an extensive menu. For those able briefly to abandon indulgence, the hotel is within walking distance of all the attractions in the Old Town.

First class

Grand Hotel Tallinn Toompuiestee 27, tel: 667 7000, fax: 667 7001, email: reservations@grandhotel.ee, web: grandhotel.ee
This hotel opened as a Mercure in 1999 but the French owners have now withdrawn. Their Estonian successors plan to extend the wine list out of France and to reduce prices somewhat to attract more groups. Its location below the Old Town and near the station suits both tourists and business visitors, particularly those eager for quieter evenings than some other big hotels can manage. Regular visitors may remember the Hotel Tallinn that used to besmirch this site. Luckily all traces of it have been removed and should never return.

Metropol Mere Pst 8, tel: 667 4555, fax: 667 4600, email: booking@metropol.ee, web: metropol.ee
In 1999, when this large four-star hotel opened, the location amongst abandoned warehouses seemed most inept. By 2001, it should be surrounded by glass offices and large car parks. In its provision for non-smokers, the allergic and the disabled, it is also looking far forwards. Tourists enjoy it for now; business visitors may well soon supplant them given its proximity to the new financial quarter of Tallinn.

Olümpia Livalaia 33, tel: 631 5315, fax: 631 5675, email: hotel@olympia.ee, web: reval.ee
Built originally for the Olympic Games in 1980, this hotel is now the firm favourite of foreign business visitors to Tallinn. With the range of restaurants and conference facilities it offers, some never leave the hotel during their stay in Tallinn. They are often joined by the local ex-pat community which has a particular affinity for the 60s' music played in the Bonnie and Clyde nightclub. At weekends and during the summer, rates drop to attract tourists paying their own way. All 400 rooms are now at least of four-star standard and reception staff work very quickly during the arrival and departure 'rush hours'. The restaurant on the top floor offers excellent views of the Old Town and many rooms do so as well. The newspaper shop always stocks up-to-date British newspapers, a rarity in Tallinn. The hotel operates its own bus service to the airport, particularly useful for passengers arriving on late night flights when taxis at the airport are in short supply. Tourists who want to arrive or leave in greater style hire the hotel's 9m-long Lincoln which costs about £50/US$80 an hour .

Palace Vabaduse Valjak, tel: 640 7300, fax: 640 7299, email: palace@scandic-hotels.ee, web: www.scandic-hotels.com
The hotel brochure claims it has offered 'excellent service since 1937' and this is probably true. Although many other hotels now match its facilities, Estonians are very loyal to it as the hotel was one of the few links from the first independence period that remained throughout the Soviet era. Embassies were briefly set up in the hotel in 1991 before foreign legations could reclaim their pre-war buildings. It is now equally

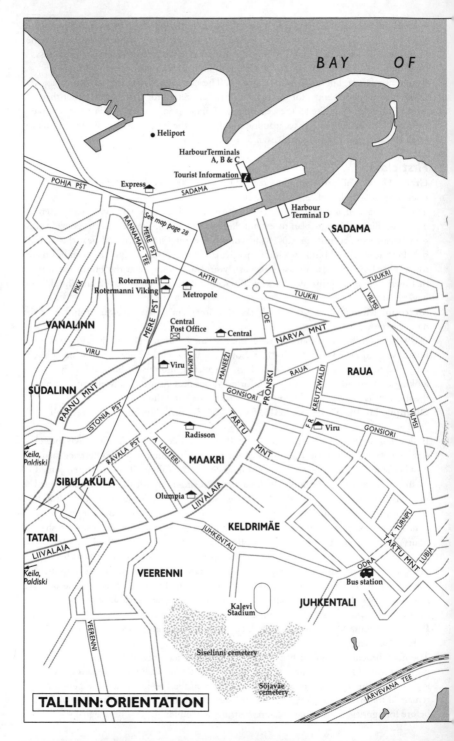

BAY OF

Heliport

HarbourTerminals A, B & C

Tourist Information

Express

SADAMA

Harbour Terminal D

SADAMA

POHJA PST

RANNAMAE TEE

MERE PST

See map page 28

AHTRI

TUUKRI

TUUKRI

VILMSI

PIKK

Rotermanni

Rotermanni Viking

Metropole

JOE

VANALINN

Central Post Office

Central

NARVA MNT

VIRU

A LAIKMAA

MANEEZI

PRONSKI

RAUA

KREUTZWALDI

RAUA

SÜDALINN

Viru

GONSIORI

F R

Viru

GONSIORI

I VILMSI

PARNU MNT

ESTONIA PST

TARTU

MNT

Keila, Paldiski

RAVALA PST

A LAUTERI

Radisson

MAAKRI

SIBULAKÜLA

Olümpia

LIIVALAIA

KELDRIMÄE

K. TURNPU

TARTU MNT

LUBJA

TATARI

JUHKENTALI

LIIVALAIA

Keila, Paldiski

VEERENNI

ODRA

Bus station

VEERENNI

Kalevi Stadium

JUHKENTALI

Siselinni cemetery

Sõjaväe cemetery

JARVEVANA TEE

TALLINN: ORIENTATION

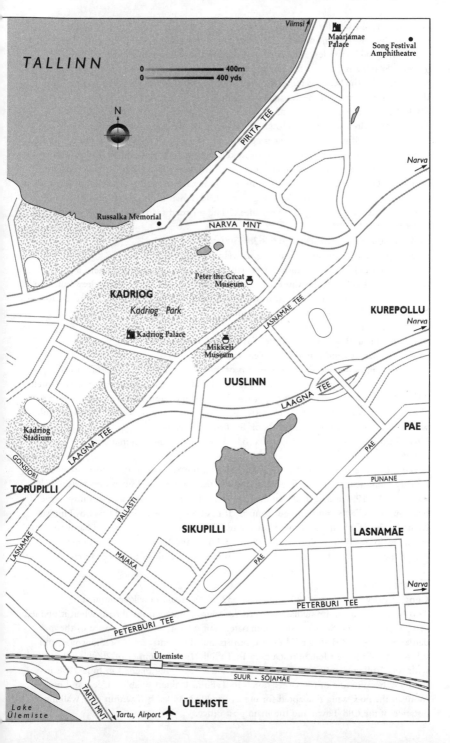

conveniently situated for tourists interested in the Old Town and business visitors needing the government ministries. In 1997 President Meri opened the new Presidential Suite which will doubtless remain one of the most expensive in Tallinn at £250/US$400 a night, but the remaining 86 rooms are more modestly priced. The hotel is run by the Scandic Hotel Group that also operates the Santa Barbara in Tallinn, the Ranna in Pärnu and the Karupesa in Otepää.

Park Kreutzwaldi 23, tel: 630 5305, fax: 630 5315, email: park@parkhotel.ee

Formerly the dreaded Kungla Hotel which could barely claim two-star status, the site transformed itself within a few weeks during the summer of 1997 and has never looked back. It has pioneered rooms for non-smokers, for the disabled and for those with allergies as well as round-the-clock gambling, fortunately in a casino with a separate entrance. Rooms are larger here than in most other hotels, and the restaurant has very low prices for excellent food. Walking to the Old Town is just about possible, and essential as the surroundings are very bleak. The guarded car park is free of charge to hotel guests.

St Petersbourg Rataskaevu 7, tel: 628 6500, fax: 628 6565, email: stpetersbourg@consul-hotels.com, web: consul-hotels.com.

The St Petersbourg (spelt as in the Estonian) is under the same management as the deluxe Park Hotel and suits those who want a comfortable Old Town address but who do not miss luxury. Its location near to many famous clubs and restaurants appeals to visitors who can dispense with sleep for much of the night. It is one of the very few hotels in Tallinn to offer a baby-sitting service.

Santa Barbara Roosikrantsi 2a, tel: 631 3991, fax: 631 3992, email: stbarbara@scandic-hotels.ee, web: scandic-hotels.com.

An austere limestone façade from the turn of the century hides a very professional operation which is run by the Scandic group who also operate the nearby Palace Hotel. The cellar restaurant is completely German, with no intrusion from Estonia or anywhere else. It has 53 rooms so staff get to know all the guests, many of whom are now regulars, which makes the hotel difficult to book for first-time visitors.

Viru Viru Valjak 4, tel: 630 1390, fax: 630 1303, email: reservation@viru.ee, web: www.viru.ee.

Being the centre of the tourism trade for much of the Soviet era, the enormous Viru initially found it hard to redefine its role in the face of competition and ever-rising standards. By 1997 it had finally undergone a complete renovation and can now serve both business clients and fastidious tourists. It has become very biased towards Finnish clients, some of whom can provide unwanted liveliness late on Friday and Saturday evenings. Its location is excellent for the Old Town and for local shops. Tourists determined to have a bath rather than a shower are more likely to succeed here.

Tourist class

Central Narva mnt 7, tel: 633 9800, fax: 633 9900, email: hotell@central.ee.

This hotel became an immediate favourite of tour operators from abroad when it opened in 1995 as it had no Soviet past to eliminate. Staff were immediately aware of the demands and eccentricities of Western tourists and the Primavera Restaurant was, and still is, one of the best Italian restaurants in Tallinn. In the summer of 2000 a full meal with wine still cost only 275EEK a head. When a new wing opened in June 1998 it suddenly became one of the larger hotels in Tallinn. It offers disabled access and one room in the new wing is adapted for use by disabled guests. It is within easy walking distance of the Old Town and the main post office.

Dzingel Manniku 89, tel: 610 5201, fax: 585411.
Situated in Nomme, Tallinn's most exclusive suburb, the Dzingel is in fact one of its simplest hotels. Regular long-stay visitors find its facilities perfectly adequate in view of the low prices charged, and many tourists are happy both in winter and in summer with its quiet location beside a pinewood. The bus journey into the town centre takes about 20 minutes. It is one of the few hotels where the staff happily and openly speak Russian although they can manage basic English. The restaurant is dull and surprisingly expensive. There is a late-night supermarket in the same block which can provide the ingredients for a varied picnic.

Mihkli Endla 23, tel: 666 4800, fax: 666 4888.
As one of the first tourist-class hotels to open near the town centre, and with only 50 rooms, success came too easily and the service still reflects this. Everything works smoothly but the human element on the hotel side is often missing. The restaurant and bar are, however, a pleasant contrast and prices are low.

Rotermanni Tel: 613 7900, fax: 613 7999, email: rothotel@infonet.ee; and
Rotermanni Viiking Tel: 660 1934, fax: 613 7901, email: viiking@anet.ee.
These two hotels share the same address, Mere pst 6a, and are very similar. Just 200m from the Viru Gates, this modest complex opened in summer 1998 and immediately became popular amongst individual tourists. It has been converted from an abandoned factory site and both hotels have about 35 rooms. Fortunately only the exterior shows signs of this past. Estonia, like Britain, is rapidly replacing losses in manufacturing with profits in tourism.

Susi Peterburi 48, tel: 630 3200, fax: 630 3400, email: susi@online.ee.
An estate agent would probably describe the location as 'unprepossessing' since it is surrounded by factories and a petrol station, and is on the wide St Petersburg motorway. It is literally the high-point of Tallinn at 55m above sea level. On May 14 1343, the St George's Day rebellion took place here. It had started further north on April 23 and this was the nearest point to Tallinn that Estonian forces would reach. Over 10,000 were killed in a desperate attempt to overthrow the Teutonic Knights. A plaque in the hotel lobby commemorates the battle. The hotel is more comfortable and more modern than any of the other tourist-class hotels outside the centre and is easily accessible by tram. The pictures displayed on its staircase put many of Tallinn's museums to shame. There are oils, lithographs, and watercolours showing contemporary and historical Tallinn; other pictures are of country scenes. They are well-lit and sensibly framed and of course can be seen 24 hours a day. Should the lift break down, this gallery is more than adequate compensation.

Wam Maria Asunduse 15, tel: 611 9500, fax: 611 9502, email: wammaria@online.ee.
The suburb of Lasnamae where this hotel is situated has really nothing to offer. The surroundings are horrendous – dreary tower blocks interspersed with abandoned fields – but with 120 modernised rooms and very reasonable prices it suits groups with a coach or visitors on a budget planning a long stay. Many rooms have baths, a rarity in Tallinn. The opulence of Kadriog Park is a walk of 15 minutes away.

Food and drink

There is now such a choice of restaurants in Tallinn that it is invidious to attempt a short list. Every major nation is represented, and more unusual ones include Argentina, Georgia, Lithuania and Scotland. Hawaiian and Thai food appeared for the first time in 2000 and Russian food also staged a come-back then, having been completely rejected in the years immediately following independence.

Detailed descriptions of restaurants appear in *The City Paper*, shorter ones in *Tallinn In Your Pocket*. A dark entrance, down poorly maintained stairs in a side street, is usually a clear lead to good food and value. Bright lights at street level should be avoided. Exploration need no longer be limited to the Old Town; competition there is driving many new entrants to open up in the suburbs. At the time of writing, nobody has opened a revivalist Soviet restaurant, though the success of such ventures in Riga and in former East Berlin must in due course tempt some embittered members of the Russian-speaking community in Tallinn. Pleasant cafés have been mentioned when they coincide with a walking itinerary, as most fortunately do. Most of the following restaurants have been open for several years and are popular with tourists, ex-pats and local residents. Apologies in advance to the many other excellent restaurants which with more space would also have been included.

Balthasar Raekoja Plats 11, tel: 627 6400. Garlic dominates every course here, even the ice-cream, but above all in the salads. Whilst other dishes do appear on the menu, they tend to be as appetising as a vegetarian option in a steakhouse. Opening in early 2000, the restaurant took over the top floor of the former pharmacy (see page 33) and has kept as much of the original wooden furnishings as was practical. With its views over the Town Hall Square, it is tempting to linger here but it also offers a quiet respite over lunch between morning and afternoon sightseeing tours. The range of short drinks at the bar can be equally tempting at other times of day.

Eeslitall (The Donkey's Stable) Dunkir 4, tel: 631 3755. In the early days after independence, this restaurant was an immediate indication of changing times. Whilst its easy-going service, French sauces, enormous menus and wine-lists may now seem normal for Tallinn, it then set a trend which other restaurants took several years to emulate. Young and old both dine happily here (an unusual combination in Tallinn), although only the young would consider staying in the spartan hostel of the same name upstairs.

Eesti Maja Lauteri 1, tel: 645 5252. Do not expect quick service here or even staff with much English, but instead be ready for enormous portions and rich food at each course. It will be hard to spend more than £6/US$10 a head and many eat their fill for much less. The vegetable soup makes a good meal in itself at lunch time. The building also houses *Global Estonian*, an English-language bi-annual magazine well worth buying for the tough interviews they give to local politicians willing to meet them.

Exit Sauna 2, tel: 644 2031. This restaurant has clearly found a market for those who like Georgian cuisine but prefer Estonian hours and prices together with a calmer ambience than is normal in Tbilisi. Vegetarians and anyone who can tolerate bland food should stay away; others will be amply satisfied. Georgian wines are served, but hopefully a wider selection can soon be available.

Karl Friedrich Raekoja Plats 5, tel: 627 2413. The grand location on Town Hall Square might suggest ostentation and prices to match but fortunately this has not happened. Each floor caters for a different age-group but it is the top floor that is recommended. Oldies should book well in advance for a table overlooking the square and enjoy a lingering lunch or dinner. Its fish salads are to be recommended and it has its own beer, called Karl Friedrich. The long walk up and down is well worthwhile.

Klafira Vene 4, tel: 667 5144. If Soviet Russia has been banished for good from Estonia, the Tsarist aristocracy is making an effective come-back here instead. Perhaps they were wise to wait until 2000, nine years after the re-establishment of Estonian independence, before doing so. Their food is strictly Russian, their wine is sensibly French. That rich Estonians are firstly willing to come and then secondly even to speak Russian to the staff shows the high standards the restaurant has set. Allow a full evening here and do not consider the cost beforehand. It will be expensive by Estonian standards, but not by London or New York ones.

Olde Hansa Vanaturg 1, tel: 631 4241. Ignore the silly name and enjoy the candles (there is no electric light). Some tables are for two, but don't come here for a quiet, intimate evening. This is really a party venue so come as a group and with a very empty stomach. Portions are enormous, even for soup and ice-cream.

Primavera Narva 7, tel: 633 9891. The bland façades that still blight much of this road out of Tallinn hide a number of bars and restaurants. This one has already been mentioned under the Central Hotel as it is in the same building, but a second listing needs no apology. Mediocre Italian food is spreading across Estonia at an alarming rate, but standards here for all courses remain excellent, even if the quality of the wine does not always match that of the food.

Toomkooli Toomkooli 13, tel: 644 6613. Those who are not deterred by the awkward location at the back of the Old Town are rewarded on arrival with an extensive international menu and wine list but prices that have stayed Estonian. Minimal music and very heavy wooden chairs give a more formal air to the surroundings than is now common in many Tallinn restaurants, but in a town now so geared to the young, this should be taken as a compliment.

Vanaema Juures (Grandma's Place), Rataskaevu 10/12, tel: 631 3928. This is probably Tallinn's most famous restaurant, but not even a visit from Hilary Clinton has gone to its head. The valid and repeated descriptions – good home cooking, a traditional décor, a cosy atmosphere – degenerate into cliché but few would dispute them. The furnishings and photographs from the previous independence period (1918–40), together with discreet music from that time, deter the young and raucous, but others will immediately appreciate the originality of total Estonian surroundings.

Zeppelin Tartu 6, tel: 661 2099. This restaurant was probably the last one in Tallinn to switch from an analogue phone number to a digital one. As it is not the sort of place that would expect advance bookings, this probably did not matter. Its Lithuanian potato dumplings are the main culinary feature but the company is as intriguing as the food here. Old Russian labourers drop in for a snack and beer, rich and poor Estonians tend just to drink here. Their dress and drinks order will typecast them immediately. The former will choose Western spirits and cocktails, the latter Estonian vodka or even tea. A black décor and striplights predominated in 2000 but it is the sort of place that might decide on a new provocation in 2001.

Entertainment

Young people congregate at Linnahall, the Concert Hall beside the Heliport near the harbour. Live pop music is staged most evenings.

Classical concerts are held in the Old Town Hall, the Estonia Concert Hall, the House of Blackheads and in St Nicholas Church. In most cases tickets are only sold on the day or the day before the concert so there is no need to prebook from abroad.

Films are always subtitled and never dubbed so tourists can see films missed at home without any problem. The Soprus Cinema in the Old Town at Vana-Post 8 is easily accessible from many hotels.

Shopping

Monday to Friday most shops open 10.00–18.00 and on Saturday they close earlier, usually around 16.00. On Sunday they stay closed. However, those in the Old Town of interest to tourists open in the summer 10.00–19.00 seven days a week. Supermarkets open seven days a week, usually 09.00–21.00. For books and postcards, the Tourist Information Centre on Town Hall Square (Raekoja Plats 10) has a good selection, all reasonably priced. The widest selection of books in English on Estonia is at Kupar, Harju 1, just below St Nicholas Church.

A one-stop shop for souvenirs, since it stocks linen, woolen jerseys, ceramics, and wooden toys is Puupood, Lai 5. Although in the Old Town, it is just off the main tourist circuit so prices are very reasonable.

For those who can restrict themselves to wooden dolls, Nukupood on Town Hall Square (Raekoja Plats 18) is conveniently located and has an enormous choice.

Kaubamaja is Tallinn's largest department store and is situated halfway between the Viru and Radisson Hotels at Gonsiori 2. It will supply any forgotten toilet article or item of clothing, and is worth visiting for its CDs of Estonian music and for its porcelain.

Medical services

Emergency services Fire: 112; Ambulance: 112; Police: 110.
Dentist Kentmanni Hambaravi, Kenmanni 11a; open 09.00–19.00 seven days a week.
Hospital Tallinn Central Hospital, Ravi 18.
Pharmacy None are open 24 hours, but Koduapteek, in the Kaubamaja Department Store, is open seven days a week; Mon–Fri 10.00–21.00, Sat 10.00–20.00 and Sun 10.00–18.00.

Embassies

Canada Toom-Kooli 13, tel: 627 3311, fax 627 3312
Latvia Tõnismägi 10, tel: 646 1313, fax: 631-1366
Lithuania Uus 15, tel: 631 4030, fax: 641 2013
UK Wismari 6, tel: 667 4700,fax: 667 4723
USA Kentmanni 20, tel: 631 2021, fax: 631 2025

Places of worship

Church services are held in English every Sunday at the Holy Ghost Church (Puhavaimu). There is no synagogue in Tallinn.

WHAT TO SEE

Tourists tend to concentrate on the Old Town but many modern buildings are of interest too. The main sights in the Old Town can be covered in one day but more time would be needed for other visits. A route for a day-long walking tour is suggested and then another day should be allowed for Pirita and Kadriog. Several sights outside Tallinn warrant a half-day on their own.

Museums usually close on Mondays though some close on Tuesdays as well. Opening hours tend to be 11.00–17.00, but for pre-booked groups they can open specially on closed days. Admission charges vary between 5EEK and 30EEK so are still quite low by Western standards.

A walking tour through Tallinn

The tour starts at the final Soviet architectural legacy to Estonia – the **National Library** (Eesti Rahvusraamatukogu) – begun in 1986 and completed in 1993. It is situated on the intersection of Endla and Tõnismägi close to the Mihkli and Santa Barbara Hotels. Its predecessor was opened in 1918 in the parliament building on Toompea and had 2,000 books, a number that only increased to 6,000 during the 1930s. After World War II, the history of the library mirrored that of the country as a whole. Its bleakest period was until 1953 when most of the collection was of Russian books translated into Estonian. On Stalin's death, the library was renamed after one of Estonia's most famous authors, Friedrich Kreutzwald, a clear sign of a more liberal climate. By 1967 funds were specifically allocated for books in the Estonian language and in 1988, shortly before this new building was supposed to open, it was renamed the National Library and the formerly restricted sections were opened to all. The design seems to symbolise *glasnost*: light streams in through many massive windows, and large open shelves display a wide cross-section of the two million books stored there. It will remain a grandiose memorial to massive public sector investment. Yet it was almost not completed. The fading Soviet government was not eager to continue funding projects outside Russia and the new Estonian one was faced with bills it could not pay. On June 28 1989, between four and five thousand volunteers joined the building works under the slogan 'Dig a grave for Stalinism'. The director, Ivi Eenmaa, later to become mayor of Tallinn, single-handedly fought Moscow and then each new Estonian government for adequate funds and was finally able to open the library on February 22 1993, two days before National Day.

Day tickets can be bought in the entrance hall, which is decorated with prints by one of Estonia's most famous contemporary artists, Eduard Wiiralt. To encourage regular use, the library has several music rooms, shops, a café and even piped music. On a bitter winter's day, tourists may wish to await a change in the weather amongst the many English-language books and journals now available there. As one of Estonia's many preparations for entry into the EU, there are also large French, German and Scandinavian reading rooms. Normally, however, visitors should head straight for the 8th floor to view two contrasting Tallinns. To the north and east is the Tallinn of the posters – the spires, turrets and golden domes. In the other direction is a part of the town best seen at this distance, consisting of abandoned factories and fading tower blocks, with minimal intrusion of any colour.

Cross the road to **St Charles's Church** (Kaarli Kirik). In its almost Episcopalian simplicity, it is the perfect antidote to what is to come later in the walk. It is a massive and austere late 19th-century limestone building which seats 1,500 people and is the centre of the Estonian Orthodox Church. At a time when Russian rule was becoming more oppressive, its size discreetly symbolised Estonian nationalism. The name comes from an original wooden church built in the late 17th century during the reign of the Swedish King Charles XI. Although the church took 20 years to build, the large altar fresco was completed in ten days in 1879 by the well-known artist Johann Koler.

Upper Town

On leaving the church, turn right into Kaarli and then take the first road on the left, Toompea. At the first crossroads, note the simple **monument** to August

TALLINN: OLD TOWN

20 1991, the date Estonia declared independence during the failed Moscow coup. Had it been necessary, Estonians were ready to use the walls and towers to defend the Old Town from possible Soviet attack, but the quick collapse of the coup and the immediate recognition by the USSR of Estonian independence prevented this. Looking ahead is a monument that dates from the 15th century, **Pikk Hermann** (Tall Hermann Tower). It has withstood numerous invasions and remains intact. Its height of nearly 50m is supported by foundations 15m deep. The first Estonian flag was flown from here in 1884, 34 years before the country was to become independent. Subsequent conquerors always marked their success by raising a flag here. A German guidebook printed in 1942 lists 12 major dates in Tallinn's history, the last being August 28 1941 when the German flag was raised over Pikk Hermann. During the Soviet occupation, the Estonian SSR flag was flown, but the Estonian national flag returned in 1989. It is raised at sunrise and lowered at sunset, except at midsummer when it is not lowered at all on the night of June 23/24. The blue in the flag represents the sky, black the soil, and white the aspirations of the Estonian people. There are plans to open the Tower to visitors in 2001.

Turn right down the hill (Komandandi) to **Kiek in de Kok** ('Peep in the Kitchen'). The reason for the name becomes obvious as one climbs the 45m to the sixth floor and peers into more and more houses; only the steeples of St Nicholas and St Olaf are higher. From the initial construction in the 15th century until the late 17th century, the tower grew in height and width with walls and floors as thick as 4m, but ironically, after a Russian attack in 1577, it never saw military action again. The last time it was prepared for war was in the 1850s when the Russians feared a British invasion during the Crimean War. On the top floor, note the model of the 'plague doctor' with a waxed tunic and cape impregnated with herbs. He carries a cane to touch patients to avoid any risk of infection. The main exhibition on the top three floors covers Tallinn's military history. The lower floors are now used as an art gallery. Kiek in de Kok does not have any catering, but the nearest tower to it, Megedi, can be recommended in this respect. This tower, like most in the city wall, dates from the late 14th century and was continually enlarged during the 15th century. From around 1800 when its defensive potential declined, it was converted into a barracks. In 1980, the top floor became a **café** which uses the name Megedi, and the ground floor a **restaurant**, called Neitsitorn.

On leaving Kiek in de Kok turn back up the hill and turn right into Toompea which ends in the square between the parliament building and the **Alexander Nevsky Cathedral**. The juxtaposition of these two buildings appropriately contrasts official Estonian and Russian architecture. The one is simple, small and functional, the other elaborate, and deliberately powerful. Ironically, the Tsarist power that it represented was to last only a further 17 years. Entering the cathedral represents a symbolic departure from Estonia. No-one speaks Estonian and no books are sold in Estonian. It is a completely Russian architectural outpost dominating the Tallinn skyline and was built between 1894 and 1900 at a time when the Russian Empire was determined to stifle the burgeoning nationalistic movements in Estonia. It was provocatively named after Alexander Nevsky since he had conquered much of Estonia in the late 13th century. The icons, the mosaics and the 15-ton bell were all imported from St Petersburg. Occasionally plans are discussed, as they were in the 1930s, for the removal of the cathedral as it is so architecturally and politically incompatible with everything else in Toompea, but it is unlikely that any government would risk the inevitable hostility that would arise amongst the Russian-speaking population of Tallinn.

The **Parliament building**, most of which dates from 1921, is one of very few in the Old Town to have seen frequent reconstruction, the last time resulting from a fire in 1917 which may have been started by the Bolsheviks. The façade is a simple classicist one, and all the stone and wooden materials are local. Earlier buildings on this site had usually served as a governor's residence although, in the late 19th century, the building became a prison. The earliest fort was built on this site in 1227 and the northern and western walls date from this time.

Continue up the hill along Toom-Kooli with the post office on your right. By the end of 2000, this street should be completely restored, the first one to be back to its 1920s' glory. Straight ahead, on Kiriku Square, is the **Dome Church** (Toomkirik), sometimes called St Mary's Cathedral. Work started soon after the Danish invasion in the early 13th century and the first church was consecrated by King Waldemar II in 1240. It was slowly enlarged over the next four centuries as funds became available, but much of the interior was destroyed in the fire of 1684 which devastated the whole of the Old Town. The Swedish King Charles XI imposed a special tax for the rebuilding of Tallinn so within two years the church had been largely restored. The baroque spire was added in 1778 so in all the church has an architectural history of over 600 years. The altarpiece, painted in 1866, is the work of the Baltic German artist Eduard von Gebhardt. The organ, probably the most powerful in Estonia, was made in Frankfurt-an-der-Oder in 1913 so is the last to have been imported from Germany before World War I.

The **Dome Church** was the religious centre for the main families of the Tallinn Baltic German community; their coats of arms cover the church walls, their tombstones cover the floor, although a few tombstones are of Swedish origin. At the back of the church are two tombstones commemorating the butchers' and the shoemakers' guilds. The most impressive tomb, which is beside the altar, is that of the French mercenary Pontus de la Gardie, who served in the Swedish army in many battles with the Russians. In the north aisle is a monument to Samuel Greig, a Scots admiral who served in the Tsarist navy from 1763 until his death in 1788. The inscription expresses the sorrow of Catherine II at his death. Like many Scots predecessors and successors, he had a distinguished career in this navy. He helped to destroy the Turkish fleet at the battle of Chesme in 1770 and to build up Kronstadt into a major naval base. Next to this monument is one to Adam von Krusenstern, the Baltic German who led the first Russian expedition to sail around the world, in 1803. Note the two globes, both of which omit New Zealand.

Turning left out of the church, the **Estonian Art Museum** dominates the opposite side of Kiriku Plats. Although it looks as though it was built as an art gallery, it was first used in the 19th century as the headquarters of the Estonian Knighthood, a major business guild. During the first independence period (1920–40) it was the Foreign Ministry and for much of the Soviet period served as the National Library. The names of the 19th- and 20th-century artists displayed here are sadly unknown outside Estonia, but many styles will be recognised by visitors. Both in the Tsarist period and under independence, most Estonian artists of note studied in Paris so the prevalent style there is reflected in their pictures. Konrad Magi (1878–1925) is the most famous landscape artist and his pictures here are of many regions in Estonia.

Lower Town

Turning sharp right from the museum along Toom Ruutli leads, after 150m, to the main **viewpoint** across Tallinn. It is inevitably crowded during the tourist season so an alternative can be recommended along Rahukohtu, on the corner of Ruutli. Rahukohtu also starts on the right-hand side of the gallery. To reach the lower town, it is necessary in either case to return along Piiskopi towards the Russian cathedral and then to walk down the steps of Luhike Jalg ('Short Leg'), rather a misnomer as there are in fact about 100 steps. At the top, though, are several tempting **cafés**, **souvenir shops** and well-maintained toilets which can provide a respite before continuing the walk. Before starting the descent, look to the left along Pikk Jalg ('Long Leg'). The façade which commands one of the best views over Tallinn is modelled on the main building of Tartu University. Perhaps appropriately in view of the current strength of the Estonian economy, this imposing building houses the Ministry of Finance.

On the right at the end of Luhike Jalg is the **Adamson-Eric Museum**. Adamson-Eric (1902–68) was without doubt the most famous Estonian artist who worked during both the independence period and the Soviet era. This house has no links with him, although before being used as a museum it did have workshops for coppersmiths. The museum opened in 1983 and the collection is based on around 1,000 works bequeathed by his widow. These cover his whole life in both painting and applied art. Gifts from abroad have recently been added to the collection. Labels are in English.

Adamson-Eric's parents were able to pay for long periods of study during the 1920s in both Paris and Berlin. Elements of Fauvism and Cubism can be seen in many of his pictures but he was equally drawn to the Bauhaus and worked closely with Walter Gropius, George Grosz and Otto Dix. On his return to Estonia he first specialised in portraits, then added landscapes and broadened into applied arts. In this field, his work became as diverse as his painting. Around 1930 he began with tapestries and textiles and then added ceramics and metalwork to his range. Shortly before the war, he diversified even more, starting to work with leather and to design stage sets. He retreated with the Soviet army in 1941 and managed to maintain his artistic integrity despite the stringent demands of Soviet officialdom. With the inevitable lack of materials for applied art at this time, he concentrated again on painting.

In 1949 the political tide finally turned against him and he was expelled from the Communist Party, forced to give up his posts and sent into factory work. Although released in 1953 on Stalin's death, his health had deteriorated and he suffered a stroke in 1955. His reaction was simply to learn to paint as well with his left hand as he had previously done with his right! His health slowly improved and he was able to add porcelain painting and tile design to his work in the field of applied art. He remained active until shortly before his death in 1968.

Continuing down the hill, the steps become a road which continues to a junction. To the left is Rataskaevu and to the right, Ruutli, both roads which house some of Tallinn's most famous **restaurants**. On the corner of Luhike Jalg and Rataskaevu is Bakhos, one of Tallinn's best-value wine merchants. Many are the angry tourists who have shopped abroad at a so-called duty-free shop only to find the same bottle here at half the price. Ahead is **St Nicholas Church** (Niguliste). It is unusual in Tallinn in having been a military installation as well as a church with ample hiding places and secret exits to the city walls. In common, though, with other churches, it was first built in the 13th century and then expanded over the next 400 years. The original spire dated from 1696 and, being outside the town walls, the church was spared from the 1684 fire. It was, however, badly damaged during the Soviet air raid on Tallinn of March 9 1944 and the spire was only restored in 1984. Fortunately the carvings, chandeliers and pictures, many dating from the 16th century, had been removed before the raid. They are all now on display again and are particularly valuable given that so much similar work was either destroyed in the 1684 fire or suffered from neglect in more recent times. The interior of the church was slowly restored during the Soviet period from 1953 onwards. A small exhibition describes this work but captions are only in Russian and Estonian. St Nicholas has kept its role as a museum and concert hall so has not been reconsecrated. The life of St Nicholas is portrayed in the altarpiece, over 6m wide and painted in Lübeck by Herman Rode between 1478 and 1482. Note the one very modern addition – a stained glass window by the contemporary artist Rait Prääts whose glass can also be seen at the National Library and the Sakala Conference Centre.

On leaving the church, turn right to the **memorial** to the writer Eduard Vilde (1865–1933). The illustrations depict scenes from his novels and plays. The two stones represent an open book. Proceed down the steps to Harju and then turn right again. This bombed site has deliberately been left as it was after the raid of March 9 1944. The inscription commemorates the 463 people killed by the raid. Returning along Harju and then Kullassepa brings one into Raekoja Plats, or Town Hall Square. Just before reaching the square, it is worth turning right for a few minutes into the small alley, Raekoja. The building on the right, which now houses the **Photographic Museum**, was the town's main prison until the early 19th century. Estonia has always had a strong photographic tradition and this museum displays not only cameras produced in the country but photographs from the 19th and early 20th centuries. It is fortunate that many pictures from the first independence period have survived. The basement is a gallery for the display and sale of contemporary photographs.

Town Hall Square (Raekoja Plats) is similar to many in northern Germany as it was the commercial centre for the Baltic Germans. In the 16th century, the Germans accounted for about 1,500 of Tallinn's total population of around 5,000. They maintained all positions of authority, ruling from the Town Hall and the surrounding buildings. The square was the centre for all major events in the town, happy and tragic. Carnivals, weddings and Christmas have all been regularly celebrated here and the Tallinn Old Days Festival, held each year in early June, recreates the carnival atmosphere with its musical and artistic events. What was probably the world's first Christmas tree was displayed here in 1441. Yet the square was also the site for frequent executions and floggings, its grimmest day being in 1806 when 72 peasants were executed following a failed uprising.

Nowadays it is hard to imagine such a background, as work and punishment have given way to total relaxation. **Cafés** surround the square and spread into it during the summer. The Café Tristan and Isolde, in the Town Hall building but with an entrance from the square, is hardly noticed by tourists so offers a quiet respite from all the activity elsewhere, as well as much lower prices. One of the few buildings on the square that kept its original function until recently was the **Pharmacy** which dates from 1422. Tour guides often like to point out that this is 70 years before Columbus discovered America. The coat of arms of the Burchardt family, who ran the **pharmacy** for 400 years, can be seen over the entrance. Amongst the medicines they dispensed unlikely to find contemporary favour were fish eyes, lambswool and ground rubies, but patients were at least offered these potions with a glass of hot wine to help digestion. In 1725 Peter the Great summoned Burchardt to St Petersburg, but he died before Burchardt could reach him. In late 1998 the pharmacy was under reconstruction. In 2000, the ground floor was opened as an antique shop and the first floor as a restaurant but much of the original design remains.

The **Town Hall** is the only late Gothic building still intact in Estonia, dating largely from the 15th century. The exterior and the interior are equally impressive. It was the administrative and judicial centre of the town and the extensive range of woodwork and paintings in the Council Chamber mainly reflect judicial themes. Six centuries of Tallinn's history have been determined in this room and, with the restoration of independence, its role will now increase. For much of this time, there were clearly ample funds in the public treasury, as is shown by the opulence of the candelabra, the money-chests and the size of the wine cellars. One of the carvings on the magistrates' bench of David and Goliath is often taken to symbolise the relationship between Tallinn Council and its nominal masters on Toompea in the Old Town. The Council Chamber has always been heated, unlike the neighbouring Citizens Hall; dancing, eating and drinking at winter receptions have to be particularly vigorous to compensate for this lack. The original weathervane on the top of the spire, known as Old Thomas, was destroyed in the 1944 raid but the rest of the building was spared. German architects, artists and craftsmen were employed for the Town Hall and all documents were written only in German, even during the long periods of Swedish and Russian rule. Only the tapestries have a non-German origin, being Flemish. It is sometimes possible to climb up the spire; the view from the top offers excellent shots of the Old Town for photographers but the stairs are steep and in poor condition so this is only recommended for the fit and determined.

Across the square, opposite the Town Hall, are several short streets which lead to Pikk. Saiakaik is the smallest street in Tallinn. Take any of these and turn right to the junction of Pikk and Pühavaimu for the **Holy Ghost Church** (Pühavaimu). That it does not face due east suggests that there was already a complex street layout by 1300 when building began. It was the first church to hold services in Estonian and the first extract from the Catechism in the Estonian language was printed for use here in 1535. The 1684 fire destroyed much of the interior and the original spire but the current spire is now the oldest in Tallinn, dating from 1688. Of the same age inside the church is the large wooden clock on the north wall, carved by Christian Ackermann from Königsberg. Spared from the fire was the folding altar carved in 1483 by the

Lübeck artist Bernt Notke. Only the organ is modern, dating from 1929; it is one of the few in Tallinn's churches built by an Estonian and not imported from Germany.

Cross Pikk for the Ajaloomuuseum, the **Estonian History Museum**. The building is as impressive as any of the contents, perhaps more so. Dating from 1410, it was the headquarters of the Great Guild and has changed little since. Visitors who arrive when the museum is shut can at least be consoled by the sight of the 15th-century door knockers. Exhibits inside are well labelled in English and concentrate on archaeology and costumes. Of more contemporary interest is the coin collection and a section on the founding of the local freemasons in the late 1770s. They were later banned by Alexander I in 1822.

As you turn left into Pikk, the new Russian Embassy is on the left and on the right is Maiasmokk, a café that has deliberately stayed old-fashioned both in decor and in prices. Tea in 2000 was 6EEK and cakes 8EEK. The name translates appropriately as 'sweet tooth'.

Pikk has two of the few notable **Jugendstil buildings** in Tallinn, both designed by Jacques Rosenbaum. Number 18, next to Maiasmokk, has a flamboyant Egyptian theme, number 25 on the corner of Hobusepea is more modest.

Number 61, built across Pagari, and probably the blandest building in the Old Town, was the KGB headquarters in Soviet times, and now houses the Interior Ministry. Unlike its opposite number in Vilnius, it has not been opened to the public.

Next on the left is **St Olav's Church** (Oleviste), named after the king of Norway and now a Baptist church. When first built in 1267, its 140m-high steeple made it one of the tallest buildings in the world. This steeple caught fire in 1820, having been struck by lightning, and its replacement 'only' reaches 120m. It is still, however, a major feature of the Tallinn skyline. Much of the interior of the church was destroyed in the 1820 fire, as it had been in an earlier one in 1625. The rebuilding, completed in 1840, provides a contrast to most other churches in Tallinn for its plain interior. Tsar Nicholas I donated a large bell in 1850 and his generosity is noted in an inscription written, with no trace of irony, in German. The organ dates from this time but the chandeliers are earlier and have been donated from other buildings.

A few yards further down on the right is **Fat Margaret's Tower** which houses the **Maritime Museum** (Meremuuseum). Outside is a plaque unveiled by Prince Andrew in May 1998 which commemorates British naval involvement in the battles between Estonian forces and the Bolsheviks in 1918–20. The tower was built between 1510 and 1529. Some walls are as much as 6m thick. In 1830 it became a prison but after being stormed in 1917 it was left as a ruin for the next 60 years. Polish restorers, famous throughout the former Soviet bloc, finally came to the rescue in 1978. Climb to the roof for very photogenic views of St Olav's and the town gates. The museum covers shipbuilding, cartography, port-construction and fish-breeding. There is a recent exhibit on the *Estonia* which sank off the Finnish coast on September 28 1994 with the loss of 850 lives. A model of one of the boats has political interest. It was named first after Viktor Kingisepp, leader of the underground Estonian Communist Party in the early 1920s and then in 1990 was renamed after Gustav Sule, who was Estonian javelin champion in the 1930s.

Turn right out of the museum and leave the Old Town on Suur Rannavarara, the continuation of Pikk. On the right is the **monument** to those who died in the *Estonia* tragedy in 1994. It can be interpreted in a number of ways, perhaps symbolising the boat breaking into two or the total divide between life and death. Cross Pohja Puiestee to the disused power station, now ironically the **Energy Museum** (Energeetikamuuseum). Built originally in the late 1920s, it then had some claim to Jugendstil influence but many subsequent alterations have completely removed any hint of beauty and style. For tourists who never had the chance to visit Tirana's 'Albania Today' or Chinese museums during the Cultural Revolution, this is a splendidly flamboyant substitute. Ironically for an energy museum, many of the lights do not work but those that do illuminate graphs that all start at zero in 1945 and shoot up to the stratosphere throughout the 1950s, 1960s and 1970s. Engineers will be interested in the various meters and generators on display. The only hint of modern Estonia is in an occasional photograph. The basement could not provide a greater contrast with all its striplights working and its displays of contemporary abstract art. Modern Estonia does indeed have energy but it is now portrayed more metaphorically than literally.

Return into the Old Town and walk behind Fat Margaret along Uus. Number 31 is the **Scottish Club**, in fact a restaurant open to all which has the best maintained lawn in Estonia. Next door is a whisky shop, a clear testimony to Tallinn's affluence and passion for Western consumer goods. It is hard to believe that until 1989 whisky was only available in foreign currency shops. Turn right into Olevimagi and then left into Vene. On the left is a smaller, but no less Russian version of the Alexander Nevsky Cathedral, **St Nicholas** Russian Orthodox church. Again no concessions are made to Estonia; everything is written, spoken and sung in Russian. It dates from the early 19th century. On the right at number 17 is the **City Museum** (Linnamuuseum). As with the History Museum, the building is as of much interest as the contents. Having escaped the fires that ravished so many buildings in the Old Town, this 14th-century merchant's house still has examples of 16th-century wooden panelling, windows and furniture. Many of the exhibits would now be regarded as politically incorrect in the West as they concentrate on the accoutrements of the rich; life below stairs and outside the guilds and churches is ignored. Nonetheless the collection shows the breadth of industry and culture developed in Tallinn from 1860 onwards. The arrival in 1870 of the railway from St Petersburg led to an increase in the population from 30,000 then to 160,000 by 1917. One anniversary the Estonians were forced to celebrate in 1910 was the 200th anniversary of the Russian conquest. This museum is well labelled in English and the postcard sets they sell are excellent value. The Museum closed for renovation in 2000 but should reopen late in 2001.

On the right are the ruins of the **Dominican Monastery**, founded in 1246 but destroyed during the Reformation in 1524 when the monks were forced to flee. Extensive archaeological excavations were carried out between 1954 and 1968 when the ruins were first opened to the public. Take a torch and wear sturdy shoes as the surviving ambulatories are poorly lit. Of most interest are the stone carvings by the 16th-century Dutch sculptor Arent Passer. Chamber music concerts take place here during the summer. On leaving the monastery, turn left into Vene and left again into Katariina Kaik. This tiny alleyway is where local ex-pats buy their **souvenirs** of Tallinn, as few tourists find it. Turn right at the end into Muurivahe, which runs below the city wall. Elderly Russians have stalls here, selling woollen sweaters, gloves and socks both in midsummer and in midwinter. The walk ends at the junction with Viru Street. To the left is the 15th-century Viru Gate, as formidable as the fortifications seen at the start of the walk. To the right is McDonald's; will it also last five centuries?

Elsewhere in Tallinn

Visitors with more time can see many other museums. Close to the Viru Gate at Vana Viru 14 and opposite the Viru Hotel is the **Fire-Fighting Museum**. Like the Energy Museum, it has not changed since the Soviet era so combines the didactic with the heroic. Dolls' houses show every possible cause of an accident in each room. Macabre photos abound of charred bodies, exploding television sets and open fires out of control. A panel lists medals awarded to local firemen until 1988 but none are listed after that year. It is a cruel comment to suggest that heroism in the Estonian fire service ceased at the restoration of independence in 1989. A number of horse-drawn and early motor fire engines are displayed. Although captions to all exhibits are only in Estonian and Russian, the staff hand out translation cards in English and German.

Back in the Old Town, in Lai, are the **Applied Arts Museum** at number 17 and the Health Museum at number 28–30. The former still sells the Soviet guidebook which boasts that the exhibits 'are really wonderful, conspicuous in their originality and can bear comparison with the best items of the world'. Exhibits from the Soviet period are now on the upper floors, and modern ones on the ground floor so visitors can judge the changes for themselves and whether such hyperbole applies to either era. In all fields the collections are extensive and show the Estonian dedication to pottery, weaving, glassmaking and woodwork that has surmounted all political regimes.

The **Health Museum** is one of the few totally contemporary museums in Tallinn and uses a range of models, toys, visual aids and colourful charts to show both adults and children the importance of healthy living. It is a brightly lit and well-thought-out display, a vivid contrast to many other museums. It may well be the only museum in the country with a hands-on element – two exercise bicycles are available for visitors.

Just outside the Old Town, behind the railway station at Kotzebue 16, is the **Dolls' Museum**. Opened in 1985 as a memorial to one of Lenin's closest colleagues, Mikhail Kalinin, it nonetheless even then had a small collection of toys. Kalinin is now forgotten and toys have taken over completely. Dolls and dolls' houses of course predominate, but there are also board games and toys from 1900 onwards, one of the few elements of Estonian life hardly touched by the changing political environment. The walk from the Old Town offers a completely changed architectural environment; Tallinn on the wrong side of the tracks becomes a town of poorly maintained wooden houses and an abandoned factory. The **market** beside the station is worth a stop of a few minutes. Excellent light refreshments are available at prices well below those elsewhere in the town and the choice of clothes, CDs, and gadgets gives a good reflection of mass Estonian taste.

A walk from the Viru Gate along either Pärnu mnt or Estonia pst, and then along Kaarli pst back to the National Library, passes the main buildings that remain from the end of the Tsarist period and the first independence period, so from 1900 until 1940. Jugendstil, neo-classicism and functualism are all represented here and it is to be hoped that developers do not get permission to make drastic changes. The **Estonian National Theatre** was in fact designed by a Finnish architect, Armas Lindgren, and opened in 1913, although the rebuilding that followed the bombing of Tallinn in 1944 was carried out under the Estonian architect Alar Kotli. The money for the original building was raised by private subscription and the Tsarist authorities attempted to block the project. They did briefly succeed in preventing the Estonian language from being used in any production. In 1918 the Estonian National Assembly met there.

On the opposite side of Estonia pst from the theatre is the **Estonian Bank Museum** which was modernised in the summer of 1998. The political history of the country is mirrored in this museum exactly through the currency. In 1928 the kroon was tied to the British pound but it floated after 1933 when Britain had left the Gold Standard. The current building dates from 1935 and manages to combine elements of neo-Gothic, neo-Renaissance and functualism. In its predecessor, Estonian independence was proclaimed on February 24 1918 and in this one, a temporary government was formed in September 1944 between the German and the Russian occupations.

The **Sakala Conference Centre** behind the bank is best known for the stained glass of Rait Prääts whose work can also be seen in St Nicholas Church and in the National Library. This area is likely to be developed soon with many office and hotel projects now under consideration. On Vabaduse Valjak (Freedom Square), the Palace Hotel and the Town Hall beside it both date from the 1930s. Their size and the imposing nature of similar buildings along Pärnu mnt testify to the confidence of the regime at the time. Behind them are a number of functualist buildings that survived the 1944 bombing raid.

A walk again from Viru Gate across Viru Square gives an appropriately unflattering picture of the construction that took place between 1960 and 1980. Looking back towards Narva mnt, the **Viru Hotel** is a major eyesore and the inevitable result of conflicting Soviet policies in the early 1970s. On the one hand tourists needed to be admitted to Tallinn to boost the country's international image, on the other they must not be allowed serious contact with the local population. An isolated tower block was obviously the answer, and until 1980, when some of the Olympic Games' events were held in Tallinn, the Viru was the only hotel for foreigners. Many probably only saw Tallinn from the bar on the 22nd floor. Estonians console themselves with the knowledge that the Viru Hotel did at least spare them a 'Stalinist cathedral' which was one proposal for this location, or an enormous memorial to Mikhail Kalinin which was another. Kalinin, a member of Lenin's Politburo, lived in Tallinn for three years between 1901 and 1904 whilst he was banished from St Petersburg. A Soviet guidebook published in 1987 blames the lack of 'artistic and economic means' for the failure of both projects. One published a year or two later might have given the true reason, the intense local opposition. A more modest statue of Kalinin was instead erected on Tower Square, a park between the Old Town and the railway station. Behind the Viru Hotel is a department store built somewhat earlier, in the 1960s. In the Soviet period it was crudely divided between a shop for the local population and one for foreigners. Both were flagships in their different ways. The local shop was better supplied than most in St Petersburg and Moscow and the notorious 'Berioshka', which took only precious *valuta* (hard foreign currencies) in exchange for vodka, wooden dolls and fur hats, was the only Soviet shop that thousands of tourists would ever enter. Before the war, the main Tallinn synagogue stood on this site.

EXCURSIONS FROM TALLINN
Rocca al Mare Open Air Museum

This deserves a half-day to itself, ideally in balmy summer weather. Take the 21 or 21b bus from the railway station and also take a sweater as protection against the wind on the many non-balmy days. A winter excursion on a sunny day is worthwhile to get some impression of what most Estonians used to endure month in, month out, every winter. Visitors at midsummer on June 23 can enjoy the all-night celebrations held here. The name in Italian means 'cliff beside the sea' and was given by the original owner of the estate when it was bought in 1863. The museum was founded in 1957 and first opened to the public in 1964. It now consists of around 70 buildings and when complete should have a hundred.

The aim is to show all aspects of Estonian rural architecture, with houses of both rich and poor. Most date from the 19th century but one of the chapels was built in 1699. The whole of Estonia is represented – windmills are of course from the island of Saaremaa but in contrast there are fishermen's cottages from Lake Peipsi on the Russian border. Even the poorest families managed to afford a sauna since to Estonians it is as crucial to living as a cooking pot. The interiors have all been appropriately furnished with kitchen utensils, weaving looms and chests of drawers. Amongst the more unusual buildings are a tabernacle from the Herrnhut movement, a strict offshoot of the Lutheran church. Future plans include the restoration of a Swedish cottage – about 8,000 Swedes lived in Estonia before World War II.

In bad weather, finish your tour at the Kolu Tavern. Kolu is a village between Tallinn and Tartu. The tavern still has two separate bars, one originally for the gentry and one for the peasants. It serves filling hot food such as pea soup and mashed potatoes with bacon, but do not expect any concessions to the 21st century; it remains firmly in the 19th, although a more conventional restaurant will in due course be built for more fastidious diners.

Paldiski

Since independence, an uneasy quiet has descended on to this former Soviet naval base situated 40km west of Tallinn. Unusually for Estonia, a reliable train service operates here from Tallinn, but individual tourists would be well advised to take a car and guide for a half-day excursion as several en-route stops can be made. Estonians are more than happy to see the back of the Russian sailors but have yet to find a new role for this harbour. Passenger services to Sweden and the switching of cargo from Tallinn are being considered.

Peter the Great inspected the site personally in 1715 before authorising the building of a harbour which was originally planned as the largest in the Russian Empire. He was not to live to see its final completion in 1768 as financial problems had led to frequent delays. Much of the labour was supplied by prisoners; so many died of ill-treatment that Paldiski became known as the 'second Siberia'.

In September 1939 the USSR imposed a 'mutual assistance' pact on Estonia under which Paldiski was seized as a naval base. In May 1940, shortly before the full occupation of the country, all Estonians were expelled from the town, a practice that would be repeated all too often after 1945, both here and in many other towns and villages along the coast. Paldiski is now the largest Soviet blot on the Estonian landscape; only the dustbins, brightly coloured and modelled on penguins with their beaks open, provide relief from piles of rubble, barbed wire and ransacked blocks of flats. The first building to be seen on the way into the town is the former prison but it can hardly be distinguished from much of what follows. When the Russian forces finally left in September 1995, having been granted dispensation to stay after independence, a population of around 4,000 was left with only 10% of them speaking Estonian. The remainder were Russian-speaking civilians. A curtain behind a window, an occasional light or even the sight of an occasional human being, shows that life has not totally died out here but the slogan on the town's English-language brochure, 'A Town with a Future', seems a joke in particularly bad taste.

Returning to Tallinn, two very contrasting stops can be made. Shortly after independence, a monument was erected in the forest at **Klooga** to commemorate the massacre of 2,000 Jews there on September 19 1944, just before the German withdrawal. The small Estonian-Jewish community had already been killed by then; these victims were largely from other Eastern European countries. The former village of **Tabasalu** is now the first of Tallinn's suburbs. It has a nickname of 'idiots' village' in view of those who live there, most of whom have much more money than sense or taste. The money stands out, but it is well protected by high walls and rottweilers. A few poultry farmers remain on the outskirts of the village but it cannot be long before they are bought out.

Aegna, Pirita and Kadriog

Allow a full day to visit the island of Aegna, the yacht harbour at Pirita and the park at Kadriog. Boats to and from Aegna operate out of Pirita harbour from a small jetty beside the café, not from the larger jetty beside the hotel and yacht club. Several buses serve Pirita from Tallinn town centre and the journey takes about ten minutes. Boats leave for Aegna around nine in the morning, at midday, and in the early evening. Check timings at the tourist office or via a hotel reception before setting off and do not forget an umbrella in case the weather suddenly changes. Tickets cost 80EEK for the round trip.

Aegna

Aegna is so quiet that even Estonians are prepared to turn off their mobile phones, and neither the Germans nor the Russians were able to leave their mark. Conifer trees abound, as do minute beaches, and the few open areas have been made available for camping. Much of the island can be seen in the three hours allowed by the morning boat schedule though a full day of peace and quiet is what most local visitors seek. Paths are clearly marked and a detailed map is displayed at the harbour.

Pirita

Pirita was built as the Olympic village for the yachting and sailing events of the 1980 Olympics. Over a precious three weeks, Tallinn briefly returned to being an international city. An array of consumer goods, Western newspapers and direct international telephone dialling suddenly came to Tallinn and left equally suddenly when the Games were over. Only the buildings have remained and they are so obviously of Soviet design that the harbour hardly seems to belong to modern Estonia. On returning to Pirita, visitors of Estonian origin may wish to take the 34 bus for 2km inland to Metsukalmistu, the **Forest Cemetery**. Many famous Estonians are buried in this pine forest, including the writer A H Tammsaare, the poetess Lydia Koidula and the chess player Paul Keres. Since independence, the body of Konstantin Päts, president until the Soviet occupation, has been returned and he is now buried here together with his immediate family. He died in a Soviet psychiatric hospital in 1956.

Lembit submarine

Other visitors will head for the main harbour and the entrance to the **Lembit** submarine, beside the petrol station. No brochures are available but the sailors on board speak reasonable English and their enthusiasm on meeting the few English-speaking visitors who bother to come more than compensates for any linguistic failings. Two submarines were originally commissioned from Barrow-in-Furness by the Estonian navy in 1936. *Kalev*, the second one, was sunk in October 1941, by which time both had been taken over by the Soviet navy and taken from Tallinn before it fell to the Germans. The *Lembit* saw service throughout World War II, being used mainly to attack German cargo ships en route to Sweden. It remained in service until 1955, after which it was used for training. The Soviets made no attempt to conceal the British origin of the submarine so many of the original features remain.

The walk back to the centre of Tallinn is two or three miles. Cross the main road from the harbour to the site of **St Birgitta's Convent**. Although the convent is included in most sightseeing tours, walking here can be a precarious experience as the ruins are so badly maintained. The convent lasted intact for only 170 years, from 1407 until the siege of 1577. The outline of the main body of the church, the western gable together with the vestry, cloister and refectories, is clear.

Staying on the land side of the main road, after half a mile comes the **Soviet War Memorial**. It could hardly be anything else, given its size and the military themes of the bronze statues. The Estonians carry out minimal maintenance here but, as with all Soviet war memorials, they are not removed and Russians congregate on the days of the old Soviet holidays such as May Day and November 7. The text is particularly offensive to Estonians as the monument is dedicated to 'Fighters for Soviet Power'. It was completed only in 1975. A Soviet guidebook excuses this long delay by claiming 'at last Estonian artists had enough skill and adequate economic means to complete such an ensemble'. The obelisk dates from 1960 and commemorates the hurried departure from Tallinn of the Bolshevik fleet in 1918 when German forces occupied the town.

Maarjamäe Palace

A few hundred yards further along this road is **Maarjamäe Palace**, which has probably had one of the most turbulent ownership histories of any site in

Tallinn. Maarjamäe means 'Mary's Hill' but the German name, Streitberg ('Hill of Strife'), was for many centuries more appropriate. The only consolation is that the blood shed here spared Tallinn itself from many battles. The final one took place in the early 18th century when Russia seized the Baltics from the Swedes during the Northern Wars. To set the seal on his conquest, Peter the Great established Kadriog Park as a summer residence, so many of the St Petersburg nobility felt obliged to followed suit. Those who could not immediately afford the luxury of a suitable building, subsidised it with a factory, so lime kilns and sugar refineries adjoined the manorhouses. The sugar was sold in Riga and St Petersburg and the plant was run on British coal. A fire in 1868 destroyed much of the factory here, and it was never rebuilt.

In the 1870s, when the estate was bought by Count Anatoli Orlov-Davydov from St Petersburg, the rebuilding he ordered came to deserve the title 'palace'. Terraces, a gateway decorated with copper eagles, and the Gothic tower gave it an almost regal air. The Dutch Consulate bought it in the 1920s when the Orlov-Davydovs emigrated to France and continued its use as a summer residence, though it was to lose its appeal in this role when the road to Pirita was built across the grounds in 1926, cutting off the manorhouse from direct and private access to the sea. However, the road brought with it commercial potential realised in a hotel and restaurant called the Riviera Palace. In 1937 the Estonian air force took it over as a training school and they are sadly responsible for the dreary façade at the front of the building. From 1940 until 1975, when Maarjamäe became a museum, the Soviet military used, but did not abuse, it.

During the 1980s, Polish restorers finally brought the building back to its turn-of-the-century glory, turning their attention to the chandeliers, fireplaces, parquet floors and ceilings. It is ironic that one of the last Soviet legacies to Tallinn should be the perfect surroundings for a museum which chronicles Estonian independence.

Although few labels are in English and the one available guidebook is now badly out of date, this is without doubt the best museum in Tallinn. New rooms are constantly being added, exhibits are generously displayed, layout is sensibly planned and there is a complete absence of the benign neglect that seems to permeate so many other Tallinn museums. It covers Estonian history from the mid-19th century until the present day. It amply contrasts the lifestyles of rich and poor and shows the diversity of industrial products and international contacts that the country enjoyed during the first period of independence between the two world wars. It even had a thriving tourist board whose brochures displayed here sold Estonia as 'The Cheapest and Most Interesting Country in Europe'. One room opened in the summer of 1998 is devoted to the life of Konstantin Päts, Estonia's president between the wars. On more contemporary themes, the anti-Soviet guerrilla movement and then the return to independence are covered movingly but not bombastically.

Song Festival Amphitheatre

Behind the palace is one of the few late-1950s constructions of which Estonians can be fiercely proud – the **Song Festival Amphitheatre**. It has the massive grandeur to be expected from that time but is not wasteful of materials and does not dominate the surrounding area. The parabola provides cover for 5,000 singers and up to 20,000 more have often taken part. The most famous recent festival took place in 1989, when the previously banned national anthem, the Song of Estonia, was sung by an audience of around 300,000 people, 20% of the entire population of the country.

Returning to the shoreline, at the junction of the roads to Pirita and to Narva, note the **Russalka Memorial**, which commemorates the sinking of a battleship with this name (*Russalka* means 'mermaid') in 1893. It depicts an angel looking out to sea. The sculptor, Amandus Adamson, is one of Estonia's most famous, and perhaps because of this monument he was granted official respect in the Soviet period and a memorial bronze bust of him stands in Kadriog Park.

Kadriog Park

The park is the next stage of the walk and one corner is just behind the *Russalka* Memorial. The park, and **Kadriog Palace**, which forms its centrepiece, was built immediately following Peter the Great's first visit to Tallinn in 1718 with his Italian architect Niccolo Michetti. Sadly it was not completed by 1725 when Peter the Great died and no subsequent Tsar ever showed the commitment that he did. In fact Catherine I never came to Tallinn again after his death. Perhaps the description often given of the palace as a 'mini-Versailles' is fair, as what was carried out does show some French and Italian influence. A fire destroyed much of the interior in 1750 and it was subsequently never again used by the Russian royal family. Kadriog Palace became the official presidential residence during the first independence period and then the Foreign Art Museum in Soviet times. It was closed for restoration in 1992 and finally reopened in July 2000. The current president lives and works in a smaller house in the grounds so many of the rooms here have been rebuilt as far as possible to reflect the 1930s' surroundings. The **Foreign Art Museum** has returned here, too, with an extensive Flemish collection as well as many engravings and lithographs by Baltic German artists. The early Soviet art displayed on the first floor is likely to be of most interest to foreign visitors. Painting escaped politics so in 1923 the artist Boris Kustdiev could still draw a nun. With porcelain this was not possible. A medium usually associated with affluence and gracious living here provides instead an array of factory chimneys, flags with slogans and marching, smiling armies. With the Palace buildings now open again, restoration work has begun in the gardens, the aim being to recreate the views President Päts so greatly enjoyed 70–80 years ago.

Kadriog Park is a year-round joy for local people and tourists alike. In winter the combination of sun and snow amidst the trees and sculptures offers a peaceful contrast to the hectic commercial life of Tallinn just a few hundred metres away. Spring brings out the blossom of the cherry and ash trees, summer the swans, the squirrels and the fountains, and autumn the blends of gold and red as the trees shed their leaves. A cottage in the park used by Peter the Great during the construction of the palace now poses as a museum but the paucity of exhibits perhaps redefines the word 'minimalist. A bare main room, a few photographs and some haphazard items of furniture would be best concealed from tourists entitled to expect much more.

A hundred metres back towards town, on Weizenbergi opposite the main entrance to Kadriog Palace, the **Mikkeli Museum** will quickly restore the enthusiasm of a visitor. This building was the palace kitchen but in 1997 was opened to house the collection of Estonia's most fortunate private art collector,

Johannes Mikkel. Born in 1907, he was able to start buying during the first independence period when departing Baltic Germans and Russian nobles abandoned enormous quantities of paintings, porcelain and prints. He was allowed to trade during the Soviet period and enhanced his collection with items bought in the Caucasus and Central Asia. There is no predominant theme, but the quality and taste of every item stands out, be it a piece of Kangxi or Meissen porcelain, a Dürer woodcut, a Rembrandt etching or any one of his 20 Flemish paintings. Folders in English are available in every room with descriptions of all major exhibits and modern lighting ensures that each item is viewed as well as possible.

Return to Tallinn centre

On leaving the museum turn back into town along Weizenbergi. At the corner of Poska on the left, house number 20a has some baroque imitation of the palace although it was built only in 1939. A good place to rest is the Café Omabi on the other corner. Apart from one microwave, modern Estonia has passed it by so the food is freshly prepared for each order, there is no menu in English and no piped music. Beside it is Kasitoo, a souvenir shop sensibly patronised by overseas Estonians as its prices are not geared to cruise passengers or Finnish day trippers. Weizenbergi lasts a further 300m or so before joining Narva mnt. Every house is probably now owned, or was before the war, by a famous Estonian. Ladas or small Toyotas may be parked in the street, but considerable wealth is discreetly hidden behind the lace curtains. The turn-of-the-century four-storey houses display hints of Jugendstil, whilst the wooden ones are characteristic of middle-class suburbs throughout Estonia. On a neighbouring street, Koidula, one of the largest wooden houses belonged to Estonia's most famous author, A H Tammsaare, who died in March 1940. It is now a museum in his honour but labelling is only in Estonian and Russian. The only English translations of his work were published in Moscow in the 1970s and are now out of print.

At the junction of Weizenbergi and Narva mnt there is a taxi rank and bus stop. A large Methodist church is being built on the far side; otherwise Narva mnt from here back to the Viru Gate is totally devoted to mammon. There is no point in describing any of the buildings since they are mainly being pulled down to give way to glass skyscrapers. This area will soon be Tallinn's Wall Street or Square Mile. A Japanese restaurant has already opened to ensure a serious and affluent gastronomic ambience.

Doma Baznīca, Rīga

Rīga 3

Stephen Baister and Chris Patrick

Rīga is the largest and most cosmopolitan of all the Baltic capitals and is by a long way the most interesting town or city in Latvia. It is located on the Daugava river about 15km from the point where the Daugava meets the Baltic Sea in the southeastern corner of the Gulf of Rīga. Rīga can trace its history to the beginning of the 13th century, but it was in the course of the Middle Ages that it developed into a Hanseatic city, and by the 18th and 19th century it had grown into one of Europe's leading ports and industrial centres. By the late 19th/early 20th century it had also become a cultural centre, famous for its opera, theatre and music. Rīga will celebrate its 800th anniversary in 2001 with a year-long series of special events and also with the rebuilding of the House of Blackheads (see page 79).

THE CITY

The modern city is divided into two parts by the city canal which flows through the elegant parks which separate the historic Old Town from most of the New Town, with its shops, offices and suburbs. The air of elegance and spaciousness created by the area of open space in what is otherwise the centre of a busy capital has led to Rīga being compared to Paris by a number of guide books and travel writers. There is some justification in the comparison. Even when Latvia was part of the Soviet Union, Rīga was more sophisticated than Russian Soviet cities and towns, since it had better shops and the odd decent restaurant and café. Now its medieval and art nouveau architecture and well kept parks allow the comparison to continue. There are modern international hotels, many good cafés and restaurants, and small and pleasant shops stocking local art and international brands. In 1992–3 the local authority privatised about 90% of Rīga's shops, from the old GUM

RĪGA 800

Rīga will celebrate its 800th anniversary in 2001. The slogan for the celebrations is 'Rīga, the eternal beginning'. A number of events are planned, culminating in the summer of 2001 with music from the towers of the city churches, an open-air concert and a fireworks display (17–19 August 2001). The city will also be designated one of that year's European Cultural Capitals.

(State Universal Store) in the Old Town, to the small bookshops and tobacconists.

Between 1945 and 1991 Rīga grew enormously, largely as a result of Soviet expansion which generally took the form of building enormous, drab, low-quality blocks of flats in the suburbs. One of the first, called Kengarags, can be seen along the Daugava and plenty can also be seen on the trip from the airport to the city centre.

The present population is estimated at just under 800,000, but even now about 40% is Latvian and about 55% Russian (the balance is made up of Poles, Belarussians and Ukrainians). Over half the population (about 54%) is female.

Until Latvia's independence from the Soviet Union in 1991 Russian was the predominant language heard in Rīga. Now, as can be seen from the signposts, Latvian is regaining ground, but Russian is still widely spoken (as are English and German, as second languages).

History
Foundation
Archaeological excavations indicate that the area now occupied by Rīga was probably inhabited and operated as a trading centre as early as the 2nd century BC. The first mention of the modern city can be traced to 1201 when Bishop Albert von Buxhoevden (or Buksherden) of Bremen established the locus Rīga and the first German fortress. Thus Rīga will celebrate its official 800th anniversary in 2001, though the *Chronicles* of Arnold of Lübeck, for example, refer to the founding of an episcopal see of Livonia in a place called Rīga in 1186. Whether 1201 was really the date of its foundation is doubtful for other reasons also, since Bishop Albert had been preceded by Abbot Berthold (who in turn had taken over from the Augustinian Meinhard) whose death in battle in 1198 marked the initial repulse of German invaders. Albert had come to restore German rule with the aid of 23 ships of merchants, sailors and armed men. In 1202 Albert founded the Fratres Militiae Christi, the Knights of the Sword, whose aim was to win over the territories occupied by the Livs, Latgals, Zemgals and Cours to Christianity. By 1207 Livonia was established as part of the German empire, when Albert was formally given it by Philip of Swabia as an imperial fief.

In 1201 the Cours attacked Rīga but failed to defeat the Germans, who held the town firmly. However, it was primarily in the towns (notably Rīga, Reval – present-day Tallinn – and Dorpat – present-day Tartu – the latter two in what is now Estonia) that the Germans were strong, not the surrounding countryside. Rīga was constantly under attack from hostile outside elements. A major setback in German domination occurred in 1236 when the Knights of the Sword were defeated by an army of Zemgals and Samogitians (a tribe in what is now Lithuania) at the battle of Saule (or Šiauliai). However, in 1237 the weakened Knights of the Sword amalgamated with a stronger order of knights, the Teutonic Order, to form the Livonian Order. As a result, German control of Livonia was firmly established. It was to last for the next three centuries.

In spite of the fact that during the 13th century Rīga suffered from no fewer than five major fires (in 1215, 1264, 1272, 1293 and 1297), which eventually gave rise to a law prohibiting the construction of wooden houses inside the town walls, the town prospered as a trading centre, joining the Hanseatic League in 1282.

Despite the prosperity, there was constant tension between the citizens and their rulers, giving rise to numerous battles and reprisals. In 1300 the Pope was obliged to intervene and promise that no more than ten knights would be stationed in Rīga at any one time. However, the knights simply took control of the shipping on the Daugava. A battle ensued, entailing a 13-month siege at the end of which (March 18 1330) Rīga capitulated again to the German knights, promising them a new castle.

The foundations of the new castle were laid in 1330 but building continued until 1353. In 1483–4 the castle was again stormed by the people of Rīga who tore it down stone by stone; however, by 1491 the knights had reasserted themselves and again a new castle was built.

The Reformation
In 1521 St Peter's Church began to operate as a centre for Reformation doctrine; in 1524 the first Latvian Evangelical Lutheran congregation was formed at St James' Church. In 1525 Walter von Plettenberg secured permission for the Lutheran doctrine to be taught, and preachers such as Andreas Knopken and Silvester Tegetmeyer taught the new Reformation theology so that Lutheran teachings gained a foothold in Rīga. Catholicism retreated: Catholic churches were demolished, and religious paintings and carvings were destroyed. In 1562 the last Master of the Livonian Order left the castle, and the Livonian state gradually shook off the German influence. By the end of the Livonian wars (1558–83) Rīga had fallen to the Russians.

The end of the 16th century marks a period of instability, and Russia (under Ivan the Terrible), Poland, Denmark and Sweden all laid claim to the city. An attempt by the Polish king, Stephen Bathory, to stage a counter-reformation in 1582 failed, although a Polish–Lithuanian kingdom prevailed for a short period until the Polish–Swedish war.

The Polish-Swedish War
The Polish-Swedish War of 1599–1629 ended as far as Rīga was concerned when it fell to Gustavus Adolphus II in 1621. Following the Peace of Oliva of 1660, Rīga became the second capital of Sweden. Again there was a period of commercial success and prosperity. In 1663 a water supply was established using wooden pipes. In 1681 Rīga's first newspaper, the *Rigische Nouvellen*, was established. In 1685 the first Bible was printed in Latvian. In the same year a number of large rocks that blocked navigation of the Daugava were removed by explosion. In 1701 a pontoon bridge was built over the Daugava – it was the longest in the world.

The Northern War
1700 saw the beginning of the end of Swedish rule. This was the year in which the so-called Northern War started between Russia, Poland, Denmark and Sweden. The Northern War lasted until 1721 when Sweden ceded Estonia, Livonia and Karelia to Tsar Peter I (the Great) of Russia under the terms of the treaty of Nystadt. However, the war ended much earlier for Rīga. In 1709 the city's food supplies were severely depleted as a result of unprecedented flooding (most food was stored in cellars). In July 1710, after an eight-month siege, the Russian general, Count Sheremetyer, was able to enter the city,

which was forced by plague and hunger to present him with the keys. Under the terms of the Treaty of Nystadt, Peter I guaranteed to leave the rights of Rīga and the surrounding provinces unaffected, so the people continued to enjoy freedom of religion and education, and the guilds and livery companies remained unaffected.

Rīga in the 18th century

This period was by no means a bad one for Rīga. Peter I married the fourth daughter of Ernst Glück, the Lutheran pastor who translated the Bible into Latvian. She became Catherine I of Russia. Writing in German of the time he spent in Rīga between 1764 and 1789 Johann Gottfried Herder (see page 78) wrote, 'I lived, taught and behaved in such a free and such an unrestrained way in Livonia such that I can hardly imagine living and behaving again.' In 1743 street lighting was introduced. In 1782 a theatre was established (where Wagner conducted in 1837–9). Rīga was also a place of intellectual and scientific enlightenment in the 18th century. In 1798 Dr Otto Herr introduced vaccination against smallpox, and in 1802 the Latvian pharmacist Grindels founded the Society of Pharmacy, which started a trend for the formation of a whole range of medical and scientific associations. In 1801 torture was abolished as part of the legal process, as was public execution.

The 18th century also saw a growth of Latvian cultural awareness. Whilst Herder wrote his *Fragmente über die neuere deutsche Literatur* ('Fragments Concerning Recent German Literature') while in Rīga, in 1774 he published a number of Latvian folk songs in German translation, and in 1796 G H Merkel published his *Latvians, particularly in Vidzeme, at the end of the Philosophical Century* in which he described the misery of serfdom.

Rīga in the 19th century

Rīga avoided the effects of the Napoleonic Wars; although Napoleon had threatened to attack 'this suburb of London', he never reached it. As Napoleon's troops under the leadership of the Prussian field marshal, York, approached Rīga in 1812, the governor-general of Rīga set the wooden houses of the Rīga suburbs on fire to deflect the invaders. In the wake of the French Revolution, the wave of liberation that swept across Europe made itself felt in Rīga, too, and in 1817 serfs were emancipated, 40 years before Russia. In 1830 farmers gained the right to live in the cities. In 1840 a rural education law was passed. Soon an educated rural class grew up, starting up trade in Rīga and other towns. Jews were only given residency rights in Rīga in the mid-19th century, before which most were itinerant traders. By the outbreak of World War I in 1914, their numbers in Rīga had reached about 100,000 and they were active both in commerce and in the academic world.

In 1857–8 the town walls were dismantled to allow expansion. In 1861 the railway came and the postal service was expanded. Rīga gradually developed into a major industrial centre and the first shipyard opened in 1869. Telephones arrived in 1877; horse-drawn trams appeared, and a major bicycle factory was established. In 1887 an electric power generation station was built. This industrialisation also brought a huge increase in the population of Rīga: in 1767 the town had 16,300 inhabitants; 100 years later the population had grown to 102,590 (of whom 20–25% were Latvian). By 1897 the population doubled to 255,879, but the Latvian proportion now accounted for almost 50%. A prosperous Latvian working class and middle class began to emerge.

Parallel to this industrial expansion came a growth in Latvian nationalism. Latvian newspapers, notably *Tas Latviešu Laužu Draugs* ('Friend of the Latvian People'), had appeared since the 1820s and 1830s, but Russian remained the language of education, government and the legal system. However, Krišjānis Barons' work in collecting Latvia's *dainas* and the establishment of a folk song festival in Rīga in 1873 gave impetus to the movement called the Latvian Awakening, which grew out of the Rīga Latvian Association. The Latvian Association published a Latvian encyclopedia, founded a national opera and a national theatre. The folk song festival gave birth to a national anthem, *Dievs Svēti Latviju*, 'God Bless Latvia'.

The thrust of the National Awakening Movement was, however, primarily anti-German and somewhat pro-Russian. It turned its back on the architecture of Germany (manifest in the castle, the cathedral and the churches of St Peter and St James) yet did not object to the construction of Orthodox churches. It did, however, demand equality of treatment for the Latvian language.

Riot and revolution

The end of the 19th century was also a time of growing working-class political awareness. In 1899 women workers at the Džuta textile mill went on strike. The police intervened, and before long demonstrations began in the course of which five workers were shot dead and 31 wounded. A full-scale riot soon ensued.

In 1900 Lenin set up his revolutionary magazine *Iskra* ('Spark') in Zürich, and in 1904 the Latvian Social Democratic Party was formed, the most significant movement of its kind in Imperial Russia.

On January 13 1905 a demonstration of the poor and working classes was put down with force in Moscow. The demonstrators had wanted to show solidarity with demonstrators who had gathered four days earlier in front of the tsar's palace in St Petersburg to hand in a petition seeking political reform. A demonstration in support also began in Rīga, but again it was put down by force of arms and over 70 people were killed. The Social Democratic Party began to organise resistance, and by October Rīga was in the grip of a general strike. Armed peasants attacked German landowners, and other strikers attacked the prison, aiming to free a number of political prisoners.

Before the end of the year Russian troops moved to regain control, putting the revolution down with particular brutality in which over 900 peasants and teachers were executed under martial law, and thousands were exiled to Siberia. The Russian authorities aimed their vengeance especially at teachers who were known for their social-democratic leanings.

Many Latvian intellectuals only escaped by fleeing to the west. The writer, Jānis Rainis, fled to Switzerland, Kārlis Ulmanis, the chairman of the Peasants' Party, who was later to become president of Latvia, sought refuge in the United States.

A new 1906 Latvian constitution gave limited recognition to Latvian nationalist aspirations by allowing, for example, Latvian to be used for teaching in schools.

World War I

The outbreak of World War I drove Latvia into the arms of the Russians with whom they allied themselves against the German foe. In 1915 German forces were approaching Rīga. In a manic evacuation, the Russians moved Rīga's industry and about 96,000 workers to Russia. Even the power station was dismantled and moved. In all, about one third of the total population of Latvia was forced to leave the country. In 1917 German troops crossed the Daugava, and the capital surrendered to the Germans.

In the same year, however, the Russian Revolution was making its consequences felt. Whilst some political elements in Rīga sought the annexation of Latvia to the German Empire, others were looking to Soviet power to free their country from the Germans. In spring 1918 Latvia was split into three: Kurzeme and Rīga went to Germany, Latgale to Russia, and the rest of Vidzeme was left unmolested. However, following the defeat of Germany, on November 18 1918, in the Rīga national theatre an independent republic of Latvia was proclaimed, and Kārlis Ulmanis was given the task of forming a provisional government. A period of what amounted to civil war ensued, the Russians supporting Latvia against the persistent exercise of German military force. Only on August 11 1920 was a peace treaty signed between Latvia and the Soviet Union following the final expulsion of German troops from Latvia in December 1919.

Latvian independence

The period between the two world wars is often referred to as the first period of Latvian independence. The 1920 treaty provided for the Soviet Union and Latvia to recognise each other as states. In 1922 Latvia adopted its own constitution and issued its own currency. Jānis Čakste was elected as the first president of the republic.

Rīga was not immune to the depression that gripped most of Europe during the 1930s and unemployment rose to high levels. On May 15 1934 Ulmanis mounted a coup and formed an authoritarian administration. Democratic socialists were imprisoned, political parties of both left and right were banned, and freedom of the press was curtailed. Ironically, in 1935, the Freedom Monument was erected in the centre of Rīga.

World War II

Under the terms of the pact between Hitler and Stalin of August 23 1939 it was agreed that the Baltic states would fall under the sphere of influence of the Soviet Union. By the end of that year the Soviet Union had already begun to establish a military presence in Latvia.

On June 17 1940 Soviet troops marched in to take over the country and establish a pro-Soviet regime. On July 21 'elections' were held under Soviet auspices and a new government and parliament declared Latvia to be a republic of the USSR. Ulmanis was deported, as were thousands of citizens from Rīga and elsewhere in Latvia, many of them to Siberia or central Asia.

In June 1941 the USSR was forced to join in the war when it was attacked by Germany. Latvia was unprepared, and on July 1 1941 Hitler's troops arrived in Rīga to 'liberate' it from Stalin's USSR, causing the Russians to retreat, leaving devastation in their wake. Stalin had murdered or deported a substantial proportion of the Jewish population in Rīga as enemies of the people; Hitler imposed his anti-Semitic policies, massacring Jews at Rumbula and Biķernieki, and establishing concentration camps.

The German occupation continued until May 1945 when the Red Army arrived again to 'liberate' Rīga from the Germans. The retreating Germans destroyed houses, factories, roads and bridges, and thousands of Latvians fled to the west.

Soviet rule
After the end of World War II the USSR provided immense economic assistance to Latvia, and Russian immigrants took the places left by the fleeing or slaughtered native Latvian population. However, the Soviet 'liberators' were not welcomed: many Latvians formed resistance groups and fighting ensued until Stalin intervened with his usual brutality, deporting some 44,000 Latvian nationalists to exile in Siberia where many died.

However, Latvian nationalism, whilst repressed, was not extinguished. In 1988 5,000 demonstrators gathered in Rīga on June 14 to commemorate the deportations, and on August 23 10,000 demonstrators gathered to mark the anniversary of the Hitler–Stalin pact. In the meantime in June at a meeting of the Latvian Writers' Union a resolution was passed that led to the founding of the Popular Front of Latvia in October 1988 that was to campaign for political, cultural and economic independence.

Liberation/Independence
In 1989 Latvia experienced its first free elections of deputies to the Supreme Soviet of the USSR. This event was followed by the passing of laws in the Latvian Supreme Soviet proclaiming the sovereignty of the Latvian Soviet Socialist Republic and declaring Latvian the official language of the country. Latvia was again on the road to independence. On November 18 1989 over 500,000 people gathered on the banks of the Daugava in Rīga to mark the 71st anniversary of Latvia's independence.

On May 4 1990 the Supreme Soviet of Latvia met in the pre-war *Saeima* building and passed a resolution on 'the renewal of independence of the Republic of Latvia'. A period of instability followed as the Latvian Communist party endeavoured to take back the helm of government, staging a coup in January 1991 which, however, failed. A plebiscite held in March 1991 resulted in three-quarters of the population voting to secede from the Soviet Union.

On August 25 1991 Iceland became the first country to recognise the new independent Baltic state, but others soon followed, and by the end of the year the Republic of Latvia had been granted admission to the UN. A new constitution proclaiming Latvia as an independent democratic republic was adopted in 1992. Rīga was once more the capital of an independent democratic state.

PRACTICAL INFORMATION
Communications
Telephones
The country code for international calls to Latvia is 371. Rīga numbers with seven digits do not require an additional area code. Six digit numbers require the area code 2. To call foreign numbers from Latvia the international access code is 1 00 which should be followed by the relevant country code.

Post office
The main post office (*Latvijas Pasts*) is at 19 Brīvības iela and is open 24 hours. It sells phonecards and postcards, and can help with international calls. Other post offices are at Stacijas laukums (Station square), 41–43 Elizabetes iela and 22 Aspāzijas bulvāris.

Internet cafés
Internet cafés have arrived in Rīga in the form of **Bilteks** at 20 Jēkaba iela, tel: 732 2208, web: www.binet.lv, and the internet café at Versia Ahitektu 1, tel: 721 0909, web: www.vernet.lv. A recent one to open is **Latnet** at 29 Raina bulvāris, tel: 721 1241, web: www.latnet.lv

Banks and money
Changing money in Rīga is not a problem: most banks have a bureau de change. In addition, there are exchange booths (*valutas maina*) in many streets and in shops in the city centre, and of course most hotels will change money. All are reliable, although rates do vary, so it can be worth shopping around, especially if you are changing a large sum. Hotels tend not to give such a good rate as the bureaux.

There is a 24-hour currency exchange bureau called **Ahāts** at 26 Brīvības bulvāris, 90 Brīvības iela and on Stacijas laukums, the square in front of the railway station. The other, **Marika**, has branches at 14 Basteja bulvāris and 30 Brīvības iela.

Cash machines are also becoming more common in Rīga, and a large number accept Visa and Mastercards. (Most machines have English-language instruction options.)

Eurocheques and **travellers' cheques** can be changed at many banks, but will not generally be accepted in restaurants. It is best to carry a certain amount of cash for drinks and to pay admission charges, but almost everything else can be put on a credit card.

Tourist information
After a year without a tourist office, Rīga has now reopened one on the Town Hall Square beside the House of Blackheads. It is open daily 10.00–19.00, tel: 704 4377. The following publications should also be consulted:

Rīga in Your Pocket is published five times a year and is printed by the Jāņa Sēta Printing House in Cēsis. Its address is PO Box 615, 4 Pils laukums (room 112), Rīga, tel: 722 0580, fax: 722 3416, email: riyp@mailbox.riga.lv. It is widely available, costs Ls0.60, and is invaluable. It also has a website: www.inyourpocket.com.
Rīga This Week (the official city guide) appears six times a year and is free. It is published by the Rīga-Inform Publishing House, tel/fax: 728 3565, email: rinform@mail.eunet.lv. It, too, is available on the internet: www.eunet.lv/riga.
Rīga Guide is also published six times a year by Lu & Ka Ltd, 28 Aspāzijas bulvāris, tel/fax: 722 9856, email: rg@guide.riga.lv. It too is free.

All the above contain **maps** of central Rīga. Maps of the main areas you are likely to visit also appear on pages 71 and 86–7 of this book. **Jāņa Sēta** (83–85 Elizabetes iela) is the best place to buy the maps that they publish and also for locally produced guidebooks. The best detailed map of Rīga is their *Rīga City Map*. They also sell maps and English-language guidebooks to the neighbouring Baltic states and for Russia.

Lattelkom provides an information service which can be obtained by calling 118. The service costs Ls0.09 a minute. Operators speaking Latvian, Russian and English can give the usual directory enquiries kind of information, but also give out information on what is on in theatres and cinemas and so on; you can also dial the number to obtain directions if you are lost.

Public holidays

Good Friday	
Midsummer	June 23–24
Independence Day	November 18
Christmas	December 24–26
New Year	January 1

Tours

A number of firms offer city tours by coach. It is probably best to organise these through your hotel if you are staying in one that offers this facility. Otherwise you can contact one of the agencies below:

Latvia Tours 8 Kaļķu iela, tel: 708 5057 or 708 5001, fax: 782 0020, email: latviatours.lv; also at 13 Marijas iela, tel: 724 3391. Does city tours and also offers trips to the Open Air Musuem, Rundāle Palace, Sigulda, Cēsis, Kurzeme and Latgale. Bookings can also be made at the Hotel Latvijā (tel: 722 1040) and at the Hotel de Rome (tel: 721 6168).

Rīga City Tour by double decker bus, leaves from Raiņa bulvāris, just by the Freedom Monument, every day at 10.00, 12.00, 15.30 and 18.00 for a city tour of 2½–3 hours.

Lauku Ceļotājs 11 Kuģu iela, tel: 761 7600 or 761 7024, fax: 783 0041.

Rīga Travel Agency 28 Aspāzijas bulvāris, tel: 722 0368 or 721 6727, fax: 722 2398.

Student and Youth Travel Bureau Lacplesa 29, tel: 728 4818, fax: 728 3064, email: sjcb@sjcb.lv.

TAS (Travel Agency Satellite) 21–22 Raina Blvd, tel: 722 2901 or 781 4045, fax: 782 0285, email: tas@blatnet.lv. Offers group and individual tours and general travel agency services.

VIA Hansa Tours 3 R Vāgnera iela (3rd floor), tel: 722 7232, fax: 782 0294, email: rīga@viahansa.com.

Trips are also offered by many of the above to Sigulda, Cēsis, Kurzeme, Latgale, Jūrmala and the Rundāle Palace.

Transport

Rīga has a well-developed transport system of eight **tram** lines, 24 **trolleybus** lines and 39 **bus** lines. The fare is charged at a flat rate of 20 santīmi a journey. Different tickets are needed for each mode of transport. Tickets can be bought on board from the *konduktors*. In addition to the bus, tram or trolleybus, there is another form of transport, the *taksobuss* or *mikroautobuss* which covers longer distances and costs more depending on the length of the journey.

The maps in *Rīga in Your Pocket* and the yellow Jāņa Sēta Rīga map contain information showing public transport routes.

Taxis are fairly reliable provided you use official ones which have a meter; some have orange and black markings. Rates are about 25 santīmi per kilometre during the day rising to 35 per kilometre between 22.00 and 06.00. The **bus station** (*autoosta*) is in Prāgas iela, close to the main market and on the other side of the railway station (under the bridge) away from the city centre. You can try to phone for information, tel: 721 3611, but may find it advisable to attend in person: timetables are on display, otherwise apply to window 1. **Eurolines** have an office in the bus station which sells tickets on all its international services to neighbouring countries.

The **railway station** is at Stacijas laukums, tel: 723 3397 for bookings and 237 2134 for information.

Airport
The airport is about 8km from the city centre and the 22 bus links the two. It runs every half hour. Taxis cost about 8 lats (£9/US$14). The terminal is constantly being extended to cater for the increasing number of flights it handles. Currency exchange offices are open whenever flights arrive and leave.

Port
The tram stop is about 100m from the terminal and trams run every few minutes. The fare for any distance is 0.2 lats (£0.23/US$0.36).

Car hire
Car hire is relatively easy to organise but is also quite expensive, as it is in the other Baltic states.

Avis Aspāzijas bulvāris, tel: 722 5876, fax: 782 0441; and at Rīga Airport, tel: 720 7353.

Eurodollar Rīga Airport, tel: 720 7710, fax: 720 7709.

Europcar 10 Basteja bulvāris, tel: 722 2637, fax: 782 0360; and at Rīga Airport, tel: 720 7825.

Hertz 15 Kaļķu iela, tel: 722 4223; and at Rīga Airport, tel: 720 7980, fax: 720 7981.

Scorpio 24 Aspāzijas bulvāris, tel: 722 7021, fax: 782 0098.

Statoil 117 K. Ulmaņa gatve, tel/fax: 740 1654; 434a Brīvības gatve, tel: 754 2306, tel/fax: 754 2358; and 9 Ziepniekkalna iela, tel: 762 7062, tel/fax: 762 7109.

Accommodation
There has been a huge expansion of hotel accommodation in Rīga since independence, so visitors are no longer restricted to staying in the soulless tower block hotels typified by the Hotel Latvijā which were imposed on the visitor in the Soviet years. Now there are hotels in every possible price range, although few in the three-star category. The good hotels are in line with international standards and the official prices reflect that, although the opening of several new hotels in 2000 reduced prices for both business visitors and tourists during the year, a trend that is likely to continue in 2001. At the other end of the spectrum there are still many cheap but sometimes shabby hotels. There are very few youth hostels (see page 60 for details). In between the two extremes, private enterprise has spawned a growing bed and breakfast market, often in private homes, offering accommodation from the equivalent of about

US$10 a night. In practice this often means little more than staying in the spare room of a Latvian family's house or flat. It follows that standards vary enormously.

An alternative to staying in Rīga is to book a hotel in nearby Jūrmala, Rīga's seaside resort. Jūrmala is about 20 minutes from Rīga by car and about 30 minutes by train.

All the quality hotels take credit cards. It is, however, advisable to book in advance, especially during the summer months and around trade fairs and festivals.

Superior hotels

Eurolink 22 Aspāzijas bulvāris, tel: 722 0531, fax: 721 6300, email: eurolink@brovi.lv.

This is actually the third floor of the Hotel Rīga (see below) but is run as a separate hotel under joint Latvian-Swedish management. It was the first four star hotel in the capital when it was first set up, and offers modern conference and meeting rooms as well as accommodation of a high standard (59 rooms) and Scandinavian cuisine in the restaurant. It is conveniently located, right next to the Opera House and within easy reach of the Old and New Towns. Single rooms cost US$91–140, doubles US$101–165 and suites US$240.

Hotel Grand Palace 12 Pils Iela, tel: 704 4000, fax: 704 4001, email: grandpalace@consul-hotels.com, web: www.consul-hotels.com.

Following the success of their Park Consul and St Petersbourg hotels in Tallinn, the Schlossle Hotel group opened this similar hotel in Rīga Old Town in May 2000. As in Tallinn, an ancient façade on a narrow cobbled street hides a hotel of discreet but extensive luxury in both the public areas and in the 56 rooms. An open fire during the winter is a hallmark of these hotels but unique to Rīga is the Orangerie where a traditional afternoon tea is served. Single rooms cost around US$220 and twins US$260, with reductions at weekends.

Hotel de Rome 28 Kaļķu iela, tel: 708 7600, fax 708 7606, email: reservation@derome.lv, web: www.derome.lv.

At the edge of the Old Town, this German-run 4-star hotel is one of the best in Rīga. The location overlooking the Freedom Monument and surrounding parks – of which there is a terrific view from the restaurant – on the edge of the Old Town but within easy reach of the New is ideal for the tourist. But it is also within easy reach of all the government offices, ministries and so on, so is also suitable for anyone visiting Rīga on official business. The standard of accommodation and public areas is high. The German Otto Schwarz Restaurant offers an excellent breakfast and first class meals at other times of day. It has 90 rooms (10 single, 60 doubles and 20 luxury suites). Prices start from about US$120 for a single room, and US$150 for a double but lower rates are available in July and August.

Konventenhof or **Konventa Sēta** 9–11 Kalēju iela, tel: 708 7501–05, fax: 708 7506, email: reservation@konventa.lv, web: www.derome.lv.

This hotel is housed in a complex of restored buildings in the heart of Old Rīga (see page 81 for an account of the restoration of the Konventa Sēta). It has 80 rooms and 61 apartments. Single rooms cost from Ls44 per night; double rooms and suites from Ls55–70 per night. The hotel also aims at the business market with its four conference rooms (34–119m^2) which can be hired from Ls90–160 a day. It is under the same German management as the Hotel de Rome.

Man-Tess 6 Teātra iela, tel: 721 6056 or 721 0225, fax: 782 1249, email: mantess-@binet.lv.
This charming hotel in the centre of Old Rīga is an elegant 18th-century house once owned by H Haberland, a Rīga architect. It has only six rooms (three doubles, one single, two suites and four offices) each one in a different style (the so-called white room is light and modern, the 18th-century room is furnished in the style of the Hanseatic period). The ground floor restaurant is exotically decorated (marble, water and even caged birds) and is one of the best in the Old Town. Prices range from Ls60 for the single room to Ls100 for a suite. There is a banquet/conference hall on the fifth floor.

Maritim Park Slokas 1, tel: 706 9000, fax: 706 9001, email: parkhotel@apollo.lv.
This was for many years the rather seedy Hotel Turist but it closed as such in autumn 1999 and reopened as a totally new four-star hotel with 240 rooms in May 2000. Its location 'over the river' may put off some visitors but others will appreciate the extra space, the quieter environment, the access to cheap local shops and above all its much lower prices. The Old Town is in any case only a ten-minute tram-ride away and in the summer this is a pleasant walk of half an hour. Standard rooms cost around US$90 for a single, US$120 for a twin.

Metropole 36–38 Aspāzijas bulvāris, tel: 722 5411, fax: 721 6140, email: metropole@brovi.lv, web: brovi.lv.
Run by the same Latvian-Swedish management team as the Eurolink, the Metropole is suitable for both tourists and the business traveller. Built in 1871 the Metropole is the oldest hotel in Rīga. It has 80 rooms and was completely refurbished before reopening in 1992. Again, it is conveniently located next to the opera house and within easy reach of the Old and New Towns. Single rooms cost US$109–160, doubles US$129–185 and suites about US$240. All rooms are equipped with satellite phone and cable TV.

Radisson SAS Daugava Hotel 24 Kuģu iela, tel: 706 1111, fax: 706 1100, email: radisson@com.latnet.lv, web: www.radissonsas-rīga.lv.
This is the leading business hotel in the Baltics and claims to be the only real conference hotel. It is an international standard business hotel with 361 large rooms and suites, including two floors of executive rooms which have their own lounge for drinks and fully equipped business centre. There is security parking, 24-hour room service and cable TV. With 10 air-conditioned conference rooms the hotel can arrange meetings for up to 360 delegates. A business service offers translation, secretarial and other commercial services. The Grill Room restaurant is highly recommended, as is the buffet breakfast. There is a modern fitness centre, sauna, large swimming pool and shop. The Radisson is very much a business hotel, and published prices (US$155–175 for a single room and US$175–195 for a double) reflect this, but tourists can get excellent rates at weekends, and in July and August. Agents who specialise in the Baltics can often offer competitive prices year-round. The building is a rather unimaginative white block on 'the wrong side' of the Daugava away from the main part of the city, but it is quiet and has spectacular views over the river. For these reasons, together with the size of its rooms, it has now attracted a regular clientele of business visitors and tourists. It offers free transfers from the airport and an hourly shuttle bus to the Old Town.

Ridzene 1 Reimersa iela, tel: 732 4433 or 732 5171, fax: 728 2100, email: park.hotel@ridzene.lv, web: parkhotelridzene.com.
Formerly a Soviet guesthouse, this hotel was totally renovated during 1999 and reopened that autumn as a business-class hotel. Its location behind the American

Embassy is convenient for many ministries and also for the Old Town. It is a medium-size hotel with 95 rooms all of which provide every possible convenience, although they are smaller than might be expected in a hotel of this class. The underground car park is of great help in the winter. On opening, room prices were around US$225 for a single and US$275 for a double, but these started to fall during 2000 when several new business-class hotels opened.

Rīga Hotel 22 Aspāzijas bulvāris, tel: 704 4222, fax: 704 4223, email: info@hotel.riga.lv, web: www.lvnet.lv/hotel/.

Next door to the Metropole, so again close to the National Opera and the Old and New Towns, the Rīga is slightly cheaper than the hotels above. Single rooms cost Ls55, doubles Ls80 and suites Ls92–106. With its 243 rooms the Rīga is one of the largest hotels in the capital. The rooms are comfortable and it has been refurbished to a high standard since communist times. However, it still has a slight tinge of the atmosphere of the Soviet era with its *dezhurnaya* on every floor, long corridors and vast hall of a restaurant. Very good value, particularly for groups.

Medium-range hotels

Brigita 11 Saulkalnes, tel: 762 3000; fax: 762 3190. Clean and modern, the Brigita is a privately owned hotel that is used a great deal by business travellers and those wanting a long stay. It has a café and bar as well as a sauna, but is about 25 minutes by trolleybus from the centre of Rīga. It has 22 rooms and prices range from Ls25 for a single room to Ls34 for a double room and Ls41 for a suite consisting of two rooms and a study. Very good value if a central location is not essential.

Hotel Centra Audeju 1, tel: 722 6441, fax: 750 3281, email: hotel.centra@delfi.lv. This welcome addition to the small hotels in the Old Town opened in June 2000 with 19 rooms so is well suited to individual travellers. Access by taxi is easy as it is near one of the Old Town entry points and the baths in every room will be welcomed by many. Good sound-proofing fortunately protects guests from the lively night-life in the surrounding streets. Photographers should try for a room on the higher floors, to get a novel angle on the Old Town streets.

Karavella 27 Katrīnas dambis, tel: 732 4597, fax: 783 0187. With 70 rooms this is a fairly large hotel situated about 10 minutes by car (2km) from the centre of Rīga towards the harbour (it is 1km from the marine passenger terminal). Some rooms overlook the city. It is modern, but is in a fairly run-down part of the city. Single rooms Ls25–30, doubles Ls35–40, suites Ls45–70. Excellent rates for groups and ample parking for coaches and cars.

Kaspars 19 Mūkupurva iela, tel: 42 4269, fax: 42 4755. A clean and comfortable hotel about 5km from the city centre. It is not easy to get to unless you have a car, but it has the advantage of being in a peaceful location and having tennis courts, a sauna and indoor swimming pool. Prices are Ls17 for a single room and Ls28 for a double.

Laine Hotel 11 Skolas iela, tel: 728 8816 or 728 9823, fax: 728 7658, email: laine@com.latnet.lv, web: www.laine-apollo.lv.

A small hotel (28 rooms) in an elegant art nouveau house, the Laine has the advantage of being centrally located, not far from the Hotel Latvijā. With room prices ranging from Ls15–35 for a single room to Ls22–40 for a double (the cheaper rooms require you to use communal showers), the Laine is exceptionally good value.

Hotel Latvijā 55 Elizabetes iela, tel: 722 2211 or 721 1755, fax: 728 3595 or 782 0240, email: admin@latvija.hotel.lv, web: www.latvija.hotel.lv/hotel.htm.

This was the hotel in which Intourist put its customers in the days of the USSR. It is a huge, impersonal skyscraper of a building, typical of Soviet hotel architecture in the way it dominates its surroundings. It has over 350 rooms and numerous bars, cafés and restaurants, but it has to date lacked any sort of charm. Two advantages are its location in the New Town just five minutes from the Old Town, and the views from its upper storeys. In early 2000 rooms cost from US$70 a night for a single and US$229 for an apartment and a whole range in between the two. Discounts of up to 25% were available at weekends. It closed in June 2000 and is due to reopen in May 2001 under Norwegian management.

Māra 186 Kalnciema iela, tel: 790 1316, fax: 790 1315, email: mara@mailbox.riga.lv. Part of the Best Western chain, the Māra has 24 rooms at prices from US$125–175 per night. It is out of the centre on the way to the airport but operates a shuttle bus to both the airport and the city centre. More of a business hotel than one for tourists.

Oma 33 Ernestīnes iela, tel: 761 3388 or 761 2388, fax: 761 3233. A former private house in what was one of the more fashionable quarters of Rīga before the war, this tastefully converted hotel has just 17 rooms plus meeting rooms for business clients. Located about 15 minutes from the city centre by bus and 20 minutes from the airport, this hotel is again more likely to appeal to the business user than the tourist, although long-stay visitors will appreciate the lower prices and the quiet location. Room prices range from Ls25–50.

Radi un Draugi 1–3 Mārstaļu iela, tel: 722 0372, fax: 724 2239. This is a 49-room hotel right in the centre of the Old Town in a superb location. Room prices range from Ls24–36 depending on the type of room and the level of occupancy (there are some rooms for three sharing). With an Irish pub and a British pub beside it, noise can be a problem in the evenings.

Tia 63 Kr Valdemāra, tel: 733 3918, 733 3035 or 733 3396, fax: 783 0390, email: tia@mail.bkc.lv. A clean and comfortable hotel near the centre with rooms from Ls28 for a single to Ls50 for a top of the range double. The building looks austere from the outside but the rooms have all been modernised.

Viktorija 55 A Čaka iela, tel: 701 4111, fax: 701 4140. This small hotel (with only seven single rooms at US$44 per night, 24 doubles at US$68 and three luxury rooms at US$92) sometimes appears in the budget hotel category (it has a few rooms at the very low price of US$16–24). In spite of its rather gloomy entrance it has been renovated in recent years, and although not quite central (about 10 minutes by car from the central station and a bit further to the Old Town), it is not too far to walk.

Cheaper hotels

Almina 2a Ieriķu iela, tel: 256 9278. Rather run down with shared rooms at Ls2 per person per night, doubles Ls5–7.

Arēna 5 Palasta iela, tel: 722 8583. One of Rīga's cheapest hotels, with basic rooms (showers and toilets in communal hall area), the Arēna's location makes it popular because of its proximity to the Dome. Single rooms from Ls3 per night, doubles from Ls6.

Aurora 5 Marijas iela, tel: 722 4479. Close to the station, so relatively central. The Aurora offers basic rooms at prices ranging from Ls3.50–7.80 according to whether they are singly, doubly or triply occupied. Communal toilets and showers.

Baltā Kaza 2 Ēveles iela, tel: 237 8135. The name means 'White Goat'. Located some way out of Rīga, this small and simple hotel looks grim but is fairly clean. It has

35 rooms plus dormitories and bunk bed accommodation at prices from Ls3 per person per night.

Baltija 33 Raiņa bulvāris, tel: 722 7461. Very primitive but cheap with room prices Ls4.70–12.40 per night.

Elias 14 Hamburgas iela, tel: 251 8117. A small hotel with only seven double rooms near Lake Ķīšezers reached by taking the number 11 tram from Kr Barona iela or the number 9 bus from the station. Rooms are Ls16 per night.

Latavio at the airport, tel: 720 7149 or 720 7375. Next to the airport, so unprepossessing in location as well as appearance. Rooms Ls9.28–25.52.

Latgale 4 Aviācijas iela, tel: 718 8882. The hotel has 20 double rooms at Ls15 per night.

Linga 2 Līču iela, tel: 734 8403. Rooms from Ls7.5–25. All rooms have TV and shower or bath. Take the number 11 bus from near the circus on Merķeļa iela.

Mežaparks 19 Sakses iela, tel: 755 7988, fax: 755 7964. Known as the hotel which used to accommodate Latvian sportsmen, the hotel is located near Ķīšezers lake. To reach it take the No 2 trolleybus to the last stop. Prices from Ls7 for a single room to Ls17 for a luxury double room.

Oskars 9a Krustabaznīcas iela, tel: 755 6955. Formerly used by Soviet troops, the hotel is now run by the Latvian army and is still used to put up military visitors. It has 64 rooms, eight 6-bed dormitory rooms, 23 single rooms (Ls6–8) and 25 double rooms (Ls8); there are also luxury double rooms (at Ls16–21 a night). It has excellent sporting facilities, including a swimming pool, gymnasium, sauna and solarium. The accommodation itself is plain but clean. Because the hotel is still used for military purposes, local sources recommend that foreigners book in advance.

Pļavnieki 26 Salnas iela, tel: 713 7040. Located in the suburbs some distance from the centre (take the number 52 bus from the central market and get off at the Baltinavas stop), this hotel offers small apartments with TV, shower and toilet at Ls8.35–14 per night.

Saulīte 12 Merķeļa iela, tel: 722 4546 or 722 8219. Located near the station; good value with rates Ls4–18 for a single room and Ls7–20 for a double.

Sports 5 Gogoļa iela, tel: 722 6780. Centrally located between the station and the central market, this is a run-down hotel with almost no amenities. Rooms from Ls4 (single) to Ls6.40 (doubles).

Valdemārs 23 Kr Valdemāra iela, tel: 733 2132 or 733 4462; fax: 733 3001. Centrally located in an art nouveau building, the Valdemārs is clean and spacious. Room prices Ls14–23 for a single, Ls28–38 for a double.

Apartments

As an alternative to hotels, especially for long-term visits, there are a number of organisations that rent apartments.

Magda 24 Smilšu iela, room 609, tel: 722 5049.
Patricija 22 Elizabetes iela, office 6, tel: 728 4868.

Rīga Tourist Information Bureau will also help (see page 52).

Bed and breakfast

Patricija 22 Elizabetes iela, office 6, in addition to organising apartments will put you in touch with people offering bed and breakfast. Phone number as above.

Youth hostels

For up-to-date information, contact the **Hostel Association** at 2a Laimdotas iela, tel: 755 1271.

Placis 2a Laimdotas iela, tel: 755 1824. Prices are Ls3–6 a night. There are double and single rooms. Take the number 4 trolleybus or the number 1, 14 or 32 bus to the Teika stop.

Studentu Kopmītne 10 Basteja bulvāris, tel: 721 6221. Student rooms above the Baltika travel agency at Ls3–4 per person per night.

Technical University Hostel 22a Āzenes iela, tel: 203395 or 613843. Basic accommodation at Ls3 per person per night. Located on the Ķīpsala island, take the trolleybus (number 7 or 21) across the Daugava.

Turība 68 Graudu iela, tel: 790 1471. 158 beds at Ls5–7 per night. Take the number 8 trolleybus from Strēlnieku laukums to the Graudu stop.

Food and drink

Restaurants can now be found in all parts of the city. The current situation is very different from the Soviet era when finding anything to eat (or even a coffee) outside the tourist hotels was difficult, indeed almost impossible. However, the new spirit of enterprise does not always bear fruit, and restaurants come and go, so visitors are advised to check that any restaurant recommended is still in operation before turning up. Bookings are rarely necessary, except where stated – supply outstrips demand.

For obvious reasons the list below is eclectic and makes no claim to being comprehensive. Standards are generally high, so if a restaurant looks clean and decorated it is reasonable to assume that the food will be good.

The overwhelming majority of restaurants take the usual credit cards.

Expensive

Boulevard N20 20 Aspāzijas bulvāris, tel: 721 6061. Located in a basement next to the Hotel de Rome, this restaurant established in 1998 offers mainly steak, pizza and pasta.

Columbine Metropole Hotel, 36–38 Aspāzijas bulvāris, tel: 721 6161. Part of the Metropole Hotel, this is rated as one of the best restaurants in Rīga, offering international cuisine of the highest standard. Its Swedish breakfasts are famous. Expect to pay Ls25 or thereabouts for dinner.

Eurolink Restaurant Eurolink Hotel (on the third floor of the Rīga Hotel – see above). Good food with a Scandinavian emphasis. Dinner Ls15 per head.

Grill Room Radisson SAS Daugava Hotel, 24 Kuģu iela, tel: 796 1111. This restaurant has a high standard, but being part of a large international hotel lacks atmosphere. Expect to spend about Ls30 a head. The Grill Room is closed on Sunday and Monday.

Lielāis Kamielis 3 Vecpilsētas iela, tel: 721 2614. The 'Big Camel' is a well established restaurant in the cellar of a former merchant's house and comes highly recommended as a place serving good Latvian food. Booking is advised.

Lolo Pub 51 Elizabetes iela, tel: 728 1849. Not a pub, but a sophisticated restaurant serving European food and said to be frequented by diplomats. Budget for about Ls20 a head.

Man-Tess 6 Teātra iela, tel: 721 6056. Although many of the restaurants in the upper price bracket belong to hotels and suffer from all that that means in terms of atmosphere, the Man-Tess restaurant is different because the hotel is so small. The restaurant is on the ground floor of this attractive building in the Old Town. Booking is advised since it has only five or six tables. Expect to pay about Ls20–25 a head.

Otto Schwarz Hotel de Rome, 28 Kaļķu iela, tel: 708 7623. Located on the top floor of the hotel, this is a restaurant in the international mould but with an emphasis on German cuisine. Excellent views over the Freedom Monument. Vegetarian menu. Prices are international so allow about Ls20 a head.

Palete 12–14 Gleznotāju iela, tel: 721 6037. Opened in 1998 in an elegant building in a narrow street in the Old Town, the Palete is worth a visit. Atmospheric and elegant with unobtrusive piano music and good value at about Ls12 per person for a full meal with wine, much less if you just have a snack. The name means 'palette' and comes from its location in Painter Street.

Raibais Balodis Konventa Sēta, 9–11 Kalēju iela, tel: 708 7501. Part of the Konventa Sēta Hotel. Good food in an attractive setting and well located in the Old Town.

Symposium 84/1 Dzirnavu iela, tel: 724 2545. A well known and respected restaurant in the Berga Bazars area serving Mediterranean food. About Ls15 a head.

Vēja Roza TV tower, 3 Zaķusalas krastmala, tel: 710 8643. 'The Wind Rose' is the name of the restaurant 93 metres up in the TV tower. Expensive, as one might expect for this sort of location.

Vincents 19 Elizabetes icla, tel. 733 2634 or 733 2830, fax: 783 0206, email: ritins@mbox.rīga.lv, web: www.vincents.lv. Vincents (the name comes from the van Gogh reproductions which decorate it) is an atmospheric restaurant in the New Town offering Latvian, French, Italian, Asian and Mexican cuisine – at least that is what it claims. It has an attractive terrace for open-air eating in summer. Expect to spend about Ls15 a head.

Zivju Restorāns 4 Vāgnera iela, tel: 721 6713. Rīga's best fish restaurant is relatively expensive and generally used by expense-account diners. When we visited, the president was holding a reception in a private room at the back of the restaurant. Ls25 a head.

Medium price

Arve 12–14 Aldaru iela, tel: 721 6452 or 722 0649. Cellar restaurant, moderately priced. Conveniently located near the Swedish Gate in the Old Town.

Bordo 23 Kr Valdemāra iela, tel: 724 0388. Basic setting, but good value.

Kalanda 8–10 Jāņa iela, tel: 722 9775. Extremely pleasant restaurant located in an old house with an attractive courtyard. It is divided into different rooms which give it an intimate feel. Convenient for the Old Town.

Livonija 21 Meistaru iela, tel: 722 8093. Another cellar restaurant offering Latvian cuisine.

Mežonīgā Plūme 79 Ģertrūdes iela, tel: 724 4160. The name means 'Wild Plum'. Not central, but convenient if you are in the New Town, it serves a wide range of dishes in generous portions. Excellent value.

Oāze 2a J Alunāna iela, tel: 732 1920. Located opposite the British Embassy in an art nouveau setting, the Oāze serves Latvian food.

Pie Kamina Hotel Latvijā, 55 Elizabetes iela, tel: 721 2381. Location in the unprepossessing Hotel Latvijā is compensated for by the fact that this restaurant (the name means 'At the fireside') is on the 25th floor, so the views are terrific. A favourite in the Soviet era, it now serves decent food at moderate prices.

Pūt, Vējiņ! 18–22 Jauniela, tel: 721 2291. The bar downstairs serves drinks and modest food, but there is an excellent restaurant upstairs serving a good variety of well cooked food in pleasant surroundings. Highly recommended. The name means 'Blow, the Winds'.

Rozamunde 8 Mazā Smilšu iela, tel: 722 7798. A traditional Latvian restaurant on the first floor in a former student fraternity house. The café on the ground floor is more modest.

Senā Rīga Hotel Rīga, 22 Aspāzijas bulvāris, tel: 721 6869. Latvian restaurant forming part of the Hotel Rīga. Traditional Latvian interior; staff wear national costume.

Sirdsmīļa 11 Aldaru iela, tel: 721 2585. The name means 'sweetheart' in Latvian, and this is an intimate restaurant: it only has four tables, so booking is advisable.

Staburags 55 Čaka iela, tel: 299787. Traditional Latvian.

Others

American Café Radisson SAS Hotel, tel: 733 4672. American 50s' style café in the Radisson Hotel. Serves crêpes and sandwiches as well as a range of American-style food.

Aragats 15 Miera iela, tel: 373445. An Armenian restaurant that comes highly recommended in local sources.

Dickens 11 Grēcinieku, tel: 721 3087. An immediate success on opening in late 1999 with the large British community in Rīga, both for the beer and for the food.

Divi Laši 8 Tirgoņu iela, tel: 722 8214. Self-service fish restaurant. The name means 'Two Salmon'.

Faetons 41 Lacplesa, tel 728 0167. Probably the best of the five Armenian restaurants in Rīga but still reasonably priced.

Feniks 54 Kaleju, tel 722 8009. A reasonably priced Chinese restaurant.

Grieķu Restorāns 10–12 Skārņu iela, tel: 721 1026. Rīga's only Greek restaurant, conveniently located in the Old Town. Excellent atmosphere, and a menu you would expect to find at a Greek restaurant anywhere.

Jever 6 Kaļķu iela, tel: 722 7078. Specialises in German fare.

Mārrutku Maizītes 4 Krāmu iela. A Soviet-theme café serving Russian food. The name means 'horseradish sandwiches'.

Murphy's Pub 12 Teātra iela, tel: 721 6961. One of Rīga's many 'Irish' pubs. Serves food, although it is not especially Irish. Central location; good value.

Paddy Whelan's 4 Grēcnieku iela, tel: 721 0249. A pleasant 'Irish' pub, Paddy Whelan's serves good food and is popular with locals. It is a short walk from the Hotel Rīga, the Man-Tess and many other central hotels.

Paldies Dievam 11. Novembra, Krastmala 9, tel: 750 3964. Rīga had to wait until 2000 for its first Caribbean restaurant and cocktail bar but early reports are positive.

Petergailis Peterbaznīcas iela (alongside St Peter's Church), tel: 721 2888. The unprepossessing exterior conceals a sophisticated restaurant inside.

Verdiņš 11 Mazā Pils iela, tel: 722 1339. French, but not necessarily expensive, as Verdiņš serves crepes and cheaper food as well as its standard French food.

Zelta Panda 54 Kalēju iela, tel: 722 1339. Good Chinese food, moderate prices, conveniently located near the Centrs department store. The name means 'The Golden Panda'.

Zilais Putns 4 Tirgoāu iela, tel: 722 8214. 'The Blue Bird' on the Dome square serves Italian food.

Vegetarian

Andalūzijas Suns 83–85 Elizabetes iela, tel: 728 8418. The 'Andalucian Dog', as this café is called, must take its name from the Buñuel-Dali film *Chien Andalou*. The menu is Japanese inspired.

Fast food

American Fried Chicken 33–35 Tērbatas iela.

McDonalds 18 Basteja bulvāris.

McDrive 434 Brīvības gatve, 101 Krasta iela, and 76a Lubānas iela.

Pizza Lulu 27 Ģertrūdes iela and 145 Kr Valdemāra iela.

Ņujorkas Pica (New York Pizza), 8 Blaumaāa iela.

Pīrāgi 14 Kr Barona iela (entrance in Elizabetes iela), serves *pīrāg* (small pies or pasties stuffed with cabbage or meat and onion).

Cafés

Rīga is full of cafés where you can drink tea and coffee and eat cakes, pastries and snacks and can also order modest meals and alcoholic drinks. The Latvian café can be compared in that sense with cafés in Germany or Holland. Most of them are open from the morning (when they serve breakfast) until late at night (generally at least until 22.00 or midnight).

Anre 30 Aspāzijas bulvāris, serves cheap food and drink.

Café Opera 3 Aspāzijas bulvāris, is an elegant café in the opera house; 19th century interior.

Coffee Bar Centrs, 16 Audēju iela. Pleasant café in the Centrs department store.

Favorite 52 Kr Barona iela. Candle-lit café which serves exotic drinks.

Ice Queen 20 Ģertrūdes iela. Ice-cream café.

Jautrais Jēkabs 4–IIc Torņa iela.

Jautrais Maiznieks 95 Brīvības iela.

Kafijas Veikals 6 Mazā pils iela.

Kolonade 26 Brīvības iela, serves good tea, coffee and pastries.

Leduspuķe 28 Vaļņu iela.

Lolo Café 51 Elizabetes iela (entrance Baznīcas iela). An elegant café in the Viennese tradition serving excellent breakfasts and good-quality cakes and pastries.

Mednieks (The Hunter), 24 Peldu iela.

Monte Kristo 27 Ģertrūdes iela. Coffee and cakes.

Operas Galerija 28 Kaļķu iela (Hotel de Rome). Elegant café/bar.

Osiris 31 Kr Barona iela. Next door to the bookshop.

Sala 85a Elizabetes iela. The name means 'island'. First-class cakes and pastries.

Smāragds 18 Jāņa iela. A pleasant café serving a range of drinks, cakes and snacks.

Vēja Stundā 53 Dzirnavu iela. 'The Hour of the Wind' is a cosy basement café close to the Hotel Latvijā.

Bars

There are hundreds of bars in Rīga. Arguably the classification 'bar' is not a helpful one in Latvia, since restaurants, cafés and bars often overlap. You can drink alcohol in all three, often without having to order food. The bars mentioned below are a small and random selection. Bear in mind that all the major hotels also have one or more bars.

Ala 11 Audēju iela, tel: 722 3957. The name means 'The Cave'. Good cocktails at moderate prices.

Kalanda 8–10 Jāņa iela, tel: 722 9775. A bar serving a wide range of drinks. Also a restaurant.

Lido Alus Bārs 76 Dzirnavu iela, tel: 728 6204. A beer bar with a medieval atmosphere that will appeal to some and not to others.

Lidojoūā Varde 31a Elizabetes iela, at the corner of Antonijas iela, tel: 732 1184. 'The Flying Frog' advertises widely in local magazines and serves food as well as drink. Flamenco night on Tuesday, jazz on Thursday. It serves excellent food at cheap prices. Handy when exploring Rīga's art nouveau buildings.

M6 Mārstaļu iela, tel: 721 2640. A pleasant bar located behind a gallery.

Murphy's Pub Irish pub – see *Restaurants* above for details.

Ordenis 5 Jāņa Sēta, tel: 722 8223. A pleasant bar, well located in St John's Courtyard in the Old Town.

Paddy Whelan's Irish pub – see *Restaurants* above for details.

Piebalga 7 Laipu iela, tel: 722 4253. A beer bar known for the wide range of local beers.

Pie Zviedru Vārtiem 11 Aldaru iela, tel: 721 0184. A pleasant bar close to the Swedish Gate from which it takes its name.

Pulkvedim Neviens Neraksta 26-28 Peldu iela, tel: 721 3886. 'Nobody writes to the Colonel' is said to be one of Rīga's trendiest venues. This bar and restaurant also has live DJs and a dance floor. Advance booking is advised.

Runcis Jāņa Sēta, tel: 722 4198. 'The Tomcat' is a noisy bar located in the St John's Courtyard (Jāņa Sēta) part of the Old Town and has a cat theme.

Sams 40 Brīvības iela, tel: 728 8256. A popular bar where it can be hard to get a table.

Vēja Brāļu Ordenis 25 Marijas iela, tel: 728 9026. The name means 'The Order of Brothers of the Wind'. This bar was originally designed for the members of a motorcycle club, a fact reflected in the decor.

Entertainment

Jazz and music clubs

Blūzs 170 Brīvības iela.

Cita Opera 21 Raiņa iela. The name means 'Alternative Opera'.

Kabata 19 Peldu iela, tel: 951 6517. 'Pocket' is a basement club, and extremely fashionable at the moment.

Karakums 18 Lāčplēša iela, tel: 728 2287. Popular dance bar.

Ligzda 59 Maltas iela, tel: 731 2207.

Reformātu Club & Restaurant 10 Mārstaļu iela. Rīga's best-known club of its kind is also famous for its first-class food. The entrance is in Alksnāja iela.

Rothmans 1 Tilta iela.

Saksofons 43 Stabu iela, tel: 29 6678. Look for the saxophone sign outside.

Nightclubs

7-Up Club 130 Kr Barona iela.

Aeroplāns 6 Lomonosova iela, tel: 724 1508. Dancing, billiards, gaming machines, disco and bar.

Aladins 32 Čaka iela, tel: 728 8781. Bar, casino and 'adult' entertainment.

Bimini 67–69 Čaka iela, tel: 29 0610. Billiards and slot machines.

Dailā Impērija 31 Brīvības iela, tel: 721 2552. The dancing on Thursday, Friday and Saturday nights make this one of Rīga's most popular venues.

Groks Stacija 22 Kaļķu iela. Dance club designed in the form of an underground station platform – complete with graffiti.

Jockey Club 49 Elizabetes iela, tel: 722 8844. Scandinavian nightclub, open 24 hours: restaurant, night club, floorshow (at least that is what it advertises).

Klubs 3 22–24 Grēcinieku iela, tel: 722 6750. 'Adult' entertainment.

Monte Kristo 8 Merģeļa iela. Open 24 hours.

Ole 1 Audēju iela, tel: 722 3206. Billiards and café on the first floor, night club on the second floor.

Panna 2a Laimdotas iela, tel: 731 2362. Dance club.

Ratuža Pagrabs 2 Krāmu iela, tel: 721 2355. Discos organised by the Technical University on Thursday, Friday and Saturday nights.

Slepenais Eksperiments 15 Skūņu iela, tel: 722 7917. The 'Secret Experiment' is a techno-design music club, but many people come here for its cheap lunch during the day. Open until 05.00.

Super FM 12 Bezdelīgu iela, tel: 610106. Teenage-oriented disco organised by a local radio station. Closes at 23.00.

Underground 1 Slokas iela, tel: 615456. Dance club.

XXL 63 Bruņinieku iela, tel: 273883. Topless bar.

Zero Zone 27 Kandavas iela, tel: 458062. Claims to be the biggest night club in Rīga: disco, bar and pool.

Casinos

The term 'casino' covers a great deal, from places which offer little more than gambling machines to places offering real card games.

Admirāļu Klubs 12 Audēju iela, and 8 Blaumaņa iela. Advertises widely in hotels and elsewhere.

Aladins 32 Čaka iela, and 5 Tērbatas iela. Cafés with gambling machines. Also has branches in other Latvian towns.

Casino Latvijā 24 Kaļķu iela.

Doms Casino 5–7 Tirgoņu iela.

Jack Spot 2 Avotu iela.

Karo 72 Brīvības iela.

Klondaika 1 Grēcinieku iela.

Labrints 32 Aspāzijas bulvāris.

Mirage 22 Aspāzijas bulvāris, is part of the Hotel Rīga: food, drink, dancing and gambling.

New York 16 Audēju iela, is also a bar restaurant, disco and night club.

Regency Palace 24 Kuģu iela.

Royal Casino 55 Elizabetes iela.

Tornis 7 Smilšu iela.

Theatres

Club Hamlet 5 Jāņa Sēta, tel: 722 9938. Not really a theatre but a club organised by the Latvian Actors' Association. Live performances every Wednesday, Friday, Saturday and Sunday.

Dailes Theatre 75 Brīvības iela, tel: 727 0278.

Kabata Theatre Studio 19 Peldu iela, tel: 951 6517 or 951 6779.
National Theatre 2 Kronvalda iela, tel: 732 2759.
Rīgas Jaunais Teātris (New Rīga Theatre) 25 Lāčplēša iela, tel: 728 0765.
Puppet Theatre 16–18 Kr Barona iela, tel: 728 5355.
Krievu Drāmas Teātris (Russian Drama Theatre) 16 Kaļķu iela, tel: 722 4660.
Skatuve 108–110 Maskāvas iela, tel: 722 2281.
Youth Theatre 1 Ropažu iela, tel: 755 1801.

Music
Opera and ballet
Latvian National Opera 3 Aspāzijas bulvāris, box office 10–12 Teātra iela, tel: 722 5747, fax: 722 8240.

Concert halls
Concerts are held at the places mentioned below and at a number of Rīga churches, for example, St Peter's. The organ recitals in the Dome are world famous. The Latvian National Symphony Orchestra enjoys a high reputation. The Ave Sol and Wagner Hall are used for chamber music; orchestral concerts generally take place in the Great Guildhall or the Dome.

Ave Sol 7 Citadeles iela, tel: 327 670.
Dome Cathedral Doma laukums, tel: 721 3498. The box office opposite the cathedral has closed. Tickets can be purchased just inside the porch of the main entrance or at the Filharmonijas Kase, 6 Amatu iela and in the Wagner Hall, 4 R Vāgnera iela.
Lielā Ģilde (Great Guildhall) 6 Amatu iela, tel: 721 3798.
Mazā Ģilde (Small Guildhall) 3–5 Amatu iela, tel: 722 3772.
Vāgnera Zāle (Wagner Hall), 4 R Vāgnera iela, tel: 721 0814 or 721 3426.

Cinemas
For information on what is on in English telephone 118 777 0777 or 118 722 2222. Many films are in English with subtitles in Latvian and Russian.

Daile 31 Barona iela, tel: 728 3854.
Kino 52 52–54 Lāčplēša iela, tel: 728 8778.
Kinogalerija 24 Jauniela, tel: 722 9030.
Oskars 2 Skolas iela, tel: 733 3643.
Palladium 21 Marijas iela, tel: 728 1610.
Rīga 61 Elizabetes iela, tel: 728 1105.

Shopping
Shopping in Rīga is good: you can buy almost anything you are likely to need. Below, however, are the names of some shops selling items which are peculiar to Latvia or Rīga. Amber and jewellery are popular purchases, as are traditional wooden toys and linen. Latvian art is popular, especially ceramics. Consult *Rīga in Your Pocket* and the other Rīga city guides for details of local commercial galleries and what they are showing. *Laima* sweets and chocolates and the traditional Black Balsam drink in its distinctive bottle are also popular souvenirs.

Generally, shops are open between 09.00/10.00 and 18.00/19.00 on Mondays to Fridays, closing an hour or so earlier on Saturdays. Most are closed on Sundays, although those catering for tourists now tend to open every day. Food shops open a little earlier and some stay open until 21.00 to 22.00 It is still common, particularly for small shops, to close for lunch, often from 14.00 to 15.00.

Antiques

Note that a licence from the Inspection Board for History and Culture and the Protection of Monuments is generally needed before you can export antiques or valuables. There are no customs duties if goods are exported to EU countries, and reduced rates are payable on export to certain designated countries (for example, Australia, Canada and Russia). For further information, consult the Board at 22 Pils iela, tel: 721 4100.

Antiqua 20 Kr Valdemāra iela, tel: 728 4377.
Antiqua 4–IIc Torņa iela, tel: 732 1199.
Antikvariats 8 Baznīcas iela.
Bonus Antiks 6 Merķeļa iela, tel: 722 6903.
Galerija 53 Dzirnavu icla, tel: 728 2978.
Lade 53 Ģertrūdes iela, tel: 728 1975.
Raritets 45 Čaka icla, tel: 275157.
Tango 66 Dzirnavu iela, tel: 728 9286.
Volmar 39 Brīvības iela, tel: 728 3436.
Volmar 13 Mazā pils iela, tel: 732 5432.

Bookshops

The **Valters un Rapa** bookshop in Aspāzijas bulvāris at the corner of Teatrā iela, opposite the main entrance of the Hotel Rīga, is good for maps, language books, art books, postcards and stationery. It has a large Russian section. The **Jāņa Sēta** bookshop is excellent for maps and guidebooks. The **Jāņa Rozes**, next door to Jāņa Sēta, is one of the best sources of foreign-language books in Rīga.

Aperto Libro 31 Kr Barona iela.
Daina 38 Brīvības iela.
Globuss 26 Vaļāu iela.
Jāņa Rozes 85a Elizabetes iela; branches also at 5 Kr Barona iela, 90 Brīvības iela, 'Dole', 375 Maskavas iela, 57 Dzirnavu iela and 4a Visvalža iela.
Jāņa Sēta 83-85 Elizabetes iela.
Planeta 5 Tērbatas iela.
Valters un Rapa 24 Aspāzijas bulvāris.

Jewellery

A & E 17 Jauniela.
Dimants 66 Brīvības iela.
Senās Baltu Rotas 4 Krāmu iela.

Music

CDs and cassettes are cheap, but watch out for pirated and counterfeit products.

Bass 23 Ģertrūdes iela.
Bel Canto 5 Vāgnera iela.
D.S.M. 22 Grēcinieku iela.
M-Daile 31 Kr Barona iela.
Mikrofons 6 Audēju iela.

Souvenirs

A & E 17 Jauniela. Specialists in amber.
Amatnieku Darinājumi 5 Amatu iela.
Dailrade 28 Vaļņu iela.
Ezerciems 7–9 Kaļķu iela.
Livs 15 Jauniela.
Māksla 35 11. Novembra krastmala.
Māra 9–11 Kalēju iela.
Nordwear Amberfree Souvenirs 1 Grēcinieku and 2 Kaļķu.
Pine 4 Torņa iela.
Rota 9–11 Kalēju iela.
Sakta 32 Brīvības bulvāris.
Senā Klēts 28a Kr Barona iela.
Tautas Mākslas Salons 25 Vaļņu iela.
Vecpilsēta 7–9 Kaļķu iela.
Ventus 9 Torņa iela.
Ženēva 5 Vāgnera iela.

Food

Food shops are easy to find. The **central market** (see page 92) is good for fresh food. The **Rimi** department store has a large food department on the ground floor (see below for details). The following food supermarkets can also be found in central Rīga:

Interpegro 18 Elizabetes iela (open 10.00–22.00; closes 19.00 on Sunday); branch also at 33 Raiņa iela (entrance in Marijas iela).
Maksi Markets 110 Deglava iela (open 09.00–21.00; closes 18.00 on Sunday).
Rimi 16 Audēju iela (Universalveikals) (open 08.00–22.00; 09.00–19.00 on Saturday and 10.00–17.00 on Sunday).

There are 24-hour shops designated by the sign *diennakti* ('day and night'):

Ābolītis 17 Kr Barona iela.
Aga 25 Kr Valdemāra iela.
Diennakts Veikals 11 Vaļņu iela.
Elida-L 10 Grēcinieku iela.
Visbija 68 Brīvības iela.

Specialities

Laima chocolates are sold at 22 Miera iela, 16 Smilšu iela, 16 Marijas iela, and at other branches in Rīga (and throughout Latvia).
Latvijas Balzams 1 Marijas iela, and other branches in Rīga. More than 50 different types of Latvian alcoholic drinks, including the well-known Black Balsam.

Latvijas Bite 13 Ģertrūdes iela, is the honey shop of the Latvian Association of Beekeepers and specialises in honey and related products.
Symposium Vini 84 Dzirnavu iela (in the Berga Bazars), is one of Rīga's best-known wine shops.

Medical services
Hospital Gailezeva; Hipokrata 2
Dentist Elladent; Vilandes 18 (open 09.00–23.00 Mon–Fri; 09.00–14.00 Sat–Sun).
Pharmacy There is a 24-hour emergency pharmacy (aptieka) service (ring the bell) at the Karmēlijas aptieka, 74 Brīvības iela, tel: 293514 and at Krastmala aptieka, 29 11. Novembra krastmala, tel: 722 3065.

Embassies
Canada Doma Laukums 4, tel: 722 6315, fax: 783 0140.
Estonia Skolas 13, tel: 781 2020, fax: 781 2029.
Lithuania Rūpniecības 24, tel: 732 1519, fax: 732 1589.
Russia Antonijas 2, tel: 721 2579, fax: 783 0209.
UK Alunana 5, tel: 733 8126, fax: 733 8132.

Places of worship
The majority of churches are Lutheran, Orthodox churches coming in second place. Few offer services in languages other than Latvian or Russian.

Church of England St Saviour's, 2a Anglikāņu iela (service in English 10.00 Sunday).
Lutheran The Dome (Sunday 12.00); St John's (Sunday 10.00); other Lutheran churches abound.
Old Believers Grebenščikova Church, 73 Krasta iela (service in Russian 08.00 Sunday).
Orthodox The Orthodox Cathedral, 23 Brīvības iela.
Roman Catholic St Jacob's, 7 Jāņa iela (the Roman Catholic cathedral); Our Lady of Sorrows, Lielā Pils iela.
Synagogue 6–8 Peitavas iela (Hebrew services at 09.00 and sunset on Saturday).

WHAT TO SEE
It is best to see Rīga on foot. The Old Town is a relatively small area, and if pushed for time, you could walk around most of it in a day, although that will only give you a superficial impression. To see the Old Town more thoroughly and to see something of the New Town, you should allow two days. A car is not much use: access to the Old Town is restricted for cars, and parking in the New Town can be hard to find.

Old Town
The majority of sights are in the Old Town (*Vecrīga*), which is the area of the city located between the Daugava river and the city canal (*pilsētas kanāls*). The Old Town contains a wealth of historic buildings from the medieval town walls dating back to the 13th century to the grey modernity of the flats and offices built when Latvia was part of the Soviet Union. Between the two extremes there are buildings of almost every period and style, classical, Gothic,

art nouveau and modern. Much of the Old Town suffered neglect when Latvia was part of the USSR, but a great deal of restoration and reconstruction has been undertaken in the years following independence (the reconstruction of the Konventa sēta area being one of the best examples).

The best way to see the Old Town is on foot: the area is relatively small, but in any event, large parts of the Old Town have been made traffic-free zones (there is access for vehicles, but you have to buy a pass), while other parts consist of narrow streets, making vehicle access impractical. Many of the streets are cobbled and others suffer from lack of maintenance, so you have to keep your eyes open for holes and uneven road and pavement surfaces. Wear sensible walking shoes.

The main sights of the Old Town are described below by reference to two suggested walking routes covering the Old Town sights on either side of Kaļķu iela.

Walk one
Our first walk starts from the Hotel de Rome at the corner of Kaļķu iela and Aspāzijas bulvāris, not far from the Freedom Monument. Take the road leading away from the Freedom Monument and the parks along the side of the hotel and you will find yourself almost immediately at Vaļāu iela, a pedestrianised street of shops, bars and cafés. Turn right into Vaļāu iela. At the end of the street you will see one of the major landmarks of the Old Town, the Powder Tower.

Powder Tower
The **Powder Tower** (*Pulvertornis*) is one of the oldest buildings in Rīga. Its name is derived from the fact that it was once used to store gunpowder, although at times it was also referred to as the Sand Tower after Smilūu iela (Sand Street), the road that leads past the tower and which was once the main road to Pskov in Russia. Records of the tower can be traced back to 1330. The tower is the sole survivor of what used to be 18 towers that formed part of the city fortifications. Because it was used to store gunpowder it had to be dry, well ventilated and secure, hence the walls which are 2½m thick. They were relatively effective: nine cannonballs are said to be embedded in the walls, relics of the Russian invasions of 1656 and 1710. Only the lower parts of the tower are original. The tower was substantially destroyed by Swedish forces in 1621 and restored in 1650.

Since it ceased to have any military significance, the Powder Tower has been put to various uses. In 1892 it was used as the headquarters of a German student fraternity called Rubonia. After World War I it was turned into a war museum. In 1957 it became the Latvian Museum of the Revolution and functioned as such until independence. Now it houses the War Museum.

Smilšu iela
Smilšu iela itself is one of Rīga's oldest streets. Some say it got its name from the sand of which the road was made; others say the name comes from the Kubes Hill and nearby sand dunes which were levelled in the 17th century. If you stand in Smilšu iela facing the Powder Tower and look across Basteja bulvāris you can just see the remains of Bastion Hill (*Basteja kalns*), one of the fortification towers dating back to the 17th century.

RĪGA: OLD TOWN

VANŠU BRIDGE

✈ Airport,
Jūrmala

CITADELES

VALDEMĀRA

KRONVALDA

VINGROTĀJU

National Theatre

Riga Castle

PILS
LAUKUMS

TORŅA

Canal

Our Lady
of Sorrows

BASTEJA

POĻU

ANGLIKĀŅU

PILS

MAZA PILS

KLOST.

JĒKABA

ALDARU

St Jacob's

St Saviour's

Grand
Palace

The Three
Brothers

Powder Tower

MŪKU

SMILŠU

DOMA
LAUKUMS

MAZA SMILŠU

VALŅU

Dome

ZIRGU

New Town

Arena

History &
Navigation
Museum

PALASTA

Concert Hall
& Guildhalls

ŠĶŪŅU

AMATU

MEISTARU

BRĪVĪBAS

Former Palace of Peter I

JAUNIELA

Technical
University

KAĻĶU

Russian Drama Theatre

Hotel de Rome

Tourist Information

ℹ

Blackheads'
House

Occupation
Museum

Konventenhof

ŠĶŪŅU

Decorative &
Applied Arts Museum

Convent
Courtyard

VAGNERA

KALĒJU

Pharmacy
Museum

Rīga Hotel/Eurolink

AKMENS BRIDGE

GRĒCINIEKU

St Peter's

St John's

St John's
Courtyard

Man-Tess

TEĀTRA

National Opera

II NOVEMBRA

KUŅGU

PĒLDU

JĀŅA

Mentzendorff
House

Radi un Draugi

The Reiter House

AUDĒJU

Hotel
Centra

VALŅU

ASPAZIJAS

MĀRSTAĻU

ALKSNAJA

Monument to those
who fought in 1905

MISTEREJAS

Metropol

Daugava

KALĒJU

Station

0 ━━━━ 100 m
0 ━━━━ 100 yds

↓ Main routes out of Rīga

Torņa iela
Behind the Powder Tower is Torņa iela (Tower Street), a well restored, traffic-free street. Next to the tower is the entrance to what is now again the **War Museum**, (*Latvijas Kara Muzejs*) (open 10.00–18.00 except on Monday and Tuesday). The museum is devoted to the military history of Latvia and concentrates heavily on recent history with permanent exhibitions devoted to the World War I, the 1905 revolution and the liberation struggle of 1918–20, and the fate of Latvia during World War II.

Further along Torņa iela you come to part of the city wall (best seen from the parallel Trokšņu iela). Rīga was protected by a wall from the early 13th century. Eventually it extended to a length of some two kilometres. By the 14th century the walls were 1.8m thick. The arches between the pillars would be filled with stones and sandbags to provide reinforcement when the city was under siege; in peacetime they were emptied again and used for storage or as stables or even accommodation. The income derived from letting the arches was used to raise money to pay for the upkeep of the city's defences.

Swedish Gate
At the corner of Torņa iela and Aldaru iela (Brewer Street) is the **Swedish Gate** (*Zviedru Vārti*), so called because it was built when Rīga was under Swedish rule and because it was the gate through which the Swedish king, Gustavus Adolphus, entered the city in 1621. It is the only city gate still left intact. According to legend, the citizens of Rīga abducted a young Latvian woman who had unwisely fallen in love with a Swedish soldier and was meeting him secretly near the gate, and walled her up in the gate as a warning to others. The Swedish Gate is unusual in that it passes through a whole house (number 11 Torņa iela). The house at number 11 is the first recorded house in private ownership in Rīga. It is recorded as belonging to Ivan Martin Serpentin who acquired it on April 2 1679. The first floor was let to a man called Kordu, the town lamplighter, who paid a rent of six taler per annum.

Executioner's House
Although it is not possible to visit them, there are several attractively restored **historic houses** on Torņa iela of which the most notorious is the one now at numbers 7–9, a large pink house that was once occupied by the city executioner until the position was abolished in 1863. Number 5 Torņa iela was the site of the prison built in 1685 by Rupert Bindenschu, the architect who also worked on the reconstruction of St Peter's Church.

Jēkaba laukums and the Arsenal
At the end of Torņa iela you come to Jēkaba iela (Jacob or James Street) and to the right Jēkaba laukums (Jacob or James Square), where concrete barricades were erected during the struggles of January 1991. The square, which was first laid out in the 18th century, was once used for military parades and exercises, but gradually fell into disuse and neglect. It was restored in 1924 and new flowerbeds and a play area for children were added.

On the side of the square closest to Jēkaba iela is a row of low buildings. The middle building, taller than the others, is the former Arsenal. Built in 1828–32 to designs by I Lukini and A Nellinger on the site of what was once part of the town wall, the arsenal that stood here was replaced by a customs house. Now the building is a gallery (the **Arsenals Museum of Fine Arts**, *Mākslas Muzejs 'Arsenals'*) where modern painters exhibit (open 11.00–17.00 every day except Mondays).

Castle Square and Rīga Castle

Close to the end of Torņa iela is a green which forms part of Pils laukums (Castle Square). The large building on the corner on your right is the **Bank of Latvia**, built in 1905 to designs by the Latvian architect, Reinbergs. Number 2 Pils laukums was, until recently, a Red Army museum but is now part of the Museum of Literature and Art History described below and is used for temporary exhibitions (open 11.00–17.00 except Monday).

The main building on Pils laukums is **Rīga Castle** (*Rigas pils*), a large yellow building with a red roof. The present structure is the last of three which have stood here. Its predecessors were two Livonian castles, the first of which was built in 1330, the second in 1515. The leader of the Livonian Order lived in Rīga castle up to 1470 when his residence was moved, eventually to Cēsis. The people of Rīga destroyed the castle in 1487 but were forced to build a replacement by Walter von Plettenberg, the last head of the Livonian Order. It was completed in 1515 and included the so-called Lead Tower (*Svina tornis*) which still stands. The castle was extended in the 18th century by the addition of a new wing which became the residence of the Russian governor, and from 1918–40 that of the president of Latvia. It also underwent substantial restoration in 1938 which included construction of the 'Three Stars Tower', easily recognised by the three stars on its top. In the early part of the 19th century Wilhelm von Kester built an observatory on the main tower from which Alexander I of Russia observed the solar eclipse of April 23 1818.

Now the castle houses three museums: the **Latvian History Museum**, *Latvijas Vēstures Muzejs* (open 11.00–17.00, except Monday and Tuesday), which traces the course of Latvian history from 9000BC to the 20th century; the **Latvian Museum of Foreign Art**, *Latvijas Ārzemju Mākslas Muzejs* (open 11.00–17.00, except Monday and Tuesday), the biggest collection of foreign art in Latvia; and the **Rainis Museum of Literature and Art History**, *Raiņa Literaturas un Mākslas Vēstures Muzejs* (open 11.00–17.00, except Monday).

The Museum of Foreign Art is odd, since many of the oldest exhibits (sculptures from Greece and Rome and artefacts from ancient Egypt) are mixed up with modern works; the more conventional galleries exhibit paintings by 17th century Dutch artists, German works dating from the 16th–19th centuries and Belgian painting of the 20th century. There are almost no works of great distinction.

The Rainis Museum was founded in 1925 and is devoted to Latvian literature. Exhibits include photographs, manuscripts and texts relating to the history of Latvian literature from its earliest times right up to the 20th century. Recent additions are two exhibitions devoted to Gunārs Freimanis (1927–93) and Voldemārs Zariņš (1917–81), both of whom were persecuted by the Soviet authorities. Freimanis spent 10 years in the Russian *gulags*; Zariņš was sent to forced labour in the coal mines of Tula. The museum is interesting as an example of how Latvia is trying to emphasise its cultural and national identity after independence. Unfortunately, all the information (except for a short pamphlet) is in Latvian.

To the right of the castle, in the direction of Kr Valdemāra iela, is the old stable block (unused at present).

Our Lady of Sorrows

Leaving Castle Square (Pils laukums) and crossing the cobbled area of the square (the opposite end to the one at which the stables are located, in the direction of Lielā pils iela) you come to a church, the Roman Catholic **Church of Our Lady of Sorrows** (*Sāpju Dievmātes baznīca*). The location was already the site of a humble Catholic chapel in the 18th century, but the present building owes its existence to the Austrian emperor, Joseph II, who persuaded the Russian tsar, Paul I, and the king of Poland, Stanislav August, to donate money for the construction of the present church which was built in 1784–5.

St Saviour's Church

Just beyond the Catholic church is Rīga's only Anglican church, **St Saviour's**, which stands in Anglikāņu iela, just off Lielā pils iela. This red-brick church, the largest Anglican one in the Baltic states, was built in 1857–9 to cater for the spiritual needs of the English seamen and merchants who came to Rīga. The main door leads on to a small porch that overlooks the Daugava. The bricks used to build the church were imported from England, as was a layer of soil on which the church was built, although construction was supervised by the Rīga architect, Johann Felsko. During the Soviet era the church was used as a discotheque by the students of the Technical University, but it was returned to the Church of England when the Archbishop of Canterbury visited Rīga in 1994.

The Three Brothers

Returning to Lielā pils iela, turn right into Mazā pils iela, heading away from the tower of Rīga Castle. The three houses at numbers 17, 19 and 21 Mazā pils iela are known collectively as '**the three brothers**' (*Trīs brāļi*). The oldest is the right-hand house with the Germanic step-gable and dates back to the 15th century. It is claimed that it is the oldest domestic building in Rīga.

Little is known about its history except that in 1687 it is recorded that it was used as a bakery. Numbers 19 and 21 were built later in the 17th and 18th centuries respectively. In 1966 repair work began with a view to restoring the buildings after years of neglect. Number 17 is set back from the street: when it was built there was less pressure on building land in Rīga so a small area was left for stone benches to be installed by the main entrance; but by the time the other houses were built land had become more expensive, so they were built closer to the road and with more storeys so as to maximise land use. The house at number 19 now houses the **Museum of Architecture**, *Latvijas Arhitektūras Muzejs* (open 09.00–17.00 Sunday–Friday, Saturday 12.00–16.00).

Note also the house at 4 Mazā pils iela where the Baltic historian Johans Kristofs Broce worked from 1742–1823 as rector of what was then Rīga's imperial lycée.

St Jacob's Church

Opposite the three brothers is Klostera iela (Monastery Street) which leads to **St Jacob's Church** (*Jēkaba baznīca*), the Roman Catholic cathedral of Rīga. (The church is also called St James', since Jacob and James are alternative translations of Jēkabs.) Originally built outside the city walls between 1225–6, the church has been rebuilt several times, although the sanctuary and naves are original. The church has changed hands on several occasions: after the Reformation it became a Lutheran parish church (the first Lutheran service in Latvia was held here in 1522); but in 1582 it was handed over to the Jesuit order; in 1621 it became a Swedish garrison church; it was finally returned to the Roman Catholic church in 1922.

The 73m high tower shows traces of restoration work carried out in the 16th and 17th centuries. The heavy buttresses are unusual for Rīga churches: shortage of land meant that most churches were built with internal buttresses.

Parliament Building

At the corner of Jēkaba baznīca, if you turn right, you come to a formidable brown building with a coat of arms and a balcony over the main entrance. This is the building where the Supreme Soviet of Latvia used to sit. In 1919–34 it was the seat of the Latvian national parliament. Now it functions once again as the **Parliament** building, the seat of the *Saeima*. It was here on May 4 1989 that parliament passed a resolution on the independence of Latvia. The building itself is in the style of a Florentine palace. Note the decoratively carved double doors and heavy lanterns. In the outbreak of crime which followed independence in the early 1990s, the bronze plaque on the front of the building was stolen.

National Library

Turn right into Jēkaba iela and walk along the back of the cathedral. The small street on the left, Mazā Trokšņu iela (which means 'the street of little noise') has formed the subject matter of many pictures by Latvian artists. Numbers 6/8 Jēkaba iela is a substantial stone building which houses the **Latvian National Library**.

Turning left back into Smilšu iela, the house at number 6 has a modern front and is now the **Commercial Bank**. The upper storeys are good examples of the Jugendstil (art nouveau) style of architecture for which Rīga is so famous. Next to it is Aldaru iela (Brewer Street) with its view back to the Swedish Gate. The large brown building that dominates the rest of Smilšu iela is occupied by ministries and government offices.

House of the Cat

Here the road forks. Take Mazā Smilšu iela (Little Sand Street) and turn right into Meistaru iela (Master Street). On your left is a large yellow building called the **House of the Cat**. Perched on each of the building's two pointed towers is an arched cat looking down on the city. The origins of this piece of architectural caprice are uncertain but inevitably there is a story. Apparently a Latvian businessman sought admission to the city guild but was refused. To spite the guild he bought the nearest property he could find to the guildhall, built the house that still stands and had two cats put on top so that each directed its backside towards the guildhall. According to the same story the spurned merchant was eventually forced to move them, hence their present position.

Guildhalls

If you continue down Meistaru iela you come to what used to be the Guild Square but is now known as the Philharmonic Park (*Filharmonijas Parks*). On a wet day it can look fairly grim but in better weather it is enlivened by kiosks selling ice-cream and drinks, and by pavement artists. There is also a long strip of wall used for announcements about local musical, theatrical and other cultural events. The **Great Guildhall** (*Lielā Ģilde*) is the large, dull yellow building at one edge of the square, at the corner of Meistaru iela and Amatu iela (Commercial Street). The **Small Guildhall** is right next to it on Amatu iela itself. These buildings represent the centres of Rīga's former glory as a Hanseatic city. The Great Guildhall was the council chamber of the merchants; the smaller one housed the council of the less influential craftsmen's guilds. The Great Guildhall was originally established in the 14th century, but has undergone substantial changes over the years. In 1853–60 it was reconstructed in English Tudor style according to designs by Beine and Scheu. The Old Guild Chamber dates back to the 16th century and is decorated with the emblems of the 45 Hanseatic towns. The so-called 'Brides' Chamber' dates back to 1521: until the 19th century it was still used on the wedding night of children of members of the guild or members themselves. However, a great deal of damage was done by a fire in 1963. Now the building is used as a concert hall. The smaller hall was built (in its present form) in 1864–6. It is also sometimes called the St John's Guild – notice the statue of St John with a lamb in one corner of the façade under the tower. Now it is used as offices.

Continue along Amatu iela to Šķūņu iela (Barn Street). On your right there is a pale green coloured building with white decoration, an excellent example of Rīga's Jugendstil (art nouveau). Note the sculptures of a boy reading (at roof level) and of frogs (by the entrance). The nearby billiards/snooker hall was once the site of St Catherine's church, built between the 14th and 15th centuries.

Rīga Dome Church

If you turn right out of Amatu iela, past Zirgu iela, you come to the cathedral square, Doma laukums. The square is dominated by the cathedral, the **Dome Church** (*Rigas Dome* – the name comes from the German *Dom*, meaning cathedral) or St Mary's Cathedral, as it is sometimes referred to, the largest church in the Baltic states (open for visitors 13.00–17.00 Monday to Friday, and 10.00–14.00 on Saturdays). The foundations of the church were laid in 1211 and consecrated in 1226. It was modelled on the cathedral at Rattenburg at the instigation of Albert, the Bishop of Rīga, although he did not live to see his plans come to fruition. The original church was cruciform, but was extended in the 15th century; the central nave was heightened to let in more light, and three chapels were added. Two towers were envisaged, but only one was actually built over what is now the main entrance. It burned down in 1547 and was replaced in 1595. That tower was replaced again in 1775–6 due to fears about its structural soundness (fears prompted by the collapse of the tower of St Peter's). The old tower was 132m high, the tallest in Europe; the new one was much smaller at 90m.

Like many of Rīga's churches the Dome became a Protestant church in the Reformation, and much of its elaborate interior decoration was destroyed in 1524 and the church lost its original name of St Mary's. Thus all that remains today as decoration are the tombs of merchants, all purchased, the price set by reference to closeness to the high altar. A whole chapel was devoted to the Tisenhausen family: note the plaque for Mary Tisenhausen who died in 1611, and the stained glass panels donated by the family in the 19th century and made in Munich in 1893. One depicts the Tisenhausen family with the Virgin Mary and angels, the other Bishop Albert, the founder of the church. In the neighbouring chapel stained glass depicts Walter von Plettenberg reading the edict proclaiming religious freedom and pledging protection from the Catholic bishops (1525). On the north side there is more modern stained-glass (by E Tode, 1902) depicting the life of St Martin, the life of St George and the lives of the apostles, Peter and Paul. The three stained-glass windows above the altar depict stories from the Old and New Testaments. The pulpit, the work of the wood carver Tobias Heincs, dates back to 1641. The angel that surmounts it was added much later in 1817 and is the work of the sculptor Imhof.

The organ of the Rīga Dome is world famous: indeed for many people the church is known as a concert hall, and in particular for its organ recitals, rather than as a place of worship. The first organ was installed in the 16th century, but the present instrument was built in 1884 by the firm of Walcker & Co of Ludwigsburg, Germany. It was first used at an inaugural recital and service on January 31 1884 when it was played by three organists, including the cathedral organist, Wilhelm Bergner. It was rebuilt and restored in 1981–4 by the Dutch organ builders, Flentrop Orgelbouw bv Zaandam. With four manuals and pedal board, 6,718 pipes (ranging in size from 10m to 13m) and 124 stops, it is large even by cathedral standards; indeed when it was first built it was the largest instrument in the world. The organ case is older than the organ itself: the work of Jakob Raab, it dates back to the 16th century, although the baroque decorations were added later in the 17th century.

The cloister and garden are at present being restored.

The tower of the Dome was used as a lookout post. The watchman would communicate with the guards on the ground below by means of a wooden ball containing a message. (The tower of the town hall was used in the same way.) Now the tower is dominated by a huge weathercock, the predecessor of which can be seen in the church itself where it was placed after 390 years of service in the open air.

Although the Dome is still used for concerts, it now also operates again as a place of worship. The first service in recent times was held there on October 9 1988 to mark the founding of the Popular Front (*Tautas Fronte*). The box office for concert tickets is in the church porch. Tickets can also be bought at the Filharmonijas box office, 6 Amatu iela, and at the Wagner Hall box office at 4 Vāgnera iela. For details of concerts see the posters in the church or consult *Rīga This Week*, *Rīga Guide* or *Rīga in Your Pocket*. They generally take place on Wednesdays and Fridays. Services are held at 08.00 every day and at noon on Sundays.

Around the Dome
Just off Doma laukums, Tirgoņu iela (Traders' Street) has a number of bars and restaurants. Behind the Dome is Jauniela (New Street): the Pūt, Vējiņ! is a good place to eat and drink (there is a bar downstairs and a good restaurant upstairs). The building at 8 Doma laukums is the **Latvia Radio Building**. It and the nearby Finance Ministry recall the architectural style of Nazi Germany and were built during the time of the Latvian president, Kārlis Ulmanis. The Radio Building was one of the buildings that was barricaded in 1991 by demonstrators resisting communist sympathisers; bullet holes in the building offer a grim reminder of the fighting. Doma laukums was heavily guarded and occupied by people lighting bonfires and erecting tents. From time to time radio staff would appear on the balcony of the Radio Building to announce the news to the people gathered in the square below. It was from the same balcony that President Gorbunovs proclaimed independence in August 1991.

Opposite the Radio Building is *Rigas Fondu Birža*, the **Rīga Stock Exchange**, a green and brown building with ornate statues. It was built in 1852–5 in Venetian style to a design by the architect Harald Bose. Unused for 50 years or so, it now operates again as a stock exchange.

Herder Square
If you leave Doma laukums passing the main door of the cathedral with the Radio Building behind you, you come into Herdera laukums, Herder Square. This small square is dominated by the statue of the German critic, writer and theologian, Johann Herder, which stands on a small green.

Turning out of Herder laukums you come to Palasta iela (Palace Street). The building that was once the clergy enclosure of the abbey attached to the Dome is now the **Museum of History and Navigation of the City of Rīga**, *Rigas Vēstures un Kuģniecības Muzejs* (open 11.00–17.00 daily except Monday and Tuesday). Founded in 1773, this is the oldest museum in Latvia. It was originally set up to house items from the private collection of Nicolaus von Himsel (1729–64) whose portrait by an unknown artist hangs in the ground floor exhibition hall. The main permanent exhibition traces the development of Rīga from its beginnings to 1710. It does so by reference to maps, plans, pictures and objects of all kinds from the everyday life of the city's inhabitants. The second main permanent exhibition is devoted to the history of navigation from ancient times to the present day.

Peter I's Palace
Further on in Palasta iela at number 6 stands a tiny building in which Tsar Peter I (Peter the Great), kept his personal carriage when he visited Rīga.

Just beyond it at number 9 is what used to be Peter's palace, from which Palasta iela derives its name. Peter bought this house from a local merchant called Henaberg and is said to have been especially fond of it because he was able to indulge in his hobby of gardening there, on either the terrace or the hanging garden on the roof. When he lived here in the 18th century it was possible to see the harbour from the windows of the palace (before it was moved further from the centre of the city). In 1745 the palace was rebuilt to designs by Rastrelli, the architect better known in Latvia for his work on the

Rundāle Palace. In 1886 it became the Russian school and until recently functioned as a Russian cultural centre. At present it is undergoing restoration.

Walk Two

Our second walk in the Old Town starts from the Riflemen's Square (Strēlnieku laukums). This large open area used to be a market square, then the site of the town hall of Rīga. The most distinguished building is the House of the Blackheads, rebuilt in 1998.

House of the Blackheads

The **House of the Blackheads** (*Melngalvju nams*), one of Rīga's most important monuments, was reopened in January 2000 as a faithful replica of the original. It is open every day except Monday. The foundations are skilfully exhibited under glass. The original house (really a building made up of two houses connected by an enclosed courtyard), with its Dutch Renaissance façade (1620), dated back to 1331 but was badly damaged in World War II. The 'Blackheads', first mentioned in 1413, were an association of unmarried merchants who lived in Rīga and Reval (Tallinn). Originally a loose association, they grew to become a powerful force. It is believed that they got their unusual name from their black patron saint, St Maurice. The Blackheads left for Germany in 1939 and because of this German association the Soviet authorities blew up the remains of the building in May 1948.

The first floor of the building was used for shops and businesses; the guildhall of the association occupied the second floor; the upper floors were used for storage and warehousing. The ground floor was a concert hall. The huge step gable was 28m high and highly decorated with statues of people and animals. The building was topped by a large figure of St George which acted as a weather vane. A statue of Roland used to stand in front of the building. A popular figure in the middle ages, and especially in Germany, the Roland statue was erected in 1897 but was damaged in World War II and the original is now kept in St Peter's Church. A replica has been erected in the square.

Riflemen's memorial

The present name of the square comes from the **memorial** to the Latvian Riflemen which was erected in 1970 to commemorate the valour of the Latvian Rifle Regiment during the Russian Civil War. The Riflemen formed Lenin's bodyguard during the 1917 revolution. Plans to change the square provide for the statue to be removed and replaced by something more politically neutral.

Occupation Museum

The ugly black cuboid building behind the memorial was also built in 1970 and used to be a museum devoted to the exploits of the regiment. Now it is the **Museum of the Occupation of Latvia**, *Okupācijas Muzejs* (open daily, all year), which contains a permanent exhibition devoted to the history of Latvia during the Soviet and Nazi occupations of 1940–91. Founded in 1993, the museum exhibits photographs and documents, maps and artefacts dealing with the period and contains a replica of a barracks room from a Soviet *gulag*. There are explanatory booklets for each part of the exhibition in Latvian,

Russian, English and German. There is considerable controversy over the continued location of the museum here. Some argue that the Soviet building disfigures Latvian Rīga and should be removed. Others say that the content of the museum is so important that it should not be moved from this central location.

Technical University

One side of the square is dominated by the long building and laboratories of the **Technical University** of Rīga. The unimaginative architecture is typical of the Stalin era. Now most of the university operates from a campus on the other side of the river on Ķīpsala island. This building is likely to be demolished in 2001, to be replaced by a new Town Hall.

Rīga's bridges

The traditional bridge with the large lantern-like lights is the Akmens tilts (Stone Bridge) which replaced the long pontoon bridge that spanned the river before World War II. A more elegant example of 20th century architecture is the dramatic modern bridge, the harp-like Vansu tilts, which crosses the river to the north.

Mentzendorff House

Leave the square by turning into Grēcinieku iela (Sinner's Street) and taking Kungu iela (Gentleman's Street). On the corner of Grēcinieku iela and Kungu iela there is an impressive building called the **Mentzendorff House** (*Mencendorfa nams*). The house once belonged to a rich Rīga merchant family and is now a museum of life in the 17th and 18th centuries (open 10.00–17.00 Tuesday to Saturday).

Walk down Kungu iela past the Mentzendorff House to Mārstaļu iela. Number 21 Mārstaļu iela is a fine example of baroque domestic architecture and was built in 1696 for another wealthy citizen of Rīga, Dannenstern and his family.

Reiter House

The house at number 2 Mārstaļu iela is the **Reiter House** (*Reitera nams*), a building that derives its name from another wealthy Rīga merchant, Johann von Reiter. The house was built in 1682. Note the six pillars that decorate what appears to be the front of the house but is, in fact, the side.

If you backtrack down Mārstaļu iela and turn left into Alksnāja iela (Alder Street) and then left into Vecpilsētas iela (Old Town Street) you may care to take a look at the buildings at numbers 10 and 11–17 which are good examples of some of the 20 or so **medieval warehouses** of the Old Town.

If you bear right around the corner passing numbers 13–15 you come to the house from which the Latvian Popular Front operated in the late 1980s.

Universal Store Building

Turn right into Audēju iela (Weaver Street). The rather grim looking **Centrs department store** was formerly the Universalveikals, the Rīgan equivalent of Moscow's GUM or State Universal Store. In fact the building itself predates the Soviet era and was actually built before World War II under the Ulmanis regime. Rīdzenes iela (Rīdzene Street) runs alongside it. The street gets its name from the River Rīdzene which used to flow here. The Rīdzene was originally called the River Rīga but became known as the Rīdzene in the 17th century. It flowed through the Old Town and on into the Daugava but eventually became overgrown and disease ridden so was covered over in the 19th century.

The interior is now a modern department store. The ground floor has an extensive supermarket and a snackbar much cheaper than any of the surrounding cafés. A wide range of foreign newspapers is also sold here.

Convent Courtyard

Turn left into Teātra iela (Theatre Street) at the end of Rīdzene iela. This brings you back to Kalēju iela. Just off Kalēju iela there is a passage that leads you to the **Konventa Sēta**, an area of beautifully restored historic buildings between Kalēju iela and Skārņu iela. The 17th century warehouses and other buildings in this area had fallen into complete decay (the area used to be known as 'the dead town') but have now been restored with the aid of German investment.

The history of the Konventa Sēta goes back, like so much of Rīga's history, to the 13th century when a castle was built on this site by the Knights of the Sword. The Convent of the Holy Spirit (from which the area then took its name) was also established here, and in due course a number of alms houses and other institutions settled nearby. Eventually commerce superseded religion and the buildings began to be replaced by warehouses. Each warehouse had its own name, but because of the associations the area had with the convent, many were given names with the word 'dove' in them (the dove being a symbol of the Holy Spirit, the third person of the trinity). The former St George's chapel became known as 'the white dove', and the building next to it 'the grey dove' and so on. Many of these traditional names have been revived as part of the restoration. One house called Campenhausen recalls the Rīga councillor who founded a home for elderly ladies here. The so-called 'grey sisters' building once served as accommodation for the nuns of the convent.

In 1989 talks began between Latvian and German architects and builders about restoring the derelict area. Before long a German–Latvian joint venture firm, REHO, was formed and the reconstruction of the Konventa Sēta began. The restored complex of buildings reopened in December 1996. A major part of the Konventa Sēta is taken up by the Konventa Sēta Hotel, a modern three/four-star hotel occupying a number of the restored buildings. Other buildings in the Convent courtyard are taken up by shops.

St John's Courtyard and Church

Close to the Konventa Sēta at the end of Teātra iela there is a part of the city wall. An archway in Kalēju iela leads to Jāņa Sēta (John's Courtyard), a cobbled courtyard with the city wall on one side and a bar, café and restaurant forming the other sides of the quadrangle.

A second arch leads out of the courtyard to **St John's Church** (*Jāņa baznīca*). Built in 1234 for the Dominicans by Bishop Nicolas, the oldest surviving parts of the church are the main door and porch. The original chapel became too small, so in 1330 it was expanded by the addition of a red brick nave with a choir and apse covered by a tiled roof and decorated with a small tower which still survives. As a result of renovation work in the 15th and 16th centuries the meshed vaulted ceilings came into being. The 35m high nave dates from the 15th century. The baroque altar is 18th century, the work of J E Meier and K E Apelbaum, and has sculptures depicting the crucifixion and SS Peter and Paul. The altar painting, *The Resurrection*, is the work of the Rīga artist, A Stiling. Several paintings of the Passion and of the apostles decorate the organ loft. The stained-glass is 19th century. The organ is a gift from the town of Uddevalla in Sweden; the old organ, which dated from 1854, was given to the church of Cesvaine in Vidzeme.

The façade was restored in 1924–26 under the supervision of the architect E Laube. On the outside, at the altar end of the church, is a statue of St John the Baptist (the patron saint of the church), and nearby is one of Salome, the daughter of Herodias who married Herod Antipas, her dead husband's brother. St John preached against the marriage, as a result of which Herodias persuaded Salome to dance for her husband and seek as her reward the head of John the Baptist.

The history of this church again reflects Rīga's turbulent past. The Dominicans were ousted in the Reformation, and for some time after 1523 the church was used as stables by the mayor of Rīga, Shulte, then as an arsenal, until in 1582 the Polish king, Stephen Bathory, seized it and handed it over to the Jesuits. However, in due course it was returned to the Lutheran church, and is still used as a place of worship, primarily by the Lutherans, but also on occasions for ecumenical services.

The façade overlooking Skārņu iela is decorated with two stone faces which are said to be the faces of two monks. One explanation for their being there is found in the story that they represent two monks who were immured at the time the church was built; the other is that they were put there as an early elocution aid – other monks were supposed to shape their mouths in the same way as the stone examples, thereby improving their own qualities as preachers.

Ekke's Convent/Waxworks Museum

Skārņu iela (Butchers' Street) got its name from the shops that were located in this part of Rīga in medieval times. Number 22, next door to St John's church, is a house known as **Ekke's convent** (*Ekes konvents*). It is believed to have been built in 1435 as a guesthouse for travellers. However, in 1592 Nikolaus Ekke, a mayor of Rīga, acquired the building and turned it into a home for widows of members of Rīga's small guild.

In recent years the building served as a tourist information centre but funds for this ran out in early 1999. It was then reopened in 2000 as a **waxworks museum** and serves as a useful introduction to Latvian history with all the country's heroes portrayed here. It is open daily 10.00–19.00.

St George's Church/Decorative and Applied Arts Museum

Further along Skārņu iela, next to number 10, the old white building with brick lined windows is **St George's Church** (*Jura baznīca*). It was the first stone church and possibly the oldest building in Rīga, built at the beginning of the 13th century and generally dated at 1202 or 1204 when it was part of a castle (Wittenstein Castle) belonging to the Knights of the Sword. The castle was destroyed in 1297 after which it became a church until the Reformation, before falling into disuse. In 1989 it became part of the **Museum of Decorative and Applied Arts**, *Dekoratīvi Lietišķās Mākslas Muzejs* (open 10.00–18.00 every day except Monday), which specialises in applied art from Latvia and abroad from the 19th century onwards.

St Peter's Church

On the other side of Skārņu iela stands one of Rīga's most famous and distinctive churches, **St Peter's** (*Pētera baznīca*). It is a large red-brick church with a simple, light interior decorated by coats of arms. The main entrance is located on Vecrīgas laukums (Old Rīga Square). The original church that was built here in 1209 was wooden and, unusually, was built not by foreigners but by the largely Christian Liv people of Rīga. No record remains of the original church which was started in 1406, although the reconstruction process went on until the end of the 15th century. A steeple was erected in 1491 but collapsed in 1666 causing considerable damage and killing the inhabitants of a neighbouring building. A replacement was completed in 1690 by the Strasbourg architect, Bindenschu, and was, in its time, the tallest in the world. However, this, too, was damaged by fire caused by lightning in 1721. Tsar Peter the Great was in Rīga at the time of the incident and ordered the steeple and spire to be restored yet again. Reconstruction was completed in 1746 under the supervision of Johann Wulbern. His steeple stood for 195 years until it was destroyed along with the rest of the church by German mortar fire in 1941, ironically on June 29, the feast of St Peter.

The latest reconstruction work began in 1963 and was completed by 1973. The present steeple, 123.5m high, is a steel replica of its predecessor. It conceals a lift which takes visitors up to two viewing platforms which provide wonderful panoramas of the city. (The lift starts from the gallery in the tower and is open from 10.00–17.00 except on Monday.) For many years St Peter's was the tallest building in Rīga until Intourist built the Hotel Latvijā which is about a metre higher.

In 1352 Rīga's first clock was installed in St Peter's. One of the church's finest objects was a marble pulpit by the Italian Giovanni Baratta, but it was destroyed in the fire of 1941 along with the German oak altar, the wooden pews and a magnificent organ.

Many of Rīga's churches have cockerels as weathercocks, and St Peter's is no exception. A golden weathercock has topped the spire for 200 years. The symbol has a special significance for this church, since it recalls how St Peter denied Christ three times before the cock crowed. The old weathercock is still kept in the church porch.

After restoration, St Peter's functioned initially only as a museum and concert hall, although it has now begun to be used again for church services.

There are two famous stories associated with St Peter's. The first is the story of the blue guard. The blue guard was a civilian volunteer unit formed in the 18th century to guard prominent citizens of Rīga. One of the guards is supposed to haunt St Peter's. An old man bet two young men that they would not dare to spend the night of the feast of St Andrew in the church and prove that they had been there by hammering a nail into the altar. On St Andrew's night the two youths entered the church just before midnight, but at the stroke of midnight the old man and his witnesses who were waiting outside the church heard a terrible cry. The people outside soon broke into the church and one of the young men managed to escape through the main door. However, his friend was found hanged from the nail, a victim of the ghost of the blue guard. The second story concerns Johann Heinrich Wulbern, the steeple builder. There was a tradition that when a new building was being topped off, the architect would go to the top and throw down a glass which was supposed to shatter, the number of shards representing the number of years for which the building would stand. Unfortunately, when Wulbern threw down his glass it was caught by a passing hay cart and therefore suffered only a minor crack. Nothing came of this evil omen, but the glass is preserved in the Museum of History and Navigation.

On leaving St Peter's, return to Skārņu iela and then turn right into Kaļķu iela. This last part of our walking tour of Old Rīga will take you past some of Rīga's newest shops and bring you back to the Hotel de Rome and a sign that Rīga is now a thoroughly 20th-century consumer-oriented city: opposite the hotel and almost in the shadow of the Freedom Monument is Rīga's first McDonald's.

New Town

The Old Town and New Town are separated by the city canal (*pilsētas kanāls*) which runs through a series of parks and gardens. The canal follows the line of part of the old city wall which was demolished in the 19th century. Through the centre of the parks, separating the Old Town from the New Town, is Brīvības bulvāris (Freedom Boulevard), a pedestrianised street that is also the site of the Freedom Monument.

Freedom Monument

The **Freedom Monument** (*Brīvības piemineklis*) dominates the centre of Rīga. Known locally as 'Milda', it was erected in 1935 and paid for by public subscription. At 42.7m high it is the tallest monument of its kind in Europe. It was designed by the Latvian architect Kārlis Zāle and consists of a tall granite column surmounted by a 9m high figure of a woman holding three golden stars above her head. The three stars represent the three cultural regions of Latvia - Kurzeme, Vidzeme and Latgale. Engraved in gold letters on the base are the words *Tevzēmei un brīvībai* ('for fatherland and freedom'). Also decorating the monument is a sculpture of Lāčplēsis, the bear slayer, a mythical Latvian hero. The monument was dedicated on November 18 1935, the 17th anniversary of the declaration of independence.

Nowadays the base is often surrounded by flowers, frequently red and white, the colours of the Latvian national flag. Flowers were forbidden during the Soviet era; indeed the Soviet authorities had contemplated removing the monument altogether, since it served as a focus of Latvian nationalistic aspirations, but thought better of the idea, fearing demonstrations and reprisals. Instead they erected a statue of Lenin. The two monuments stood back to back for decades, Lenin facing east towards Moscow, the Freedom Monument facing west. Lenin has now disappeared, but the Freedom Monument remains.

Laima clock

Close to the Freedom Monument (on the Old Town side of the park) stands the **Laima clock**, another well known landmark and a popular meeting point. *Laima* is the name of a well known chocolate manufacturer and the Latvian word for happiness or good luck (there was also an ancient deity of that name).

National Opera

Southwest of the Laima clock is a fountain, the Nymph of Rīga, which dates back to 1888. It stands in front of the stately **National Opera**, the home of Rīga's opera and ballet companies. Originally built as a German theatre, this impressive building (classical on the outside, baroque on the inside) can be seen from anywhere in this central parkland area. Founded in 1919, the National Opera was the focus of Latvian cultural life during the first independence. The first Latvian operas were performed in the 1860s, and some are still performed alongside the established international repertoire. The Rīga ballet is a company of international standing. Many of its members have gone on to be international stars, such as Māris Liepa, who was a leading member of the Bolshoi Ballet, and his son, Andris Liepa, who danced with the American Ballet Theater in the 1989/90 season.

The parks

The parks on either side of the Freedom Monument were laid out in 1853–63. The one through which Brīvības bulvāris runs is the ***Bastejkalns Parks***, so called after the 17th-century bastion that once stood here and formed a vital part of Rīga's defences.

If you walk through Bastejkalns Park you will come across a set of engraved stones near the bridge that crosses the canal (most are on the New Town side, one is on the Old Town side of the canal). On the night of January 20 1991 forces loyal to Moscow attempted to capture a number of government buildings including the Ministry of the Interior on Raiņa bulvāris, the street running alongside the canal on the New Town side. Several Latvians were shot, some say by sniper fire from the roof tops. The stones preserve the memory of five victims: Gvīdo Zvaigne, a cameraman who was filming events, Andris Slapiņš, a cinema director and cameraman, two militiamen, Sergejs Kononenko and Vladimirs Gomanovics, and Edijs Riekstiņš, a student.

The park also contains monuments to the writer, Rūdolfs Blaumanis, the composer Alfrēds Kalniņš, and the researcher, Mstislav Keldish.

Next to Bastejkalns Park is ***Kronvalda Park*** with its monuments to the Latvian writers Sudraba Edzus and Andrejs Upitis. Also set in this park are the Rīga Congress House (*Rigas kongresu nams*) and the Rīga Council Building (*Rigas dome*).

National Theatre

Close to the canal on Kr Valdemāra iela is the **National Theatre**. It is a small theatre with seating for only 890. It was here that Latvia declared independence on November 18 1918. A concert is held here every year to commemorate the event. If you are interested in the history of Latvian theatre you may care to visit the **Theatre Museum** (see page 100).

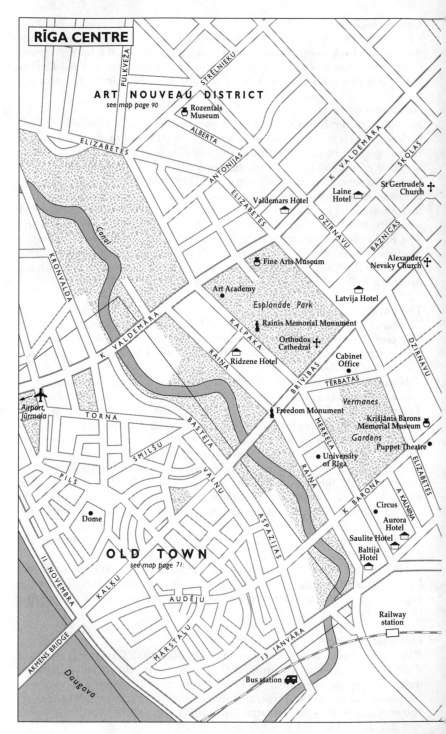

RĪGA CENTRE

ART NOUVEAU DISTRICT
see map page 90

Rozentāls Museum

PULKVEŽA

STRĒLNIEKU

ALBERTA

ELIZABETES

ANTONIJAS

ELIZABETES

Canal

KRONVALDA

K VALDEMĀRA

Valdemārs Hotel

Laine Hotel

St Gertrude's Church †

K VALDEMĀRA

SKOLAS

DZIRNAVU

BAZNĪCAS

Fine Arts Museum

Alexander Nevsky Church †

Art Academy

Esplanāde Park

Latvija Hotel

KALPAKA

Rainis Memorial Monument

RAIŅA

Orthodox Cathedral †

DZIRNAVU

Ridzene Hotel

Cabinet Office

BRĪVĪBAS

TĒRBATAS

Airport, Jūrmala

TORŅA

BASTEJA

VAĻŅU

Freedom Monument

Vermanes

Krišjānis Barons Memorial Museum

MERĶEĻA

SMILŠU

RAIŅA

Gardens

Puppet Theatre

PILS

University of Riga

K BARONA

ELIZABETES

A KALNIŅA

Dome

ASPĀZIJAS

Circus

Aurora Hotel

Saulite Hotel

OLD TOWN
see map page 71

Baltija Hotel

11 NOVEMBRA

KALKU

AUDĒJU

Railway station

AKMENS BRIDGE

MĀRSTAĻU

13 JANVĀRA

Daugava

Bus station

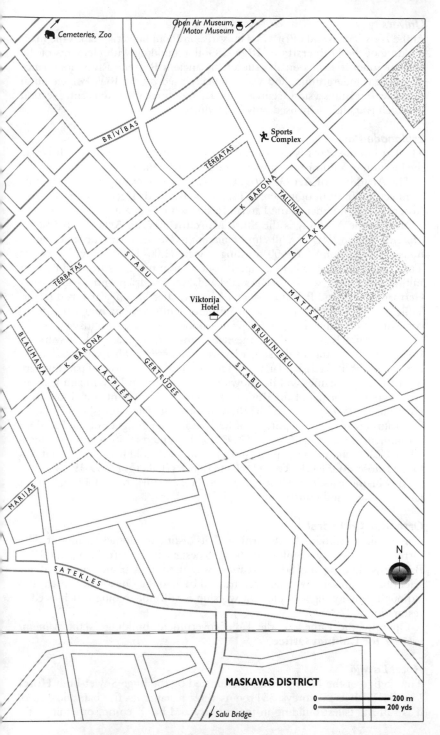

Cemeteries, Zoo

Open Air Museum,
Motor Museum

BRĪVĪBAS

TĒRBATAS

Sports
Complex

K BARONA

TALLINAS

A ČAKA

STABU

TĒRBATAS

MATISA

Viktorija
Hotel

BRUNINIEKU

BLAUMAŅA

K BARONA

LĀČPLĒŠA

GERTRŪDES

STABU

MARIJAS

SATEKLES

N

MASKAVAS DISTRICT

0 ———————— 200 m
0 ———————— 200 yds

Salu Bridge

University

At the New Town end of Brīvības bulvāris, on Raini bulvāris, stands the main building of the **University of Rīga**, a Gothic building with elements of the Romanesque. It stands on the site of the ancient Rīdzene River, long since channelled underground, and was originally used by the Rīga Polytechnical Institute. It features a stone staircase divided into three parts, the centre section of which is traditionally used only by graduates.

Esplanade Park

The **Esplanade Park** is the second major park in the town centre. It is also the location of a number of important buildings in the New Town.

The **Academy of Art** (*Mākslas akademija*) is a fine example of neo-Gothic architecture. In front of it there is a statue by Burkards Dzenis (1936) of Jānis Rozentāls, the founder of the Latvian Realist school of painting.

Next to the Academy is the **State Museum of Fine Arts** (*Valsts Mākslas Muzejs*), built in 1905 by Wilhelm Neumann in German baroque style, which houses a collection of 17,000 paintings (open 11.00–17.00 every day except Tuesday). This used to have a superb collection of paintings from all parts of Europe, including works by Ingres, Landseer, Friedrich and various early German, Dutch and Italian masters. However, after World War I its director, Vilhelms Purvītis (himself a prominent landscape painter) began to concentrate on Latvian art, and now its exhibits are almost exclusively works of Latvian and Russian origin. Inevitably, there is a great deal of work by Rozentāls (his portrait of the singer Malvine Vignère-Grīnberga painted in the last year of his life is particularly well known), but the majority of paintings are by artists whose names will be known only to experts in Latvian and Russian art. There is a portrait of the Russian writer Turgenev (painted in 1869) by A Gruzdins (1825–91), a bust of the Russian composer Moussorgsky by Teodors Zaļnkalns (1876–1928), a portrait of Kārlis Zāle (the designer of the Freedom Monument) by Ludolfs Liberits (1895–1959) painted in 1934 and showing a relaxed Zāle smoking a cigarette, and a picture of the old harbour when it was located closer to the Old Town by Jānis Roberts Tilbergs (1880–1972).

Also in the park is the monument to Jānis Rainis, one of Latvia's most famous writers and translators.

Orthodox Cathedral

The Russian Orthodox **Cathedral**, with its distinctive domes surmounted by Orthodox crosses, was built in 1876–84 to designs by Roberts Pflugs and Jānis Baumanis. During the Soviet years it was used as a planetarium and for scientific lectures. Now it has been handed back to the Orthodox church, and although functioning as a place of worship is still undergoing much-needed restoration.

Opposite the cathedral, the large government building is the *Ministru kabinets*, the **Cabinet Office**.

Hotel Latvijā

The skyline of the New Town is dominated by the huge Soviet-built **Hotel Latvijā**. With its 27 storeys, 354 rooms, three restaurants, five bars and casino, it is still the tallest building in the country and has become something of a

Above left Alexander Nevsky Cathedral, Tallinn (HB)

Above right Viru Gate, Tallinn Old Town (TH)

Left Clock on the Town Hall, Tallinn (HB)

Below Town Hall Square, Tallinn (HB)

Above View towards Rīga station and covered market (RR)

Right Art nouveau or Jugendstil door, Rīga (SC)

Below left Old Town Rīga (RR)

Below right Covered markets in what were formerly Zeppelin hangars, Rīga (RR) landmark, although many of Rīga's inhabitants regard it as an eyesore. It took about 20 years to complete. There is a story about a travel guide who was asked by someone in her group what the huge building site was. She told the person concerned and bemoaned the inefficiency of Soviet construction. The story got back to her boss who reprimanded her for her disloyalty. The next time she was asked the same question, by which time building was at a more advanced stage, she simply replied, 'I don't know what it is, but things move fast here: there was nothing there the other day'. The travel writer, Colin Thubron, describes a stay there in the 1980s in *Among the Russians*:

> The hotel itself conformed miserably to expectation. It was huge, charmless, exhibitionist. Latvians joke that these tourist ghettoes are made of sixty per cent glass, thirty per cent ferro-concrete and ten per cent microphones. All their minor fittings, all those things by which a civilization may be gauged by archaeologists after it has gone, were wretchedly poor. When I turned on the light-switch the electricity made a scuttling like rats along the curtain rails, then died. The furniture was of black-varnished pine; the shower curtains chiffon-thin. The lukewarm water which trickled from the shower was augmented by surreptitious leaks in other places, and the rain had enfiladed the double-glazed windows to stream down the frames.

Piecemeal improvements were made throughout the 1990s but the hotel was closed completely in June 2000 for renovation, being due to reopen in May 2001.

Art nouveau

If you turn left along Elizabetes iela along the front of the Hotel Latvijā, you come to Antonijas iela on the right; this in turn takes you to Alberta iela. The streets in this area are known for two architectural features. There are a number of **traditional wooden buildings** here, including some on the Brīvības iela itself. There are also some of Rīga's finest examples of art nouveau or **Jugendstil** in the surrounding streets. The house at 4a Strēlnieku iela dates back to 1905 and is the work of one of the most famous proponents of the style in Rīga, Mikhail Eisenstein (father of the film director Sergei). It was used by various schools for some years and as a student hostel between 1957 and 1993. In 1993 it was given to the Stockholm School of Economics who restored it in 1993–4. Other examples in Strēlnieku iela are 1b (note the beading design around the windows) and 2a, a simple block of restored flats with attractive balcony rails. At the corner of Strēlnieku iela and Elizabetes iela (number 21a) there is a building with an attractive yellow-grey frieze above the third floor and a plaque commemorating the architect and diplomat, Mārtiņš Nuksa (1878–1942). Another example of Eisenstein's work is the house at 10b Elizabetes iela; number 23 Elizabetes iela, opposite the Ukrainian Embassy, is another good example of the style – the plaque at the top says, *Labor vincit omnia* ('Work conquers all'). Other examples in this area are 3 Ausekļa iela (opposite the Tobago café), 14 Ausekļa iela, numbers 3 and 4 Vidus iela and the two domed buildings at the corner of Vidus and Vīlandes iela.

RĪGA: ART NOUVEAU

Jāņis Rozentāls and Rūdolfs Blaumanis Memorial Museum
Further examples of some of the area's finest art nouveau houses are to be found on Alberta iela, including the house at number 12, designed by K Pēkūens, flat 9 of which is now the **Jāņis Rozentāls and Rūdolfs Blaumanis Memorial Museum**, *Jāņa Rozentāla un Rūdolfa Blaumana Memoriālais Muzejs* (open 11.00–17.00 every day except Tuesday and Wednesday). The museum is reached from an entrance in Strēlnieku iela. Take the elaborate staircase in the rather neglected hallway to the top floor and ring to gain admission. Good photographs of Alberta iela can be taken from the Rozentāls Museum.

Jāņis Rozentāls (1866–1916) was born, the son of a blacksmith, in Kurzeme. In spite of the fact that he enjoyed only a rudimentary education, he studied at the St Petersburg Academy of Arts from which he graduated in 1894. He painted some 300 portraits, landscapes and altarpieces and did a large amount of book illustration as well as producing essays and criticism. He and his wife ran Rīga's most famous salon. He moved to Helsinki at the beginning of World War I, where he died on December 26 1916 and was initially buried. However, his remains were removed to be reinterred in the Meža cemetery in Rīga (see page 95) in 1920.

Rozentāls' wife, Elija Forsele-Rozentāle (1871–1943) was born in Finland. After studying at the Helsinki Music School and in Paris, Rome and Milan, she went on to become a renowned mezzo-soprano. She met her husband-to-be when she came to Rīga to sing in November 1902. They married in 1903 and lived in the flat that is now the museum together with their children, Laila, Irja and Miķelis. She, too, is buried in the Meža cemetery.

The painter Rūdolfs Blaumanis rented a room in the flat and lived there in 1906–08.

The museum was established in 1973. The living rooms contain pictures, photographs and artefacts connected with the life of its inhabitants. The studio and other rooms on the top floor are an art school and are used to exhibit works by the students who range from young children to mature painters.

Alexander Nevsky Church

The **Alexander Nevsky Church** on the corner of Brīvības iela and Lāčplēša iela is another Russian Orthodox church. It is named after the 13th century Russian prince who was canonised by the Russian Orthodox church in 1547 for his efforts to preserve Orthodoxy in Russia against the Germans whom he defeated at Lake Peipus (now in Estonia) in 1242. His story is now famous because of the film made by Eisenstein in 1938 with music by Prokofiev.

St Gertrude's Church

St Gertrude's Church, just off Brīvības iela in Ģertrūdes iela, is a large red brick church built in 1863–7 to designs by J D Felsko. The plain interior and pleasing woodwork and gallery are typical of so many Latvian churches.

Vērmaņu Gardens

Bounded by Elizabetes iela, Kr Barons, Merķeļa and Tērbates iela, the *Vērmaņes dārzs* (as the gardens are called in Latvian) is the most popular of Rīga's central parks. Opened in 1817, it was named in honour of the woman who donated the land to the city. Originally it was a refuge for residents of Rīga who could not get out to the countryside. It soon acquired attractions, including a bronze fountain cast in Berlin, a playground, an ice rink, a sun dial and the first rose garden in Rīga. It has an open-air theatre and a statue of Kriūjānis Barons, the writer and poet.

Berga Bazārs

Not far from the Vērmaņu Gardens, just behind the Jāņa Sēta bookshop in Elizabetes iela, is the Berga Bazārs. This area was originally developed in the late 19th/early 20th century by the builder and property developer, Kristaps Bergs (1840–1907) as a combination of commercial, residential and retail properties: the architect was Konstantins Pēkšens (1859–1928). The area fell into disrepair during the Soviet period, but reconstruction began in 1992 when ownership was restored to Berg's great-grandchildren. The new development has cafés, shops and restaurants.

The Central Station, Market and Academy of Sciences

If you take Raiņa bulvāris past the University it eventually brings you to the **railway station**. The first station was built here in 1861 and was known as the Orel or Dvinsk station. A second station, Tukum station, served Kurzeme. In 1888 a chapel called the Chapel of Thanksgiving was erected next to it to give thanks for the fact that the tsar's family escaped with their lives from a train crash near Borki in Kharkov. It was demolished in 1925. The present station was built in 1957–60. The clock tower with its digital clock marks it as a product of the sixties.

Beyond the station (under the railway bridge) is the **Central Market** (*Centrāltirgus*). In the 19th century this area was full of what used to be called 'red warehouses' (some still stand), so called after the colour of the bricks used to build them. The modern market buildings consist of five large pavilions, each one originally designed to deal with a different product. Each one is 12m high and covers an area of 75,000m^2, and was built in 1930 to a design intended for Zeppelin hangars. Apart from the formal market, the area around the hangars is full of stalls selling all manner of food, clothing and other goods.

If you continue along Gogoļa iela to Turgeneva iela you come to an excellent example of Soviet architecture of the Stalin era in the form of the **Academy of Sciences** building. Built in 1957, its nickname, 'Stalin's birthday cake', reflects its ornateness. Similar buildings can be found in Moscow and Warsaw. Note the communist hammer and sickle motifs close to the top.

By the Daugava River

The wide 11. Novembra krastmala (Embankment of November 11) is the road that runs along the bank of the Daugava between the Vansu and Akmens bridges. It commemorates November 11 1919, the day on which the pre-war Latvian flag was raised over Rīga castle. It leads on to 13. Janvara iela which turns away from the river towards the station. On the bank of the Daugava, one can see the Monument to the 1905 Revolution. It was here that the workers of Rīga held a peaceful demonstration in 1905 to show solidarity with their comrades in St Petersburg. Troops opened fire and about 70 demonstrators were killed and some 200 injured, many of them as they tried to escape the gunfire by crossing the frozen river, only to find that the ice was too thin. The statue we now see here was erected in 1960 and is the work of the sculptor Terpilovskis.

It is to the Daugava River that Rīga owes its importance. Up to the turn of the century ships still loaded and unloaded their cargoes on the quayside close to the Central Market, but by 1900 the river was silting up at this point, and new docks had to be built further upstream. The new harbour relies heavily on container traffic. The only active sign of shipping that can be seen from the Old Town these days is what comes and goes from the ferry terminal and yacht harbour at the end of Ausekļa iela.

Ķīpsala

From 11. Novembra or its extension, Eksporta iela, you look across the river to the island of Ķīpsala. There is little of interest on the island which is now occupied mainly by industrial and commercial buildings and the campus of the Technical University of Rīga. There is also a large swimming pool and sports complex, 'Alex', on the main road, Ķīpsala iela.

In earlier times the island of Ķīpsala was inhabited largely by fishermen and others who made their living from the sea. The island's historical connections with the sea still live on in the names of some of its streets, Balasta dambis (Ballast Dam), Matrožu iela (Sailor Street), Zvejnieku iela (Fisherman Street) and so on. Herder often came here to walk and study the Latvian customs still practised by the inhabitants.

In more recent times the islander Jānis Lipke (1900–87) sheltered 53 Rīga Jews in his house on the island during the Nazi occupation. As their number grew, two large cellars were dug to conceal them, and 43 survived the war.

Pārdaugava

Pārdaugava is the name for the area on the 'left bank' of the Daugava, the part of Rīga that lies on the river bank opposite the Old Town. There is little in this area to attract the visitor. It began to be inhabited only after the building of bridges across the Daugava (an iron bridge in 1871 and a pontoon bridge in 1896). Gradually it grew into an area of about 120km² of industrial and residential development. If you cross the river using the Akmens bridge you come to Uzvaras bulvāris (Victory Boulevard) which leads to **Victory Park** (*Uzvaras Parks*), so called to commemorate the liberation from German occupation. It was given this name in 1923. The smaller **Arcadia Park** (*Arkādijas Parks*) was created in 1852 by the Prussian consul general, Wehrmann (Vērmans). It was acquired by the city in 1896. Next to it, *Māras dīķis* (Mary's Pond) is a popular place of recreation. It derives its name from the mill attached to St Mary's Church which was acquired by the city of Rīga in 1573. The pond is probably the old mill pond and is sometimes referred to as Mary's mill pond (*Māras sudmalu dīķis*).

Other places of interest
Moscow District, Rīga Ghetto and Jewish Rīga
Beyond the railway station, the Central Market and the Academy of Sciences lies the Maskavas District (*Maskavas Forštate*), so called because it was a Russian area in earlier times (*Moskva* = Moscow in Russian) and the road to Moscow passed through it. Now it is often called the Latgale district, but its history reflects Rīga's historical links with Russia. The Russian character of the area is still reflected in the presence of several Orthodox churches, notably the green and white one (used by a congregation of Old Believers) still undergoing restoration in Grebenščikova iela (the street is named after the merchant whose wealth enabled the church to be built in 1814) and the Church of the Archangel Michael in Dricānu iela. The area near the junction of Maskavas iela and Kalna iela used to be known as the New Hill (*Krasraga Gorka*) and was where the Russian population of Rīga came to celebrate the first Sunday after Easter, a traditional Orthodox feast day. The traditional Russian name is barely remembered now, but the tradition remains alive in the name Sarkanā iela. Strūgu iela (between Gogoļa iela and Maskavas iela, parallel to Lāčplēša iela) also reflects the area's Russian past: the name means 'Barge Street' and recalls the days when barges and rafts sailed along the Daugava between Rīga and ports in Russia. Now the Maskavas area is very run down compared to central Rīga, and there are signs of poverty in the dilapidation of so many of the buildings as well as in the faces of many who live there.

This district was where the **Jewish ghetto** was established by the Nazis in 1941. In August 1941 the non-Jewish Rīgan citizens who lived in the district were moved to locations closer to the centre of the city, and by October an area of about 750m² had been formed taking in Lāčplēša iela, Maskavas iela, Ebreju iela (Jews' Street) and Daugavpils iela. The total Jewish population of the ghetto was about 30,000. The men in the ghetto who were fit to work were put to forced labour; the others were taken to Rumbula Forest on November 30 1941 and systematically murdered by German guards with the assistance of a significant number of Latvian collaborators. Other Jews were brought in to replace those murdered, only to suffer the same fate in the forests of Biķernieki or in Dreiliņi. The total number of people killed in this way has never been finally ascertained, but estimates indicate it to be around 50,000. On November 2 1943 the Rīga ghetto was closed following the Warsaw ghetto uprising, and the few remaining inhabitants were shot or transported to concentration camps.

No trace of the ghetto remains today, although there is a **Jewish cemetery** (*Ebreju kapi*) in the area between Tējas iela and Lauvas iela. The only **synagogue** that now operates in Rīga is in Peitavas iela. The site of what used to be the main synagogue (the Choral Synagogue) on the corner of Dzirnavu iela and Gogoļa iela is marked by a memorial (not a very impressive one) consisting of parts of the old synagogue set in a sort of park. A plaque records the destruction of the synagogue on July 4 1941. Number 29 Dzirnavu iela was also the site of a Jewish school until 1940. It opened again in 1989 as the only recognised Jewish school in the country.

There is a **Jewish Museum** and community centre at 6 Skolas iela, a short walk from the Hotel Latvijā. The exhibition covers Jewish life before World War II and full details of the Holocaust as it hit this community in Riga.

Rīga's cemeteries
Rīga has three cemeteries that are worth visiting, if time permits, since they reflect something of the history of Latvia and present a number of architectural styles. They are all close to one another in an area directly south of Meža Park and can be reached by public transport.

The Brothers' Cemetery
The **Brothers' Cemetery** (*Brāļu Kapi*) or Cemetery of Heroes on Aizsaules iela can be reached by taking the number 4 or number 9 bus from Brīvības ilea heading east (bus stops in front of the Hotel Latvijā or at the central bus station) or the number 11 tram from the stop by the National Opera.

The Cemetery of Heroes is a fascinating ensemble of architecture and sculpture in attractive natural surroundings. It was planned in 1915 when thousands of Latvians were dying in the fight against the Germans in Kurzeme, and the same year the first fallen soldiers were buried here. It took 12 years to complete the cemetery, the overwhelming part of the work being done between 1924 and 1936. There are approximately 2,000 graves in Brāļu Kapi, 300 of them simply marked *nezinams* ('unknown'). On March 25 1988 a memorial service for the victims of the years of the Stalin terror was held here, organized by the Latvian Writers' Association, and 10,000 people attended.

In Latvian folklore the oak symbolises masculine strength, while the lime tree symbolises feminine love; both of these powerful symbols are used extensively in the cemetery. The Latvian coat of arms appears over the entrance gate, while on both sides there are sculptured groups of cavalrymen. An avenue of lime trees leads to the main terrace. In the centre an eternal flame burns, flanked by oak trees. Beyond it is the cemetery itself, bordered by trees, shrubs, bushes and walls decorated with the coats of arms of all the Latvian regions and towns.

Especially moving are the *Ievainotais jatnieks* ('The Wounded Horseman') and *Divi brāļi* ('Two Brothers') sculptures. At one end of the cemetery stands the figure *Māte Latvijā* ('Mother Latvia') who looks down in sorrow at her dead, a wreath to honour her fallen sons in one hand, in the other the national flag. The sculptures are the work of Kārlis Zāle who is himself buried here.

The cemetery was allowed to fall into neglect during the Soviet period, but was restored in 1993 and has since then become a focus of Latvian national feeling.

Rainis Cemetery

The **Rainis Cemetery** (*Raiṇa Kapi*), Aizsaules iela, can be reached by taking the number 11 tram from Vermana Gardens/Merķeļa iela near the National Opera or the number 4 or 9 bus from the main bus station. Latvia's best loved writer, Jānis Rainis, died on September 12 1929 and was buried here three days later. The cemetery was renamed in his honour. An avenue of silver birch leads to his grave which is marked by a red granite sculpture. Around the monument there is a semi-circular colonnade entwined with ivy.

Alongside Rainis lies his wife, the poet Aspāzija (Elza Rozenberg who died in 1943). The cemetery is also the resting place for a great number of Latvian writers, artists and musicians, many of whose graves are decorated with a creativity to match the lives they are designed to commemorate.

Woodlands Cemetery

The **Woodlands Cemetery** (*Meža Kapi*), also on Aizsaules iela, was designed by G Kufelts, the director of Rīga's parks, in 1913. Numerous political and government figures from the period of Latvia's first independence are buried here, including the former president, Jānis Čakste, and the government ministers, Zigfrids Meierovics and Vilhelms Munters. In addition, a number of Latvian artists, writers, poets and scientists lie here, among them Jānis Rozentāls, Anna Brīgadere and Paulis Stradiņš. In April 1988 Latvia's leading human rights activist, Gunārs Astra, was buried here. Astra was sentenced to seven years' imprisonment followed by five years' internal exile by the Soviet regime in December 1983 for the crimes of possessing recordings of radio programmes, photo negatives and subversive books and for writing a manuscript of a personal nature. In his final words to the court he delivered an impassioned speech against the Soviet regime including these words:

> I fervently believe that these nightmare times will end one day. This belief gives me the strength to stand before you. Our people have suffered a great deal but have learned to survive. They will outlive this dark period in their history.

Television tower

The **TV tower** stands on Hare Island (Zaķusala). The tower is open for tours, viewing and refreshments.

Outside the city centre

Ethnographic Open Air Museum

The **Latvian Ethnographic Open Air Museum** (*Latvijas Etnografiskaja Brīvdabas Muzejs*) is located on the outskirts of Rīga by Lake Jugla about 12km from the centre of Rīga (the address is 440 Brīvības gatve). The only way of getting there by public transport is to take the number 1, 19 or 28 bus from the city centre to the stop just by the road leading to the museum (the stop bears the name of the museum, so is easy to spot). Established in 1924 (although it opened in 1932 with only six buildings) the museum now covers 100 hectares and depicts traditional ways of life from the 16th to 19th centuries. It consists of reconstructions of old farmsteads and traditional houses, windmills, fishing villages and exhibits; on occasions there are also demonstrations of traditional crafts. Note the traditional *dore*, hollowed tree trunks standing on stone bases used for bee keeping, the pub, *krogs*, and windmills; the Usma church is still used for a service on Sundays as well as for weddings.

The museum is open every day 10.00–17.00. It has an excellent self-service **restaurant** in a traditional wooden building close to the museum entrance which serves excellent typical Latvian food and drink. You should allow at least two hours for a visit, and you could easily spend a half or even a whole day here. Much of the museum was destroyed by fire in May 2000 but enough remains for a visit still to be worthwhile.

Motor Museum

The **Motor Museum** (*Rīgas Motormuzejs*) is located at 6 S Eizenšteina iela to the east of the Old Town about 8km from the centre along Brīvības gatve. It can be reached by taking the number 15 bus, but this does not run from central Rīga (alight at the Pansionāts stop in Mežciems). The number 14 or 18 trolleybuses go from Brīvības iela and Čaka iela respectively to Gaiļezers hospital, about 500m from the museum. The museum is not easy to spot: look out for what appears to be a large Audi dealership and showroom; it is a modern red brick and glass building. The entrance is reached via a bridge from the car park. It is an acclaimed collection of over 100 motor vehicles, including cars which once belonged to the Soviet leaders, Stalin, Khrushchev and Brezhnev, and Erich Honecker, the leader of the former German Democratic Republic. Wax figures of some of these former politicians and motor enthusiasts help to liven up the displays: Stalin sits in his armoured ZIS 115 (said to have done 2.5km to the litre), Brezhnev at the wheel of his crashed Rolls-Royce, Gorky stands next to his 1934 Lincoln. The Motor Museum is open every day, except Monday and Tuesday, 10.00–18.00. It has a good café, toilets and a shop selling souvenirs.

Rīga Zoo

Rīga has had a **zoo** since 1912. Covering an area of 16.4 hectares it has 2,500 animals and 400 species. It is known for its bears (brown and polar bears are represented), Galápagos turtles and Amur tigers. Rides on horseback or in carriages are alternatives to walking. It is at 1 Meža prospekts in the forest of the Mežaparks and is open 10.00–16.00 every day.

Museums

For a relatively small capital city Rīga boasts a huge number of museums covering a wide range of subjects – art, literature, theatre, history and politics, medicine and other specialist topics. The visitor to Rīga with little time to spare will not be able to visit all of them, so if time is limited, we recommend the following: the Ethnographic Museum (see page 95), the Motor Museum (see above), the Museum of the Occupation of Latvia (see page 79–80), the art nouveau houses in the New Town, especially the Jānis Rozentāls Memorial Museum (page 90), and finally the Museum of the History of Rīga and Navigation (see page 78).

The alphabetical list of museums below is not exhaustive but covers the majority of museums any visitor is likely to want to visit.

The opening hours of the major museums are reliable, but some of the smaller museums suffer from staff shortages, so it may be advisable to check opening hours locally (consult *Rīga in Your Pocket* or *Rīga This Week*, both of which also give details of temporary exhibitions, as does the *Baltic Times*) before making a long journey. Smaller museums will open for tour groups on 'closed' days by prior arrangement. The Latvian and English *Latvijas Muzeji* ('Museums of Latvia') published by the Latvian Museum Association with support from the Dutch Prince Bernhardt Foundation, is a useful booklet giving addresses, opening times and brief descriptions of the main museums in Rīga and elsewhere in Latvia.

Jāņa Akuratera Museum 6a O Vāciesa iela, Pārdaugava, tel: 619934. Open 11.00–17.00 every day except Sunday and Wednesday.
Situated across the Daugava River from the Old Town, this museum is devoted to the life of Jāņis Akuraters (1876–1937), the popular Latvian writer and rifleman. He wrote poetry and novels, his best known being *Kalps zena vasara* ('The Young Farmhand's Summer') and *Degosa sala* ('The Burning Island').

Krišjānis Barons Memorial Museum *Krišjāņa Barona Memoriālais Muzejs*, 3–5 Kr Barona iela, tel: 728 4265. Open 11.00–17.00 Tuesday, Thursday, Saturday and Sunday, 13.00–19.00 Wednesday and Friday, closed Monday.
The museum is the flat (number 5) occupied by Krišjānis Barons, the collector of Latvian oral literature, the *dainas*. The museum recreates his life and work. Examples of folk music and videos are available.

State Museum of Fine Arts *Valsts Mākslas Muzejs*, 10a Kr Valdemāra iela, tel: 735 5021. Open 11.00–17.00 every day except Tuesday.
Founded in 1869, this museum, with its 14,000 or so exhibits, houses the largest collection of paintings, drawings and graphics in Latvia. The ground floor is dominated by 19th-century Latvian and Russian works while the upper storeys are devoted to more abstract works.

Cinema Museum *Rīgas Kino Muzejs*, 22 Krāslavas iela, tel: 722 0282. Open 12.00–17.00 every day except Monday.
The building, which is in the old Russian working-class district of Rīga, used to house the secret printing press used by the communist newspaper, *Cīņa* ('Battle'). You can still visit the secret passages underneath the building and view the model printing presses.

'Dauderi' Latvian Cultural Museum *Latvijas Kultūras Muzejs*, 30 Sarkandaugavas iela, tel: 391780 or 392229. Open 11.00–17.00 every day except Monday and Tuesday.
This museum is housed in an elegant red brick house and was built in 1897–8. During the first independence it was the summer residence of the Latvian president, Kārlis Ulmanis, before he was deported. It contains a vast collection of memorabilia related to the recent history of the country brought together by Gaidis Graundiņš, a Latvian living in Germany. There are also mementos of Latvia's prewar independence, such as banknotes, stamps, photographs and so on, all collected from Latvian exiles.

Museum of Decorative and Applied Art *Dekoratīvi Lietišķās Mākslas Muzejs*, 10–20 Skārņu iela, tel: 722 2235 or 722 7833. Open 10.00–17.00 every day except Monday.
The Museum of Decorative and Applied Art opened in 1989 in the restored Jura

baznīca (St George's Church) in the Old Town. The exhibition hall still has a church-like feel about it. The exhibits include tapestries, pottery, glasswork and sculpture, and the old churchyard has been transformed into a sculpture garden.

Ethnographic Museum 440 Brīvības gatve, tel: 799 4510 or 799 4106. Open 10.00–17.00 every day.

Also called The Open Air Museum. For further details see page 95.

Museum of Fire-fighting *Ugunsdzēsības Muzejs*, 5 Hanzas iela, tel: 733 3306. Open 10.00–17.00 every day except Wednesday.

This unusual museum is appropriately housed in an art nouveau fire station built in 1912 and contains displays depicting the history of fire-fighting in Rīga. A major feature is a fire engine built during the first period of independence.

Latvian Museum of Foreign Art *Latvijas Ārzemju Mākslas Muzejs*, 3 Pils laukums, tel: 722 6467. Open 11.00–17.00 every day except Monday.

Housed in part of Rīga castle, the museum consists of three floors of paintings, sculptures, drawings and ceramics by artists from Germany, Holland, France and Belgium. For more details see page 73.

Latvian History Museum *Latvijas Vēstures Muzejs*, 3 Pils laukums, tel: 722 0586 or 722 1357. Open 11.00–17.00 every day except Monday and Tuesday.

This museum, part of the castle complex, traces the history of Latvia and Latvian culture from 9000BC to the present.

Museum of History and Navigation of the City of Rīga *Rīgas Vēstures un Kug̦niecības Muzejs*, 4 Palasta iela, tel: 721 2051 or 721 1358. Open 11.00–17.00 every day except Monday and Tuesday.

Founded in 1773, this is the oldest museum in the Baltic states. See page 78 for further details.

Jewish Museum, Community Centre and Library 6 Skolas iela, tel: 728 3484 or 728 9602. Open 12.00–17.00 every day except Saturday and Sunday.

The museum is devoted to the history of Jews in Latvia from the 18th century to World War II.

Mentzendorff House *Mencendorfa nams*, 18 Grēcinieku iela, tel: 721 2951. Open 10.00–17.00 every day except Monday and Tuesday.

The former residence of a wealthy Rīga merchant family this house is now a museum devoted to life in Rīga in the 17th and 18th centuries.

Motor Museum *Rīgas Motormuzejs*, 6 S Eizenšteina iela, tel: 709 7170. Open 10.00–18.00 every day except Monday.

See page 96 for further details.

Latvian Museum of Natural History *Latvijas Dabas Muzejs*, 4 Kr Barona iela, tel: 722 5765. Open 10.00–17.00 except Monday and Tuesday.

The museum has permanent exhibitions of geology, zoology, entomology, anthropology, and environmental protection. It also has an exhibition concentrating on the Daugava River and the effect of the construction of the hydro-electric power station on the river basin. Note the herbarium display, the work of the botanist J Ilsters.

Museum of the Occupation of Latvia *Okupācijas Muzejs*, 1 Strēlnieku laukums, tel: 721 2715. Open 11.00–17.00 every day.

See page 96 for further details.

Open Air Museum See Ethnographic Museum above and page 95 for further details.

Pharmaceutical Museum *Farmācijas Muzejs*, 13–15 Riharda Vāgnera iela, tel: 721 3008. Open 10.00–16.00 every day except Sunday, Monday and Tuesday.

Part of the P Stradiņš Museum of the History of Medicine, this branch is housed in a beautifully renovated house in the Old Town.

Latvian Photographic Museum *Latvijas Foto Muzejs*, 8 Mārstaļu iela, tel: 722 7231. Open 13.00–19.00 Wednesday and Thursday, 11.00–17.00 Friday, 11.00–15.00 Saturday. A permanent exhibition of the history of photography in Latvia 1839–1941.

Rainis Museum of Literature and Art History *Raiņa Literaturos un Mākslas Vēstures Muzejs*, 3 Pils laukums, tel: 722 1956. Open 11.00–17.00 every day except Monday. See pages 73–4 for further details.

Jāņis Rozentāls and Rūdolfs Blaumanis Memorial Museum *Jāņa Rozentāla un Rūdolfa Blaumaņa Memoriālais Muzejs*, 12–9 Alberta iela, tel: 733 1641. Open 10.00–17.00 Monday, Thursday and Sunday, 12.00–19.00 on Friday and Saturday. Closed Tuesday and Wednesday. Commemorates the life and work of two of Latvia's most famous artists. See page 90 for further details.

Gustavs Šķilters Museum *Gustava Šķiltera Memoriālais Muzejs*, Daugavgrivas iela, (across the Daugava river near Ķīpsala island), tel: 625364. Open 12.00–18.00 Wednesday to Sunday only. This museum, founded in 1971, is dedicated to the life and work of the Latvian sculptor, Gustavs Šķilters (1874–1954). There is a permanent display of his work as well as changing displays.

Museum of Space Exploration also known as Fridrich Zander's Memorial Museum (*Fridriha Candera Memoriālais Muzejs*), 1 F Candera iela, tel: 761 4113. Open only on Wednesday 11.00–16.00. Established in 1987, this museum is located in the house of the Latvian rocket designer, Fridrich Zander (1887–1933).

Latvian Sports Museum *Latvijas Sporta Muzejs*, 7–9 Alksnāja iela, tel: 722 5127 or 721 1365. Open 10.00–18.00 every day except Monday. This has a unique collection of bicycles, including a collapsible Peugeot built in 1915 and used during World War I and an English Raleigh ladies bicycle dating from 1895, as well as more conventional exhibits. It is housed in an attractive 17th century warehouse.

P Stradins Museum of the History of Medicine *P Stradiņa Medicīnas Vēstures Muzejs*, 1 Antonijas iela, tel: 722 2656. Open 11.00–16.30 every day, except Sunday and Monday and the last Friday of each month. This museum is the creation of the Latvian doctor and surgeon, Paulis Stradins (1896–1958) who collected the majority of the exhibits over a period of 30 years and presented them to the city of Rīga. The exhibits, which include medical instruments, books and papers, cover a wide range of topics, from Rīga during successive plague epidemics to how the human body copes with eating in space.

Lattelkom Museum of Telecommunications 33 Brīvības iela, tel: 724 0004. Opening times vary; check locally. One hundred and fifty years of telecommunications in Latvia.

Theatre Museum 37/39 Smilģa iela, tel: 611893. Open 11.00–18.00 (12.00–19.00 on Wednesday) every day except Monday and Tuesday. The museum is located in a building specially designed for Eduards Smilģis (1886–1966), who was an actor and director at the Daile Theatre. It contains a permanent exhibition devoted to the history of Latvian theatre.

Latvian War Museum *Latvijas Kara Muzejs*, 20 Smilšu iela, tel: 722 6915 or 722 3743. Open 10.00–17.00 every day except Monday and Tuesday.

During the Soviet occupation this museum was devoted to demonstrating how Latvia became a revolutionary Soviet state. Now it is a mainstream war museum with collections of army uniforms and other exhibits devoted to the military history of Latvia. Of particular interest are the exhibitions devoted to the Latvian Riflemen's Regiment which was known for its valour in fighting for Latvian independence.

Waxworks Museum *Vaska Figūru Muzejs*, 9 Vaļņu iela, tel: 721 6743. Open 10.00–19.00 every day except Monday.

Wax effigies of Latvian luminaries including writers Kr Barons, J Rainis, former leader K Ulmanis, the chess player M Tal, the Swedish king Gustavus Adolphus and many others from every period of Latvian history.

EXCURSIONS FROM RĪGA

Jūrmala

Jūrmala is Rīga's seaside resort (indeed the name Jūrmala means 'seaside' or 'by the sea' in Latvian) with a beautiful 30km or so of unspoilt beach. Jūrmala is actually the collective name given to a number of small towns and villages along the Baltic coast about 25km from Rīga. It can be reached by train, bus, taxi or car. Buses leave from the bus station and taxis from a special stand outside the railway station in summer. If you drive using your own or a hired car you must stop on the outskirts of Jūrmala and pay a toll of Ls1 a day to enter the area. There are frequent trains from the central railway station in Rīga, but note that there is no station actually called Jūrmala. It takes about 20 minutes from Rīga to the first station at Lielpupe, although not all trains stop there. The main stop is Majori, about 40 minutes from Rīga and the main centre of the Jūrmala area. The writer, Jānis Rainis, had his summer house here (at 5–7 J Pliekšāna iela), and it is now a museum in honour of him and his wife, the poet Aspāzija. There are a number of decent restaurants and cafés in Majori, most of them on or near the main pedestrianised shopping street, Jomas iela.

Salaspils

Salaspils is 18km south east of Rīga and can be reached by taking the tram to the station at Dārziņa and following the footpath for about 15 minutes or if travelling by car the A6 out of Rīga, turning left just before Salaspils and following the granite sign ('Salaspils 1941–44') to the memorial.

Salaspils is remembered largely as the site of the Nazi concentration camp, Kurtenhof. Built in 1941 during the Nazi occupation of Latvia in World War II, the camp operated for three years. In 1944, as the Red Army approached Rīga, the camp guards and administrators ordered the inmates to exhume and burn the thousands of bodies buried at the camp; it then was burnt to the ground by the retreating Nazis in an attempt to hide the atrocities committed there. Over 100,000 men, women and children, most of them Jews, were put to death here, among them Austrians, Belgians, Czechs, Dutch, French, Latvian, Polish and Soviet citizens. Today, lines of white stones mark the permimeter of the camp.

The Salaspils memorial, which now dominates the site of the former camp, was erected in 1967 to honour those who died there. A huge concrete wall in the shape of a long beam marks the position of the former entrance; symbolising the border between life and death, it bears the words of the

Latvian writer, Eižēns Vēveris, (a prisoner at Salaspils): '*Aiz šiem vārtiem vaid zeme*' ('Beyond these gates the earth moans'). You can actually walk the length of the wall on the inside – there is a door at each end. A series of steps takes you through a number of gloomy rooms, giving the impression of a mausoleum. There is also a small exhibition with photographs of the camp. The seven sculptures which stand in the grounds behind the wall evoke the suffering but also the spirit of defiance and resistance of those imprisoned and killed.

The stillness of Salaspils is broken only by the ticking of an underground metronome beneath the altar-like structure located to the left as you enter the ground. The noise of the ticking is a reminder of the lives spent and ended here. A narrow path leads through the woods to the place where the prisoners were executed.

Vilnius 4

Gordon McLachlan

That the name of Lithuania's largest city and national capital exists in several slightly differing versions – **Vilnius** to the Lithuanians, Wilno to the Poles, Vilna to the Jews and Russians – is a reflection of its eventful history as a melting-pot in which different ethnic groups have competed with one another for predominance. By the vagaries of fate, it is the only one of the many traditionally multi-national and multi-cultural cities of the old Polish Lithuanian Commonwealth which has preserved a mixed profile right down to the present day. Despite its key role in modern Lithuania, little more than a bare majority of its inhabitants are ethnic Lithuanians; the Russian and Polish minorities are both substantial, while there is also a significant number of Belarussians, and smaller representations of a host of other nationalities.

The diversity of the city's make-up is given a very visible expression in the Old Town, whose outstanding quality has gained it a coveted place on UNESCO's World Heritage List – as yet the only place in Lithuania to be so honoured. Although its Jewish quarter is now a sad shadow of its former self, the Old Town is otherwise substantially intact, with the domes of the Orthodox churches competing for attention with the towers of their far more numerous Catholic counterparts. Most of the latter were established by mendicant or missionary orders, and all but a few were either built or totally reconstructed in the baroque era. Vilnius boasts one of the greatest assemblages of baroque monuments outside Rome, having developed over nearly two centuries a distinctively indigenous interpretation of the style.

The re-establishment of Lithuania's independence in 1991 meant that Vilnius regained its role as capital of a sovereign state after a gap of well over four centuries. This development has inevitably led to huge changes. By no means all of these are welcome, but there have been many undoubted benefits, not least the ever-increasing number of recommendable hotels, restaurants, bars and cafés which have helped make the city a favourite holiday destination, especially for members of the (predominantly North American) Lithuanian diaspora.

THE CITY

The city of Vilnius has a population of around 580,000, which is well spread out over a municipality liberally endowed with areas of greenery; indeed, only about a third of the municipal area is built up. There are two distinct parts to the city centre. The Old Town, which is very large by the standards of its time, lies at the confluence of the Vilnia with the Neris, west of the former and south of the latter. It is now joined seamlessly to the west by the New Town, which grew up in the 19th century. Although the Old Town contains the lion's share of the city's sights, many others, including some of the most important, are scattered all over the inner and outer suburbs.

History

According to legend, Vilnius was founded in 1323 by Grand Duke Gediminas, progenitor of the Gediminian dynasty which ruled Lithuania, latterly in union with Poland, for over 250 years. The story goes that, after a successful day's hunting, Gediminas decided to pitch camp for the night at the point where the Vilnia flows into the Neris, rather than return to his castle in Trakai. On falling asleep, he had a strange dream of a huge iron wolf on the hill above, which howled with the ferocity of a pack of a hundred wolves. The pagan high priest Lizdeika interpreted this dream as a message from the gods instructing Gediminas to build a city on the hill where he had seen the iron wolf in his dream. This city would grow so great that its fame would reverberate around the world with the force of the howls of a hundred wolves.

The truth of the matter is that there was a settlement beside the Neris–Vilnia confluence at least as far back as the 1st century AD. Moreover, a wooden castle was built atop what is now known as Gediminas Hill in the 11th century. Vilnius (which takes its name from the river) was certainly a well-established town by Gediminas' time, though his role in its history is nonetheless an important one since it was in one of his letters of 1323 that it is documented for the first time, and it was probably he who raised it to the status of Lithuania's permanent capital.

Under Gediminas and his successors Vilnius occupied a small, tightly packed site protected by a fortification system which included three castles. Between 1365 and 1402 it was attacked by the Teutonic Knights on seven separate occasions, but despite inflicting considerable damage they never managed to capture it. In 1387, the year after the royal union with Poland, Vilnius was granted municipal rights, though it was only after the decisive defeat of the Teutonic Knights at the Battle of Žalgiris in 1410 that it was able to expand southwards from the confines of the original site.

Between 1503 and 1522, in response to a threat of invasion by the Tatars, the whole city was enclosed within a 2.4km-long wall. With the advent of more peaceful times, Vilnius flourished as a city of merchants and craftsmen, becoming one of the great book-printing centres of Europe. The year 1569 was one of crucial significance, as the Union of Lublin, which created the Polish-Lithuanian Commonwealth, had the inevitable consequence of Vilnius (like Kraków) losing its roles as a royal residence and administrative capital, as Warsaw, thanks to its central location, became the hub of the huge unified state.

However, 1569 also saw the arrival of the Jesuits in Vilnius, and as a result the city played a leading role in the Counter-Reformation, which saw the Roman Catholic Church recover most of the ground it had lost in Lithuania. The school founded by the Jesuits in 1570 was raised to University status in 1579, and quickly established itself as one of the great academic institutions of Europe.

It was also the Jesuits who were responsible for introducing the new baroque style of architecture, and this soon came to dominate the face of Vilnius' Old Town. Many of Vilnius' early baroque buildings were destroyed in the mid-

17th century wars with the Swedes and Russians, during which the city lost half its population, principally as a result of the plague of 1657–58. Nonetheless, it recovered well, and was embellished with a host of new aristocratic palaces, churches and monastic buildings. Initially, these were inspired by the Roman high baroque style, but in the 18th century a distinctive local style, derived from German and Central European models, was developed.

With the Third Partition of the Commonwealth in 1795, Vilnius, along with most of the rest of Lithuania, became part of the Tsarist Empire. Paradoxically, this led to it regaining its role as a capital, as it was chosen as the seat of a large administrative province. Nevertheless, there were patriotic hopes for a revival of Lithuanian independence, with the French dictator Napoleon Bonaparte, who captured Vilnius in June 1812, seen as the potential saviour. During the 19 days he spent in the city, he showed himself to be no more than a lukewarm supporter, though he did authorise the formation of a provisional government supported by an army. A dispirited Napoleon returned to the city in December of the same year in retreat from the Russians, but stayed for only a couple of hours before continuing to flee. The Russians recaptured Vilnius soon after, ending its hopes of re-establishing itself as capital of an independent Lithuania within the foreseeable future.

Throughout the failed rebellion of 1831, the authorities remained in control of Vilnius, but in the repressive measures introduced in its aftermath the city was made to suffer heavily. Its University, the most venerable in the Russian Empire, was closed down; the religious houses were dissolved, and several churches were transferred to Orthodox congregations. The next unsuccessful revolt, in 1863, resulted in the public executions of the ringleaders.

However, the 19th century also saw Vilnius develop as a major industrial centre, and it expanded greatly in size, with the construction of the New Town and suburban areas. Its population grew from 18,000 to 138,000, an increase which was in part due to an influx of Jews from elsewhere in Russia. Indeed, a census taken towards the end of the century made Jews the biggest ethnic group within the city, accounting for over 40% of the population. Poles were the next largest, at around 30%, with Russians numbering 20%, and Lithuanians little more than 2%. Language seems to have been the determining characteristic in these figures, whose significance is still much disputed: it is likely that many of the Poles (perhaps even the overwhelming majority) were ethnic Lithuanians who had, often for generations past, adopted the Polish tongue.

Despite the paucity of Lithuanian speakers in Vilnius, the city became the focal point of the national awakening which gathered momentum in the early years of the 20th century. The so-called Great Seimas, a gathering of 2,000 Lithuanians, met there in 1905 and demanded autonomy within the empire. Although nothing came of this, the city's long-dormant dream to become a national capital once more was revived as a result of World War I, which saw the Russians abandoning Vilnius to the advancing German Army in September 1915.

A census by the occupying forces the following year produced a somewhat different result from that of the Russians a couple of decades earlier. The percentage of Jewish residents was virtually unchanged, but Poles were now said to number a fraction over 50% of the population. Despite these findings, the Germans allowed a Lithuanian congress to meet in the city in September

1917. This made the formal demand for Vilnius to be made capital of a Lithuanian state, and independence was duly declared in 1918.

However, the city found itself a major bone of contention in the conflicts following World War I which saw Soviet Russia and the newly-resurrected nations of Lithuania and Poland tussle with one another for territory. In July 1920 the Soviets recognised Lithuania's right to Vilnius, and the Poles apparently followed suit by the Treaty of Suwałki of October 7. Two days later, however, ostensibly rebel troops commanded by General Lucian Żeligowski, a Polonised Lithuanian, captured Vilnius and the surrounding area. In this action, they were secretly supported by the Polish leader, Marshal Józef Piłsudski, another ethnic Lithuanian, who was determined that the city where he had grown up would become an integral part of Poland.

Following two years of somewhat half-hearted international mediation, the dispute over Vilnius was resolved in Poland's favour largely by default, there being no readily enforceable alternative to leaving it in the hands of the occupying power. From a purely objective standpoint there is no doubt that the Poles had a strong claim on the city, though for Vilnius itself the result was certainly not fortuitous, as it was reduced to a provincial role within Poland, while Kaunas was developed as the showpiece Lithuanian capital in its stead.

Following the carve-up of Poland between Nazi Germany and the Soviet Union at the beginning of World War II, the Soviets restored Vilnius to Lithuania in October 1939 as its capital in return for the right to establish military bases there, a move which paved the way for the annexation of the country the following June. The Nazi occupation of 1941–44 led to the elimination of almost all of Vilnius' large Jewish community, many of whom were murdered in the Paneriai Forest in the outskirts. When the war ended with the Soviets back in control, the city's population had fallen to 110,000, a reduction of around 100,000 on what it had been in 1939. Over the following decade, a large percentage of the local Polish population was deported to Poland. They were replaced by Russians and migrant Lithuanians, and the city's population grew steadily, with most of the newcomers housed in high-rise suburbs constructed according to Soviet principles.

For Vilnius, the Soviet decades did at least offer the compensation of its re-establishment as a national capital, albeit one under foreign occupation. It was therefore inevitable that it was in the vanguard of the successful drive towards independence, and the scene of the most dramatic flashpoint in the largely peaceful struggle – the storming of the TV tower by Soviet tanks in January 1991, which resulted in the martyrdom of 14 citizens.

Now the proud capital of an independent nation-state once again, Vilnius is gradually modernising and transforming itself in the hope and belief that this role will never again be lost. Poland formally renounced any claim to the city in the Friendship and Co-operation Treaty of 1994, though it declined Lithuania's request to apologise for having annexed it in 1920.

PRACTICAL INFORMATION
Communications
The *Baltic Times*, published weekly on a Thursday, is the best English-language source of news for the three Baltic Republics. It also lists exhibitions and concerts. *The City Paper*, published every two months, also covers the three Baltic capitals.

Telephones

Vilnius telephone numbers are of six digits, which should be prefixed by various codes depending where the call is being made from. The international dialling code for Lithuania is 370 and the area code for Vilnius that should follow this for all calls to numbers listed in this section is 2. Calls to Vilnius from elsewhere in Lithuania require the dialling code 822 then the six-digit Vilnius number.

Post and telecommunications

Central Post Office Gedimino 7. Open Mon–Fri 07.00–19.00, Sat 09.00–16.00.
Telecommunications Office Vilniaus 33. Open daily 08.00–22.00.

Banks and money

The local currency, the lit, is fixed at a rate of US$1 = 4.00Lt so in late 2000 the pound sterling was worth about 5.80Lt. Banks and exchange bureaux take all major Western currencies as well as the Baltics ones and Russian roubles. Travellers cheques can only be exchanged in banks. Cash machines are available all over the town. Most hotels and restaurants accept credit cards.

Currency exchange

Lietuvos Taupomasis Bankas Savanorių 15a or Geležinkelio 6. Open 24 hours.

Tourist Information

The English-language magazine *Vilnius In Your Pocket*, which is available from kiosks, newsagents and tourist offices, is a well-nigh essential acquisition, having attained near-legendary status among travellers, as well as the municipally-bestowed designation of *The Official City Guide*. Published five times annually, it contains comprehensive reviews of hotels, restaurants, cafés and bars; information and dates of forthcoming events and entertainment; and a host of useful listings covering professional services, shopping, transport, communications and many other subjects. Not the least of its attractions is its quirky and irreverent style, the bizarre range of idioms employed being a reflection of the contributions made by the multinational cast of people who have worked over the years on what was originally a German–Belgian venture. The text of the guide can also be accessed from its website at www.inyourpocket.com. Another highly recommendable purchase is the 1:25,000 **map** of the city, with an enlargement of the Old and New Towns and A–Z street listings, by the Latvian publisher Jāņa Sēta.

Tourist offices

Municipal Tourist Office Pilies 42, tel/fax: 620762. Open Mon–Fri 09.00–19.00, Sat 12.00–18.00. In addition to selling the usual range of maps and brochures, the office keeps piles of free information leaflets about various aspects of the city and posts up current public transport timetables.
Municipal Tourist Office Vilniaus 22, tel: 629660. Open Mon–Fri 09.00–18.00. Another branch of the above.
In Your Pocket Information Centre Airport arrival hall, tel: 999721. Open Mon–Fri 09.00–17.00, Sat 09.00–15.00. This small booth is the only public office run by the listings magazine. In addition to selling maps and guides, it books accommodation and car rental.

Tours

To book sightseeing tours on the spot, contact the tourist office at Pilies 42 which is open daily in the summer from 10.00 to 18.00. For information on tour operators to Vilnius see the *Tour operators* section (pages 4–6).

Travel agencies

Baltic Travel Service Subačiaus 2, tel: 220220, email: baltic.travel.service@post.omnitel.net.

Lithuanian Holidays Aušros Vartų 17-9, tel/fax: 312872.

Lithuanian Student and Youth Travel Service Basanavičiaus 30-13, tel: 221373, fax: 262131, email: info@lsyt.lt.

Lithuanian Tours Šeimyniškių 18, tel: 724176, fax: 721815, email: contact@lithuaniatours.com.

Transport

Airport

Rodūnės kelias 2, tel: 752588 or 306666. Reached by bus 1 or 2, the airport is situated 5km south of the stations. In the arrivals hall in the older front building are a 24-hour currency exchange, the *Vilnius In Your Pocket* information office, and the booths of several car hire companies. The airline ticket offices are all in the departure hall to the rear, with the exception of LOT, which is in the neighbouring Hotel Skrydis.

Taxis are strictly regulated at the airport and have meters. To most hotels the cost should not be more than 15Lt (£2.50/US$4.25). The local bus costs 0.60Lt (£0.10/US$0.15) for tickets bought at kiosks, or 0.75Lt if bought from the driver. The kiosk at the airport sells bus tickets. The route passes the Lietuva and New Vilnius Hotels but is too far from most others to be of use.

City trolleybuses and buses

Networks of trolleybuses and buses cover virtually the whole city, though no services actually penetrate the Old Town. As they are separately run, different tickets are required for each, which can be bought in advance from kiosks (currently 0.60Lt, 0.30Lt for pensioners and bona fide students) or, with rare exceptions, from the driver (0.75Lt). A few bus routes which run beyond the city boundaries have slightly higher tariffs, with tickets sold by an on-board conductor. Otherwise, tickets – whether bought in advance or from the driver – must be punched in one of the machines positioned throughout the bus or trolleybus. Usually these are primitive devices which make different patterns of holes, though a few buses are now equipped with computerised machines which print out the date and time that the ticket has been validated.

For visiting all but the far-flung parts of the city, the trolleybuses cover most needs, though they are prone to be uncomfortably crowded throughout much of the day, and it is often necessary to jostle with other passengers in order to be able to alight and disembark. Particularly useful services are trolleybus 2, which travels from the train station down the western side of the Old Town, the eastern part of Gedimino, then along the south bank of the Neris to Antakalnis; and trolleybus 5, which likewise begins and ends at the station and goes down the western side of the Old Town, before continuing northwards over the Green Bridge and past the Calvary Market en route to Žirmūnai. An excellent map of the whole trolleybus network can be found in *Vilnius In Your Pocket*.

Bus 1 links the train station with the airport, while the more frequent bus 2 goes to the airport from the northern inner suburb of Šeškinė via the Green Bridge and the New Town. These and many other bus routes are duplicated by minibuses, which can be flagged down anywhere. Their destination and the fare (which is normally either 1Lt or 2Lt and paid directly to the driver) are displayed prominently on the windscreen.

Taxis

Taxis are always worth considering, particularly if travelling as a family or in a group, as they are much more comfortable than the alternatives and are also very inexpensive by Western standards. They are often necessary for getting to the airport, as buses are only starting to run at the time it is necessary to check-in for some early flights. Outrageous rip-offs of tourists by taxi drivers, once commonplace, are now largely a thing of the past, though cars without meters or which do not display the name of a company should still be avoided. Ordering a taxi by telephone from one of the companies listed below, rather than picking one up at a rank, is a sure-fire way of avoiding any difficulties. Rates consist of a fixed charge of around 1.30Lt plus upwards of 1Lt per kilometre travelled; the latter figure is invariably increased at night, sometimes to as much as 2Lt.

Baltas Taksi Tel: 220909.
Denvila Taksi Tel: 444444.
Vilniaus Taksi Tel: 228888 or 229403.
Lanrija Taksi Tel: 611111.

Car hire

Avis Dariaus ir Gireno 32A, tel: 306820, fax: 306821, email: rez@avis.lt. Also at the airport, tel/fax: 262229.
Europcar Stuokos-Gucevičiaus 9-1, tel: 220207, fax: 220439, email: city@europcar.lt. Also at the airport, tel: 263442.
Hertz Ukmergės 2, tel: 726940, fax: 726970, email: hertz@auste.elnet.lt. Also at the airport, tel: 260394.
Litinterp Bernardinų 7-2, tel: 223850, fax: 223559, email: litinterp@omnitel.net.

Buses

Bus station Sodų 22, tel: 262482 or 262977. Located just south of the Old Town, this has a comprehensive network of services to other Lithuanian towns. These include at least a couple of buses an hour throughout most of the day to Kaunas, of which the fastest are the minibuses, which leave from stand 37. One or more buses per hour run to Panevėžys, while over 30 per day go to Trakai, often en route to another destination. Other approximate daily frequencies include 12 to Šiauliai, ten to Klaipėda, three to Nida, five to Druskininkai and, in season, 12 expresses to Palanga.

Among the daily international services are seven to Minsk, five to Rīga, two to Tallinn, two to Kaliningrad, four to Warsaw, one to Białystok via Suwałki and one to Gdańsk; there are also four per week to Moscow. For destinations in Western Europe, it is normally necessary to change at Warsaw. However, there are also connections to the routes passing through Kaunas as well as a direct weekly service to a range of German cities. There is a left luggage room in the terminal building. Eurolines have an office in the bus station which issues tickets that have been prebooked through travel agents abroad and also makes reservations on the spot. It is open 06.00–20.00. They operate most of the buses to Rīga and Tallinn and to Western Europe. Pre-booking before arrival in Lithuania is strongly advised.

Trains
Train station Geležinkelio 16, tel: 630086. This grand old building with a recently refurbished interior is diagonally opposite the bus station. There are 12 trains daily to Kaunas, including two expresses which are far faster than any bus. Among the other daily domestic services are seven (five at weekends) to Trakai, six to Ignalina, six to Šiauliai, four to Druskininkai via Marcinkonys, three to Klaipėda via Telšiai, Plungė and Kretinga, and one direct to Šeštokai.

There are also a number of daily international services: four to Daugavpils (Latvia), three to St Petersburg, two or three to Moscow, one or two to Rīga, one to Kaliningrad, one to Minsk and two to Warsaw, one of which continues on to Berlin. Beware that some of the Warsaw trains travel via Grodno in Belarus, necessitating the purchase of an outrageously expensive transit visa. The left luggage facility is in the station basement, which can only be reached by the stairway in front of the building.

Accommodation
There is a wide choice of accommodation in Vilnius, ranging from dorm beds in hostels to super-luxury hotels. Prices are naturally similarly variable, and are usually a fairly reliable indicator of the quality of any particular establishment.

Vilnius' stock of hotels has mushroomed since independence, and is likely to continue to expand for some years yet. The city now has plenty of highly recommendable up-market establishments, including many which offer the bonus of an atmospheric Old Town location. However, it is very noticeable that the majority of these are geared primarily towards the business traveller. Promotional leaflets tend to emphasise the provision of conference rooms, computers with email access, fax machines, photocopiers and the like. Room rates in such hotels are often comparable with those in cities of similar size in the West. There is still something of a shortage of good medium-range and (especially) budget accommodation in the city; some very dubious customers can almost invariably be found in the cheaper hotels. Prices in these categories of accommodation tend to be at least 50% higher than they would be anywhere else in Lithuania. Receptionists in the better hotels almost invariably speak adequate English; the same cannot be said for the middle and lower end of the market, though there is often a member of staff who can speak basic English or German. Discounts from the standard rates may be available in July and August at the luxury 'business-class' hotels for reservations made through their usual booking agents, but these prices may be difficult for 'walk-in' guests to obtain.

Exclusive hotels

Astorija Didžioji 35/2, tel: 220110, fax: 221762, email: vaida@radissonsas.com, web: www.radissonsas.lt. This grand early 20th century hotel in the heart of the Old Town has recently been extended by the Radisson SAS chain, and has a Business Service Centre prominent among its facilities. All rooms have hair dryer, trouser press, telephone, cable TV, safe and hot drinks machine. Prices include either a 'grab and run' or a full buffet breakfast. The Brasserie has an international menu and is among the best and most expensive restaurants in the city. Singles 760Lt, doubles 840–1,000Lt, suites 1,560–1,800Lt.

Stikliai Gaono 7, tel: 615441 or 627971, fax: 223870, email: stikliai@mail.tipas.lt; web: iti.lt/stikliai. This hotel numbers foreign royalty and other dignitaries among its clients. Occupying a 17th-century building in a quiet Old Town backstreet, it is exquisitely furnished throughout. All bedrooms are soundproofed and air-conditioned, and have satellite TV and telephone. Other facilities include a sauna, swimming pool and fitness room. The hotel restaurant serves pricey French cuisine; close by are several less formal and expensive eateries run by the same management (*see below*). Singles 600Lt, doubles 660Lt, suites 840–940Lt, apartments 1,400Lt.

Luxury hotels

AAA Mano Liza Ligoninės 5, tel: 222225, fax: 222608, email: aaa@taide.lt. Small guest house in the quiet southwestern part of the Old Town, which will arrange pick-up from the airport. All eight rooms are equipped with satellite TV. The restaurant offers a nicely varied international menu. Singles 320Lt, doubles 420Lt, suites 560–660Lt, apartments 640–740Lt.

Balatonas Latvių 38, tel: 722250, fax: 722134, email: balatonas@tdd.lt. A Hungarian joint venture, this hotel occupies a gleaming white historic villa set amid the wooden houses in the heart of the Žvėrynas district. Facilities include a sauna, swimming pool and a small café which serves full meals. Singles 330Lt, doubles 440Lt, suites 430–620Lt.

Business Guest House Saltoniškių 44, tel/fax: 722298, email: bgh@tdd.lt. Located in the north of the Žvėrynas district, this detached house overshadowed by tower blocks looks unassuming from the outside, but has a Scandinavian-style designer interior. Guests can use the sauna and swimming pool without extra charge. There is also a commercial art gallery and the expected range of business services. Singles 320Lt, doubles 400–480Lt, suites 760Lt.

CityPark Stuokos-Gucevičiaus 3, tel: 223515 or 615123, fax: 617745, email: citypark@is.lt, web: www.is.lt/citypark. Located in a recently refurbished building with a central courtyard diagonally opposite the Cathedral. All rooms have telephone, satellite TV and minibar; facilities include an express laundry, sauna and swimming pool. American-style pizza is the speciality of the hotel restaurant, Bistro 1. Singles 390Lt, doubles 480–560Lt, suites 660–700Lt.

Grybo Namai Aušros Vartų 3a, tel: 221854 or 619695, fax: 222416, email: grybashouse@taide.lt. A delightful small hotel (there are only eight rooms) in a refurbished baroque house set in a quiet courtyard at the northern end of the Old Town. The decor includes sculptures from the Congo and the former pier in Palanga. Primarily geared to tourists, it offers full travel agency services. All rooms have telephone, satellite TV, minibar, water filters and heated floors. There is a fine basement restaurant, with live classical music on Wednesday evenings. Singles 320–440Lt, doubles 420–540Lt, suite 660Lt, apartment 740Lt.

Calvary Church, Verkiai Park and Green Lakes

Trinapolis Convent and Verkiai Park

ŽIRMŪNAI

ŽVALGŲ

KALVARIJŲ

VERKIŲ

KAREIVIŲ

ŽIRMŪNŲ

ANTAKALNIO

OZO

Neris

ANTAKALNIS

ŽALGIRIO

MINTIES

KALVARIJŲ

TUSKULĖNŲ

ŽIRMŪNŲ

ANTAKALNIO

SAPIEGOS

Our Lord Jesus

ŠNIPIŠKĖS

Calvary Market

RINKTINĖS

Antakalnis Cemetery

UKMERGĖS

ŠNIPIŠKIŲ

UPĖS

ŠEIMYNIŠKIŲ

Planetarium

Žalgiris Stadium

SS Peter & Paul

St Raphael

ŽVĖJŲ

ŽYGIMANTŲ

ARSENALO

GEDIMINO

VRUBLEVESKIO

VILNIAUS

Higher Castle

Hill Park

OLANDŲ

BATORO

Genocide Musem

Cathedral

FILARETŲ

UŽUPIS

ŠVENTARAGIO

MAIRONIO

Vilnia

University

PILIES

UŽUPIO

VIČIAUS

SENAMIESTIS

PYLIMO

DIDŽIOJI

See map page 125

Bernardine Cemetery

PAUPYS

ZARASŲ

MINDAUGO

MARKUČIAI

SUBAČIAUS

SUBAČIAUS

ŠOPENO

SUBAČIAUS

Pushkin Memorial Museum

PELESOS

RASŲ

Bus station

GELEŽINKELIO

LIEPKALNIO

RASŲ

SUKILĖLIŲ

PELESOS

Railway station

Rasos Cemetery

IR

PELESOS

RASOS

GARDINO

GIRĖNO

Airport

IdaBasar Subačiaus 1, tel/fax: 622909. The guest house of this German joint venture is an offshoot of the restaurant on the opposite side of the courtyard, and has only seven rooms and two apartments for let. All have satellite TV and minibar; the apartments also have a kitchen. Single 320Lt, double 400Lt, apartments 600Lt.

Le Meridien Villon A2 highway, tel: 739600, fax: 651385, email: lemeridienvillon@post.omnitel.net, web: www.hotelvillon.lt. This huge British joint venture motel and conference centre lies 19km from the centre of Vilnius, beside the main dual carriageway to Panevėžys and Rīga. It lays on free shuttle buses to the city, and offers the services of a full holiday complex, including tennis courts, a fitness club, swimming pool, three saunas and a restaurant, Le Paysage, specialising in Gallic-influenced cuisine. The distance from town may be seen as a disadvantage by some, but many find the location beside a forest and a lake more than adequate compensation. Singles 520Lt, doubles 600Lt, suites 800Lt, apartments 1,000Lt.

Mabre Residence Maironio 13, tel: 222087, fax: 222240, email: mabre@is.lt, web: www.is.lt/mabre. Occupies the grand neo-classical courtyard buildings of a former Russian Orthodox monastery in the quiet eastern part of the Old Town. All rooms have satellite TV, telephone and minibar. Public facilities include a sauna, small pool and the Steakhouse Hazienda cellar restaurant, the city's leading steak specialist. Singles 320–380Lt, doubles 420–480Lt, suites 600Lt, apartments 800–880Lt.

Narutis Pilies 24, tel: 222894, fax: 622882, email: a.b.@narutis.lt; web: tdd.lt/narutis. This new hotel on the Old Town's main artery occupies an originally Gothic mansion which was remodelled in neo-classical style. The bedrooms are tastefully furnished, and some have 19th century murals. Other facilities include a lounge in the glass-covered courtyard, a sauna, fitness room and a cellar café-restaurant. Singles 400Lt, doubles 500–650Lt.

Naujasis Vilnius Ukmergės 14, tel: 726756 or 739494, fax: 723161, email: hotelnv@is.lt. The smaller of the two giant hotel blocks on the north side of the Neris, the former Turistas has been made over by a Swiss joint venture company into a business-class hotel with the usual support services. Recent visitors would have no idea of its Soviet past. Because of their reduced rates for tour operators, many groups from abroad and individual visitors stay here. Singles 340Lt, doubles 400Lt, suites 600–660Lt, apartments 800–860Lt.

Neringa Gedimino 23, tel: 610516, fax: 614160, email: neringa@tdd.lt. This Communist-era hotel on the main commercial street has been given a Scandinavian-style makeover, and is equipped with a gym, sauna and small pool. Air-conditioning and baths in every room, as well as its convenient location, give it a special appeal in Vilnius where such facilities are still often lacking. Singles 400Lt, doubles 500Lt, suites 600Lt, apartment 1,000Lt.

Ratonda Gedimino 52, tel: 220670, fax: 220669, e-mail: centrum@takas.lt. Despite its address, the hotel is in fact just off Gedimino so is unaffected by the neighbouring traffic noise. After opening in late 1999, it soon built up a regular clientele of business travellers and tourists who liked its family atmosphere and the good English spoken by the staff. Having 37 rooms, it is just small enough not to be impersonal. Singles 320-400Lt, doubles 500-600Lt, suites 720Lt.

Šarūnas Raitininkų 4, tel: 723888 or 724888, fax: 724355, email: info@ hotelsarunas.lt, web: www.hotelsarunas.lt. This modern business hotel near the Žalgiris Stadium is owned by Šarūnas Marčiulionis, president of the Lithuanian Basketball Federation and erstwhile player with the Sacramento Kings of America's National Basketball Association. Sportsgear and trainers worn by leading stars of the NBA decorate the informal Rooney's Bar, which serves Lithuanian and American dishes, while the formal Itališkas kaprizas offers the best and most expensive Italianate menu in town. A fitness room with weight-lifting equipment supplements the obligatory sauna. Singles 380–400Lt, doubles 440Lt, suites 560–720Lt, apartments 800Lt.

Shakespeare Bernadinų 8, tel: 314521, fax: 314522, email: info@shakespeare.lt, web: www.shakespeare.lt. Starting with ten rooms late in 1999, it will have 40 by early 2001. It is completely home from home for British country visitors with an oak-beamed lounge and worthy reading left in each bedroom, linked with the author after whom the room is named. Shakespeare joins Trollope, Dickens and Tolstoy on the doors of the more expensive rooms, cheaper ones being allocated to Goethe, G B Shaw and the Lithuanian poet Maironis. Underfloor bathroom heating and air conditioning are welcome late 20th-century features. Singles 320Lt, doubles 500Lt.

Medium-range hotels

Adelita Rodūnės kelias 8, tel: 262133, fax: 236463. Occupying the same building as the budget Skrydis hotel at the airport, this is under different management and is fully renovated, with a fitness room, sauna and café among the facilities. Whether this really makes it worth the extra cost is another matter. Singles 120Lt, doubles 200Lt.

Apia Šv Ignoto 12, tel: 223426, fax: 223618, email: apia@takas.lt. A four-room guest house in an Old Town tenement. Singles 180Lt, doubles 240Lt.

Draugystė Čiurlionio 84, tel: 236603 or 236711, fax: 263101, email: hotel.draugyste@post.omnitel.net, web: www.tdd.lt/draugyste. This high-rise hotel on the edge of Vingis Park was once favoured by Communist Party officials and visiting foreign dignitaries. The hotel struggled longer than most to put this past behind it, but has now just about succeeded. Even tourists who do not stay here should visit the café for the view from the 16th floor. Singles 190–280Lt, doubles 250–370Lt, suites 330–540Lt, apartments 470–540Lt.

Elektra Žvejų 14a, tel: 626748, fax: 723779, email: elaktra@lpc.lt. The hotel occupies the palatial former headquarters of the electricity company, whose tower is crowned by a statue of the torch-bearing Elektra, daughter of Agamemnon. Rooms all have satellite TV, telephone and mini-bar, while those facing the front command fine views across the Neris to the Higher Castle. There is also a café-restaurant. Singles 290–330Lt, doubles 350Lt, suites 460–510Lt.

Lietuva Ukmergės 20, tel: 726092, fax: 722130, email: lietuva@aiva.lt. The former Intourist hotel is much the largest and most prominent in the city. In summer 2000 the hotel was bought by the Reval group who operate four hotels in Tallinn. They plan to accelerate a modernisation programme that was already underway. Most tourist groups stay here and are happy to do so. All possible services, including a dentist, are provided under the one roof at reasonable prices, and most rooms have excellent views. Singles 180–300Lt, doubles 200–360Lt, suites 420–500Lt, apartments 740Lt.

Mikotel Pylimo 63, phone: 609626, fax: 609627, e-mail: mikotelis@takas.lt. This small haven of peace and cleanliness, opened in summer 2000, is a welcome contrast to the neighbouring market and railway station. The low prices also compensate for its ten-minute walk from the town centre. Singles 180Lt, doubles 240Lt.

Pilaitė Kalvarijų 1, tel: 752292, fax: 752269. This hotel is housed on the top floor of the mock-medieval castle overlooking the Green Bridge. The setting is undoubtedly the main draw; the rooms themselves are plain and old-fashioned. Singles 269Lt, doubles 309Lt, suites 316–359Lt.

Rūdninkų Vartai Rūdninkų 15/46, tel: 613916, fax: 220507. Named after the western gateway to the Old Town which formerly occupied the spot, the hotel is built round a

courtyard which in summer serves as an open-air extension to its café. All rooms have satellite TV and telephone; some also have a mini-bar or refrigerator. A sauna and fitness room are the other main facilities. Singles 280Lt, doubles 320–480Lt, suites 660Lt.
Sanvita Šeimyniškių 21, tel: 723428, fax: 750036. Situated right beside the Žalgiris Stadium, this is a less expensive alternative to the Šarūnas next door. A fitness centre and café are on the premises. Singles 240–255Lt, doubles 280–295Lt.
Senatoriai Tilto 2, tel: 226491, fax: 226372, email: senatoria@tdd.lt. This small low-rise hotel profits from an excellent location, being discreetly tucked away down a side street immediately to the rear of Gedimino, just a stone's throw from the Cathedral. Singles 230–350Lt, doubles 260–380Lt, suites 430–480Lt.
Victoria Saltoniškių 56, tel: 724013, fax: 724320, email: victoria@ tdd.lt. A choice of unrenovated and renovated rooms is on offer at this Swedish joint venture hotel in the northeast of the Žvėrynas district. All rooms have satellite TV and telephone, and a Scandinavian breakfast buffet is included in the price. Singles 240–272Lt, doubles 280–328Lt, suites 376Lt.

Budget hotels
Gintaras Sodų 14, tel: 738063, fax: 233881, email: hotel.gintaras@ttd.lt. Vilnius' most notorious hotel is a large Soviet-era block opposite the train station. The oft-expressed fears about room security are much exaggerated and it is a convenient place to spend the night if arriving late or departing early – even if some of the staff seem to have learned their craft from Basil Fawlty. The renovated rooms are only relatively better than the unrenovated, and not really worth the extra money. Singles 64–130Lt, doubles 95–189Lt, suites 239Lt, apartments 299Lt.
Jeruzalė Kalvarijų 209, tel: 714040, fax: 762627, email: jeruzale@takas.lt. A smallish, slightly dated hotel in the northern residential district of the same name, a short distance south of the Calvary Church. It can be reached by buses 26, 35, 36 or 50. Singles 120–150Lt, doubles 140–220Lt, suites 250Lt.
Pušis Blindžių 17, tel: 683999, fax: 721305, email: hotelpusis@mail.lt. The location, within the Agribusiness Training Centre at the far western edge of Žvėrynas, is not terribly convenient, but the rooms are good value at the price asked. Singles 105Lt, doubles 198–232Lt.
Skrydis Rodūnės kelias 8, tel: 262223, fax: 306498. Renovations at the airport hotel are proceeding at a leisurely pace and many rooms are still of the Soviet era. It is certainly worth considering for at least single-night stays if travelling by flights which arrive very late or depart early. Singles 75–160Lt, doubles 90–260Lt, suites 300Lt.
Sportas Bistryčios 13, tel: 748953, fax: 748946. Originally intended for sportsmen, but now open to all, this large and rather worn hotel is in the Antakalnis district; trolleybus 2 passes nearby. The cheaper rooms lack private facilities. Singles 59–76Lt, doubles 69–78Lt, triples 75Lt, suites 154Lt.
Žaliasis Tiltas Vilniaus 2/15 and Gedimino 12, tel: 615450 or 615460, fax: 221716, email: reservation@zaliasistiltas.lt. Considering their central locations – one overlooking the Neris, the other on the main commercial street – these two hotels charge very reasonable rates. Vilniaus has the cheaper rooms, but Gedimino is the nicer of the two, with the bonus of a modern café. Singles 80–160Lt, doubles 120–240Lt, suites 260–400Lt.

Hostels
IYHF Filaretai Hostel Filaretų 17, tel: 254627, fax: 220149, email: filaretai@post.omnitel.net. Much the larger of the two IYHF-affiliated hostels,

situated at the northeastern edge of the Užupis district, and reached by bus 34, or easily on foot. Dorm bed 32Lt, 28Lt from second night.

IYHF Old Town Hostel Aušros Vartų 20–15a, tel: 625357, fax: 220305, email: lyh@jnakv.vno.soros.lt. Despite its name, this one-room hostel with eight beds actually lies just beyond the southern edge of the Old Town, and is signposted from the train station. Dorm bed 32Lt.

Jaunujų Turistų Centras Polocko 7, tel: 611547, fax: 627742. The Young Tourists' Centre is in the eastern part of Užupis, and has a dozen rooms, each accommodating three or four people. Dorm bed 20Lt.

JNN Hostel Ukmergės 25, tel: 722270, fax: 725651, email: centras@ lvjc.elnet.lt. A short distance west of the Hotel Lietuva, this is a superior hostel in which all rooms have private facilities. Two swimming pools, a sauna, solarium and massage facilities are also on the premises. Singles 80Lt, doubles 120Lt, triples 150Lt, quadruples 180Lt; students and holders of Euro<26 cards get a 20% discount.

Bed and breakfast
Litinterp Bernardinų 7/2, tel: 223850 or 223291, fax: 223559, email: litinterp@omnitel.net. Open Mon–Fri 08.30–17.30, Sat 08.30–15.30. Offers rooms in private houses in Vilnius and Trakai, and also has some apartments for rent. Advance bookings for Kaunas, Klaipėda, Palanga and Nida can be made, and car hire, interpretation and translation services are also available. Singles 70–100Lt, doubles 120–140Lt.

Food and drink
In a welcome change from the Soviet years, Vilnius now has a huge range of restaurants, cafés, bars and pubs to choose from. Many of the leading cuisines of the world are represented, though this development thankfully has not (as it has in other capital cities of former Communist countries) resulted in any diminution in the number or quality of establishments specialising in traditional local dishes. As is the case throughout Lithuania, some places are difficult to categorise, with many bars and cafés offering a full restaurant-type menu. The main concentrations of places to eat and drink are in the Old and New Towns, though there are a few restaurants a bit further afield which well warrant the detour.

For further recommendations, particularly for formal dining, *see also* Hotels above.

Restaurants
Da Antonio Vilniaus 23. Traditional trattoria serving delicious pizzas made in a wood-fired oven, as well as a range of pasta dishes and other classic Italian fare.

Freskos Didžioji 31. Vilnius' most elegant dining room, decorated with theatre costumes and posters as well as the frescos which give it its name, occupies the rear part of the Town Hall. The international-style cuisine is prepared with a Gallic sense of flair, and while relatively expensive is good value nonetheless, the best bargains being the set lunches and help-yourself salad bar.

Geležinis Vilkas Lukiškių 3. The 'Iron Wolf' offers Lithuanian and international dishes in a curious interior which synthesises modern decor with traditional wooden features.

Geltonoji Upė Stiklių 18. Part of the Stikliai group, the 'Yellow River' is the classiest Chinese restaurant in Lithuania. Its elaborate interior is laid out and decorated in Tang dynasty style.

IdaBasar Subačiaus 1. The cavernous cellar and the hearty portions successfully invoke the culinary tradition of the German joint-owners. There are some imaginative dishes on the menu, though unfortunately the accompanying vegetables are not invariably fresh. Among the beers on tap is the celebrated Jever, Germany's bitterest brew.

Juodasis Riteris Pilies 16. The 'Black Knight' is arguably Vilnius' most pretentious restaurant, with prices to match. It has an international menu with a particularly good line in fish dishes.

Literatų Svetainė Gedimino 1. The 'Literary Salon' is a true golden oldie, and was the place from where the Nobel Prize-winning poet Czesław Miłosz witnessed the occupation of the city by Soviet tanks in 1940, an episode described in his autobiography, *Native Realm*. Well-prepared Lithuanian cuisine can be enjoyed either in the formal dining room overlooking the Cathedral, or in the more relaxed café alongside.

Lokys Stiklių 8. 'The Bear' is another stalwart of the Vilnius restaurant scene, occupying a warren of brick Gothic cellars in one of the quietest parts of the Old Town. Game dishes, particularly elk and wild boar, are its main specialities, though it has a fine all-round menu in which salads and desserts also feature strongly.

Marceliukės Klėtis Tuskulėnų 35. A traditional family-orientated hostelry just northeast of the Calvary Market, whose rustic exterior is totally at odds with the surrounding high-rise apartment blocks. Its amazing cluttered decor includes an old wooden bicycle suspended from the ceiling. Most of the staple dishes of the Lithuanian kitchen are featured on the menu, and professional folk groups perform on weekend evenings.

Markus ir Ko Žydų 4a, entrance from Antokolskio 9. Primarily a steakhouse offering a wide choice of succulent cuts, though there are plenty of other options, including salads and sweets, as well as a long drinks list.

Medininkai Aušros Vartų 8. A range of inexpensive local dishes is on offer in this restaurant, which has the benefit of a wonderful setting in a former monastery just down from the Gates of Dawn. In summer, tables are set outside in the peaceful courtyard.

Nanjing Sodų 8. Good and inexpensive Chinese restaurant offering attentive service, handily located just downhill from the bus and train stations.

Pulčinela Kalvarijų 1. A good and inexpensive Italian restaurant situated in the imposing pseudo-castle to the north of the Green Bridge. There is a range of pizzas and pasta dishes, though the award-winning speciality is stuffed rolled chicken.

Ritos Slėptuvė Goštauto 8. This celebrated restaurant founded by Chicago-born Rita Dapkutė, erstwhile spokeswoman for the *Sajūdis* independence movement, broke the mould of Vilnius' eating scene. Open until 02.00 (06.00 at weekends), it features all the favourites of American cuisine – including deep-pan pizza, hamburgers, burritos and mud pie – on the long menu, and also has a large choice of breakfast dishes. Adjoining is a bar with dance floor, while in the corridor opposite the entrance is a takeaway bakery, Ritos Krautuvė.

Ritos Smuklė Žirmūnų 68. The sister restaurant to the above is a re-invention of an old-style Lithuanian country tavern, notwithstanding its unpromising setting in a commercial district well to the north of the city centre (take bus 9, 12, 13 or 17 to Žirmūnai). Only traditional Lithuanian dishes (many of which are now rarely found elsewhere) and drinks are served; anything of Russian or Western origin is banned from the menu. Professional folk groups perform in the evenings, Thur–Sun.

Rytai Naugarduko 22. Another authentic Chinese eatery, situated in the eastern part of the New Town.

Stiklių Aludė Gaono 7. This small basement restaurant has a predominantly local menu and makes a much cheaper but still highly recommendable alternative to the posh French restaurant in the hotel next door.

Stiklių Bociai Ignoto 7. The distance of 200m or so that divides this restaurant from its management enables it to offer a more bohemian cellar environment and basic Lithuanian food and drink. The live music and the dress of the staff ensures minimal intrusion from beyond Lithuania.

Sue's Indian Raja Jogailos 11/2. Offers a wide range of dishes from the Indian sub-continent, whose spiciness may come as a welcome antidote to a surfeit of milder local fare.

Sue Kai Thai 'Thai' and 'restaurant chains' do not usually go together well but this restaurant opened at the same time as its siblings in Rīga and Tallinn. It shares the same address as the Indian Raja, above, but is otherwise appropriately different. Satay dishes predominate.

Traidenis Traidenio 39. A hybrid bar-restaurant with an international menu, located at the edge of the Žvėrynas district, just across the Neris from Vingis Park.

Trys Draugai Pilies 25a. The 'Three Friends' is on three different floor levels, and offers a variety of food, including local dishes, steaks and good though rather small-sized portions of Tex-Mex fare. Kapitonas Tenkešas in the cellars has a short menu of deliciously spicy Magyar dishes plus a decent choice of Hungarian wines.

V&G Algirdo 2. Very formal New Town restaurant serving food and wines from Georgia. Well-known Caucasian dishes, notably kebabs, are featured on the menu, though there is plenty of unfamiliar fare as well.

Fast-service restaurants

Afrika Pilies 28. A popular option for an express meal, with plenty of soups, salads and pancakes to choose from.

Čili Ukmergės 3a, also at Gedimino 23 and Jasinskio 16. Quick-service pizza restaurants which serve a few Tex-Mex dishes, and run an efficient delivery service. The Ukmergės branch is directly opposite the Hotel Lietuva.

Šavarma Aušros Vartų 6. Bright and cheerful split-level eatery serving Arab snacks such as *falafel* and *humous*.

Stiklių Stiklių 14/7. This restaurant is the bargain-price member of the eponymous chain. It offers a limited but enticing array of salads, desserts and cakes.

Trys Draugai Pilies 25. A spacious outdoor setting makes for a good break from souvenir shopping in this area.

Cafés

Alina Pylimo 49. A small Polish café just beyond the southwestern edge of the Old Town. It serves typical Polish dishes such as *bigos* (stewed fresh and pickled cabbage with chopped meats) and *flaczki* (tripe).

Alumnatas Universiteto 4. Situated alongside the university, this is a particularly recommendable choice for a summertime *al fresco* drink or snack, which can be enjoyed in the irregularly shaped triple-tier baroque courtyard to the rear.

F Aušros Vartų 5. The F stands for Filharmonija, as this café occupies the front ground floor of the city's main concert hall. It serves full meals, but is mainly of interest as a place to have coffee and cake.

Gabi Šv Mykolo 6. A delightful café with a rustic interior and a side courtyard, right next door to the Amber Museum. One of the few places in the city to have adopted a strict no-smoking policy, it offers a full menu of homely Lithuanian dishes.

Kakarieku Vilniaus 21. This is the nearest the city comes to having a Viennese-style coffee house. Salads are available in addition to the calorie-laden pastries and cakes which are the main specialities.

Magdė Basanavičiaus 3. Small country-style café-restaurant at the eastern edge of the New Town. An accordion band plays on Thur and Fri evenings.

Molinis Ąsotis Naugarduko 32. New Town café-restaurant serving typical local fare. Its well-furnished cellar is marvellously atmospheric, particularly in the evening.

Skanaus Aušros Vartų 9. Ideally located near the Gates of Dawn, many tourists take a break here from their sightseeing to enjoy a very wide range of savouries and sweet pastries. They even serve pizza for those with no imagination or interest in Lithuania.

Užupio Užupio 2. Predictably, the 'local' of Vilnius' bohemian quarter is a favourite with artists and students. Idyllically set by the River Vilnia, it has outdoor seating and a contrastingly cosy interior.

Žaltvysklė Pilies 13. A very reasonably priced café-restaurant serving both Hungarian and local dishes.

Pubs, bars and café-bars

Amatininkų Užeiga Didžioji 19/2. Plenty of inexpensive Lithuanian dishes, including a wide range of tasty starters, are available in this rambling bar with a snug cellar. However, anyone over 25 may well feel uncomfortable here, particularly late at night. Many local students manage to patronise it until closing time at 05.00.

Angaras Jasinskio 14. One of the hippest addresses in the city, offering internet access from its cybercafé and regular live music.

Betmenas Gedimino 32. The decor of this bar must be the most outrageous in the city, dominated as it is by the life-sized figure of Batman himself.

Bix Etmonų 6. Founded by the eponymous Lithuanian band as a rock music bar, though it also has a cellar with a more sedate atmosphere.

Gero Viskio Baras Pilies 34. As its name suggests, this bar is primarily known for its range of whiskies, though it also serves a menu of mostly light dishes.

Globe Bernardinų 8. Its couches make a welcome contrast to the wooden seats elsewhere and tempt many visitors to try its wide variety of drinks and snacks.

Gryčia Tilto 1. A tiny country-style bar tucked away behind Literatų Svetainė. It serves good *gira* and traditional Lithuanian cuisine.

Pieno Baras, Didžioji 21. Seemingly belonging to a bygone age, this traditional milk bar serves hot milk and home-baked cakes at very low prices.

Prie Parlamento Gedimino 46. A convincing re-creation of an English pub, though it was actually founded by a New Zealander. It is regularly full of expats and English-speaking tourists, who come to enjoy juicy steaks, jacket potatoes, and traditional pub grub such as shepherd's pie and hot puddings. Downstairs is the hugely popular nightclub Ministerija, which is open 18.00–02.00 (04.00 on Fri and Sat).

Prie Universiteto (also known as **The Pub**), Dominikonų 9. The Old Town sister establishment to the above. Although the food served is a bit more down-market, it has the advantage of an attractive galleried courtyard.

Savas Kampas Vokiečių 4. Popular café-bar with live music on Thur, Fri and Sat evenings.

Twins O'Brien Vokiečių 8. Irish pubs have mushroomed all over Europe in the past decade, and this establishment ensures that Vilnius residents do not miss out on draught Guinness and Irish stew. There are various other imported beers on tap, plus a range of bistro-style dishes.

Above University Church, Old Town Vilnius (RR)
Left Houses on Town Hall Square, Vilnius (RR)
Below left Calvary Market, Vilnius (GM)
Below right Senasis Kuapras, a Vilnius antique shop (RR)

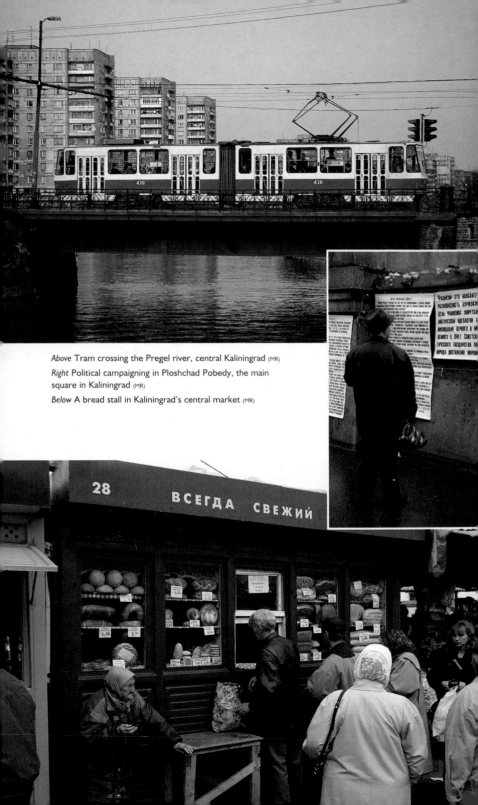

Above Tram crossing the Pregel river, central Kaliningrad (MR)

Right Political campaigning in Ploshchad Pobedy, the main square in Kaliningrad (MR)

Below A bread stall in Kaliningrad's central market (MR)

Entertainment

Theatres

Lėlė Puppet Theatre Arklių 5, tel: 628678. Housed in the baroque Oginskis Palace, this presents entertaining shows, mostly for children, though with a few pitched at an adult audience.

Lithuanian Drama Theatre Gedimino 4, tel: 629771. The city's main venue for straight dramatic fare, offering both traditional and avant-garde productions.

Opera and Ballet Theatre Vienuolio 1, tel: 620636. A varied programme of operas, operettas and ballets is staged in this huge concrete and glass building from the 1970s.

Russian Drama Theatre Basanavičiaus 13, tel: 620562. As its name suggests, it presents Russian-language performances.

Youth Theatre Arklių 5, tel: 616126. Housed in the same building as the Puppet Theatre, this company has gained a high reputation for its innovative stagings, and has made successful tours to the West.

Music

In addition to the concert halls listed below, concerts and organ recitals are held in several Old Town churches, especially the cathedral, St John and St Casimir. At the last-named, live music is normally performed every Sunday immediately after the last morning Mass ends at around 13.00. Open-air concerts – which take place in the courtyards of the university and the Chodkevičius Palace, among other venues – are a regular feature of the city's musical life in summertime.

Concert and Sports Palace Rinktinės 1, tel: 727157. The main venue for large-scale pop concerts.

Music Academy Gedimino 42, tel: 610144. In term-time, there are usually several public recitals every week by students and staff.

National Philharmonic Hall Aušros Vartų 5, tel: 627165. The country's leading concert hall presents an enticing programme of orchestral, choral and chamber concerts and organ, piano and song recitals by both Lithuanian and foreign artists.

St Christopher Chamber Music Club Šv Ignoto 6, tel: 623114. The former Jesuit Noviciate is the home of the St Christopher Chamber Orchestra, a versatile and very active body which also performs in other venues.

Festivals

Vilnius hosts an extremely varied programme of festivals throughout the year, including the following:

Užgavėnės – the climax of the carnival season celebrations is held on Shrove Tuesday (variable date in February or March) on Tauro Hill.

St Casimir's Market – the feast-day of Vilnius' very own saint is on March 6. Associated with it is a handicrafts market in the Old Town, which lasts for several days.

Skamba skamba kankliai – a colourful annual festival of folk-song and dance, held throughout the city, usually on the last weekend in May. It features invited groups from abroad as well as performers from all over Lithuania.

Rasos – the midsummer solstice is celebrated on the evening of June 23 on the White Bridge.

Summer Music Festival – throughout July, there is a wide range of concerts of all types of (predominantly classical) music. They take place at a variety of venues, many in the open air, with the majority given by Lithuanian performers.

World Lithuanian Song Festival – this massive six-day event is held in early July every four years (next in 2002). The first two days are mainly devoted to rehearsals; on the third, the participating groups assemble in Sereikiškės Park for informal performances. Each of the last three days climaxes in a spectacular open-air concert: the first, held in the Hill Park, is given by song and dance ensembles; the second, in the Žalgiris Stadium, by dance troupes (with no singing); the third, in Vingis Park, by choirs (with no dancing). The last-named makes an awesome climax, featuring up to 12,000 singers on the Song Dome stage at a time.

Day of Statehood – on July 6 there is a solemn military procession with banners to Cathedral Square, followed by an open-air concert of patriotic songs and operatic arias with orchestral accompaniment.

Vilnius International Summer Fair and Street Events Festival – the week-long fair in mid-August features a crafts market, complete with an ethnographic village, in Sereikiškės Park. During the last four days, pageants and street theatre are held throughout the Old Town.

Three Days Three Nights – a three-day beer festival on the last weekend of August in Vingis Park.

Jazz Festival – a festival of avant-garde jazz, held over three days in the first half of October.

Shopping
Opening hours
10.00–18.00 Monday–Friday, 10.00–14.00 Saturday, closed on Sunday, but in the summer many shops of interest to tourists now open for a full day seven days a week.

Amber
Amber Gallery Šv Mykolo 8. The excellent gallery has a shop alongside where authenticated pieces of amber and amber jewellery can be purchased.
Sagė Aušros Vartų 15. Another highly reputable dealer in genuine amber artefacts.

Bookshops
Akademinė Knyga Universiteto 4. Academic bookshop with a selection of English-language paperbacks, though the stock is mainly of textbooks more specifically for Lithuanians.
Lenkų Knyga Aušros Vartų 9-7. The local Polish bookshop.
Littera Šv Jono 12. With its elaborate frescoed interior, the bookshop within the University complex is undoubtedly the most attractive in the city, and has a decent representation of English-language books about Lithuania. This is also the best place to obtain copies of the English-language literary magazine *Vilnius*.
National Museum Bookshop See page 127.
Vaga Gedimino 2 and Gedimino 50. Both shops have a good selection of coffee-table books about Lithuania.
Vilniaus Gedimino 13. The largest of Vilnius' old-style bookstores. Stationery and cassettes are also on sale.

Department stores
Valstybinė Universalinė Parduotuvė Gedimino 18. A typically wide-ranging Soviet-era department store, still going strong.

Vilniaus Centrinė Universalinė Parduotuvė Ukmergės 16. The city's largest department store.

Souvenirs
Dailė Žydų 2/2. Sells a wide range of Lithuanian handicrafts.
Sauluva Pilies 22. Housed in a fine old courtyard, this is the largest souvenir shop in Vilnius, selling ceramics, glassware, woodcarvings, leather goods and many other traditional artefacts, including candle houses which are made to order.

Medical services
Baltic-American Medical and Surgical Clinic Antakalnio 124, tel: 342020, fax: 227021. A US joint venture, this is the only hospital in the Baltic states offering fully Western standards.
Medical Diagnostic Centre Grybo 32, tel: 709120. Closed Sun. There are English-speaking doctors on the staff.

Pharmacy
Gedimino Vaistinė Gedimino 27. Open 24 hours.

Embassies and consulates
Australia Karmelitų 4/12, tel/fax: 223369, email: aust.con.vilnius@post.omnitel.net.
Canada Gedimino 64, tel: 220853, fax: 220884.
France Didžioji 1, tel: 222979, fax: 224211.
Germany Sierakausko 24/8, tel: 650272, fax: 231812.
Ireland Contact the embassy in Poland, tel: (48 22) 496633, fax: (48 22) 498431.
Italy Tauro 12, tel: 220620, fax: 220405, email: ambitvilnius@post.omnitel.net.
New Zealand Jogailos 8, tel: 226467, fax: 226444.
Netherlands Didžioji 13, tel: 224085, fax: 224084, email: holhouse@ktl.mii.lt.
Russia Latvių 53/54, tel: 721763, fax: 723877.
South Africa Contact the embassy in Finland, tel: (358 9) 658288, fax: (358 9) 658365.
UK Antakalnio 2, tel: 222070, fax: 727579, email: be-vilnius@post.omnitel.net.
USA Akmenų 6, tel: 223031, fax: 312819.

Places of worship
Grace International Baptist Church Ukmergės 25/301. Service every Sunday at 11.00.
Lutheran Church Vokiečių 20. Ecumenical service on the second and fourth Sunday of each month at 12.00.
SS Philip and James Lukiškių aikštė 10. Roman Catholic Mass every Sunday at 09.00.

WHAT TO SEE
City walk
Start at the Gates of Dawn (Ausros Vartu) and walk down to the Town Hall Square past the Russian Orthodox church and St Casimirs. Continue along Pilies and turn right along Sv Mykolo, passing the Amber Museum. This leads past the Architecture Museum to St Anne's Church. Return to Pilies along Bernadinu, and turn right to face the cathedral. To the right is the castle and

the National Museum. Turning left from the cathedral into Universiteto, the Presidential Palace soon comes into view. To the left of the palace are the university buildings. The continuation street of Universiteto is Gaono which leads into the former Jewish quarter around the Stikliai Hotel. Turning left at the hotel into Stikliu, the Town Hall Square is just 300m walk. Detials of all these to follow.

Old Town

Vilnius' Old Town (*Senamiestis*) is among the most extensive in Europe, occupying a total of 255 hectares, and including over 1,000 protected monuments, among them outstanding masterpieces not only of baroque, but also of Gothic, Renaissance and neo-classical architecture. A great deal of cleaning and other restoration work has been carried out since independence was achieved, though many fine buildings languish in a semi-derelict state, a situation which is likely to persist for many years to come.

There are two distinct parts to the Old Town. The site of the original settlement, which includes the castles, the cathedral and the areas of greenery surrounding them, is no longer inhabited, and now forms an island of calm in the midst of the city centre. Across the bustling Šventaragio and Radvilaitės streets lies the much larger part of the Old Town, which came into being after the threat from the Teutonic Knights had been eliminated. Although it has become a tourist magnet in recent years, it is far from being a museum-piece. Some of it is still residential, it retains the main university campus, has plenty of shops and offices, and is well-endowed with places to eat and drink. It preserves its chaotic medieval layout, in which twisting narrow alleys are juxtaposed with a central thoroughfare divided into three distinct parts and several huge open squares. Almost every street is worth a look, and a detailed exploration of all the important sights requires several days.

Much of the Old Town is either pedestrianised or has severe restrictions on vehicular access, so it can really only be seen on foot.

Cathedral

Vilnius' **cathedral**, which is dedicated to SS Stanislaus and Ladislaus, occupies the site of an ancient pagan temple to the god Perkūnas, and originally lay within the fortification system of the Lower Castle. The first church on the site was erected in the 13th century, following the ostensible conversion of King Mindaugas. When the nation officially reverted to heathen ways, the Perkūnas temple was reinstated, but was replaced by another church when Christianity was introduced in 1386 following the royal union with Poland. Under Vytautas the Great, this was supplanted by a more splendid Gothic cathedral, which underwent repeated alterations down the centuries, before being almost totally rebuilt between 1783 and 1801 to plans by Laurynas Gucevičius. Even if its neo-classicism makes it something of an outsider in the predominantly baroque townscape of Vilnius, it is a majestic building nonetheless, one of the most important churches in the style anywhere in Europe. Under the Soviets, it served as an art gallery for 32 years, but in 1989 was restored to its role as the seat of the local archbishop.

The façade has a portico of six Doric columns and a rosette-encrusted vault. On the tympanum above is a carving depicting *The Sacrifice of Noah* by an Italian

VILNIUS CENTRE

River Neris

ŽYGIMANTU

ARSENALO

Hill Park

Neringa

VILNIAUS

TILTO

St George

Museum of Applied Arts

National Museum

Gediminas Hill

Three Crosses

Vilnia

GEDIMINO

VRUBLEVSKIO

Higher Castle

Žaliasis Tiltas

Central Post office

JOGAILOS

Academic Drama Theatre

Bank Museum

Citypark

Cathedral

Lower Castle

Sereikiškes Park

Municipal Tourist office

LABDARIŲ

TOTORIŲ

ODMINIŲ

Belfry

ŠVENTARAGIO

RADVILAITĖS

Holy Cross

Radvila Palace

LIEJYKLOS

University

BERNARDINU

Shakespeare

Sereikiškes Park

Jewish Museum

PYLIMO

Presidential Palace

UNIVERSITETO

Amber Gallery

Mickiewicz Museum

St Anne

SV MYKOLO

Jesuit Noviciate

St John

PILIES

Narutis

Museum of Lithuanian Architecture

St Michael

SS Francis & Bernardino

Theatre, Music & Film Museum

SV IGNOTO

St Catherine

KLAIPĖDOS

SV JONO

Šlapelis Museum

Mabre

Vilnia

Reformed

VILNIAUS

Holy Spirit

Stikliai

Municipal Tourist office

Piatnickaya

Holy Mother of God

DOMINIKONŲ

ANTOKOLSKIO

STIKLIŲ

UŽUPIO

ŽYDŲ

Vilnia

TRAKŲ

Vilnius Picture Gallery

St Nicholas

The Assumption

PRANCISKONŲ

Evangelical Lutheran

Post office

VOKIEČIŲ

SAVIČIAUS

Čiurlionis House

St Mary the Soothing

PYLIMO

ŠIAULIŲ

VOKIEČIŲ

ROTUŠĖS AIKŠTĖ

DIDŽIOJI

BOKŠTO

NAUGARDUKO

St Nicholas

Contemporary Arts Centre

Town Hall

St Casimir

SV KAZIMIERO

Artillery Bastion

Missionaries' Monastery

RŪDNINKŲ

Astorija

Lėlė Puppet Theatre & Youth Theatre

Visitationists' Convent

LIGONINĖS

National Philharmonic Hall

SUBAČIAUS

ARKLIŲ

Synagogue

Rūdninkų

PYLIMO

All Saints

Grybo Namai

AUŠROS VARTŲ

Holy Spirit

MINDAUGO

N

Basilian Monastery

St Teresa

DAUKŠOS

RAUGYKLOS

SV STEPONO

BAZILIJONŲ

Gates of Dawn

Central Market

AUŠROS VARTŲ

SODU

Mikotel

PYLIMO

ŠOPENO

SEINŲ

0 ___ 300 m
0 ___ 300 yds

GELEŽINKELIO

PELESOS

LIEPKALNIO

Bus station

Railway station

sculptor, Tommaso Righi, who was also responsible for the five small reliefs and the niche statues of the four apostles and the patriarchs Abraham and Moses on the entrance wall. Atop the tympanum, and visible from afar, the figures of SS Stanislaus and Casimir flank St Helena, who bears the gilded True Cross. These huge statues, which were put in place in 1996, are reproductions of the originals, which were destroyed by Soviet decree. The north and south sides of the cathedral are closely harmonised with the façade. Both have colonnades with six columns, with the former having niche statues of saints, the latter of grand dukes.

Except on Sundays and festivals, the interior is entered via the small northern side door. It is laid out in the form of a spacious hall, with a grand central area and narrow aisles with chapels. The focal point is the high altar, which is shaped like the front of a classical temple, and shelters a large painting of *The Martyrdom of St Stanislaus* by Franciszek Smuglewicz, the founding director of the Vilnius School of Art. Other furnishings of special note are an exquisite silver tabernacle from the 1620s, a painted wooden crucifix from later the same century, and the splendid 18th-century organ case (most of the pipework dates from 1969, though some 19th-century registers survive). Among the many other paintings hung throughout the cathedral is a complete series of the apostles by Smuglewicz. A cache of nearly 300 gold and silver artefacts found in the wall in 1998 is on display at the Applied Arts Museum.

It is sometimes possible to visit the vaults underneath the cathedral on application to the shop by the entrance. The best time to try is around 11.00, when pre-booked groups are often escorted round. On view are altars used for pagan worship, as well as fragments of the medieval churches which occupied the site. Particularly intriguing is a late 14th-century fresco of *The Crucifixion with the Virgin and St John*, the oldest surviving monumental painting in Lithuania.

The **Chapel of St Casimir**, which is entered via a resplendent portal from the southern aisle, is the only important part of the previous cathedral which survives in an unaltered state. In order to integrate it into his new design, Guccvičius added a sacristy on the northern side which copies its distinctive outline of a square lower storey surmounted by an octagon supporting a cupola with lantern. The chapel was built between 1622 and 1636 by the Italian Constante Tencalla in order to house the mortal remains of St Casimir (1458–84), Lithuania's patron saint. Work on the sumptuous interior, which is faced with luxuriant black, white and coloured marble, continued for a century after its construction. Much is by itinerant Italian masters. Hiacinto Campana painted the ceiling frescos, Michelangelo Palloni the side frescos of *The Opening of the Coffin of St Casimir* and *The Miracle of the Coffin of St Casimir,* while Pietro Peretti (or Perti) created the lavish stucco backdrop to the silver shrine. In front of the shrine is a curious little portrait of the saint, dating from the 1520s in commemoration of his beatification. The only painted sections uncovered by the intricate silver frame are Casimir's head – and three hands.

Katedros aikštė (Cathedral Square) is a vast paved space on the south and west sides of the cathedral which makes an ideal starting or finishing point for parades and processions. Since 1996, it has been the setting for the **Monument to Grand Duke Gediminas** – a particularly appropriate location, as it must be close to the spot where he had his legendary dream about the iron wolf. The commission for the statue was entrusted to the veteran sculptor Vytautas Kašuba, who had spent most of his career in America, and died soon after the monument was erected. That Gediminas is shown with his sword in his left hand is an allusion to his supposed preference for diplomacy over war – though in reality he used both to achieve substantial territorial gains for the Grand Duchy.

The focal point of the square is the **belfry**, a combined bell and clock tower which is a favourite local rendezvous point. It has had a curious history. Its round lower storey, which is pierced by numerous gunports, dates back to the 14th century and belonged to the fortification system of the Lower Castle; indeed, it is the only part of this which survives to this day. In the 1520s it was converted into the cathedral's bell tower by the addition of two octagonal tiers. The following century, a fourth tier was added to house a clock which still preserves its original mechanism. In 1893 it finally assumed its present appearance when it was crowned with a small steeple.

Castles

The **Lower Castle**, which in the 16th century was transformed into a splendid Renaissance-style Royal Palace for Zygmunt the Old, was the main residence of Lithuania's Grand Dukes. Unfortunately, the finest parts of the complex were pulled down by the Tsarist authorities in 1802, leaving only a number of ancillary buildings. However, highly fruitful archaeological excavations have been carried out on the site over the past decade, and these are likely to continue for a long while yet.

Among the intact parts of the castle is the 18th-century New Arsenal just to the north of the cathedral, which now houses the **National Museum of Lithuania** (open Wednesday–Sunday 10.00–17.00). The display begins with archaeological finds, while the country's later history is evoked in a collection of portraits, weapons, books, textiles, prints, liturgical objects, coins and sundry other artefacts. Those of particular aesthetic appeal include the 15th-century treasury door of the nearby Bernardine Friary, the baroque banner of the Handcraftsmen's Guild, the 17th-century vestments of a Uniate bishop, the embossed leather sleigh of the Tiškevičius family, and a Meissen vase decorated with coats-of-arms honouring the dynastic union of Saxony and Lithuania. There is also a large folk art section, which is grouped by region and features iron crosses, wooden statues, painted chests, embroidery, costumes, pottery, masks, lace, baskets and decorated Easter eggs. The museum is being regularly expanded. In 2000 new galleries were opened covering the Soviet occupation and more material added to the collections covering the 1920–40 period. The **bookshop** has the best selection in Vilnius of books in English on Lithuanian history and art.

At the northeastern edge of the complex is the 16th-century Old Arsenal, a hybrid Gothic–Renaissance building which is nowadays the home of the **Museum of Applied Arts** (open Tuesday–Sunday 11.00–18.00). The highpoint of this museum is now the gallery called 'Christianity in Lithuanian Art' which opened in December 1999. This collection of gold, silver and embroidery, dating mainly from the 16th century, was hidden in the walls of the cathedral in September 1939 to protect it from the Russian invaders. It was only discovered again in 1985 when air conditioning was being installed. The local archaeologists wisely kept their secret to themselves in case the collection was moved to Moscow. Only in 1998, when they felt certain about continuing Lithuanian independence, did they reveal their success. They are quite literally Lithuania's 'Crown Jewels'.

In the cellar, fragments of the early medieval wall of the castle can be seen. Among the objects on display in the baroque section are Brussels tapestries, porcelain, tiles, mirrors, fans, chasubles and furniture, with the most spectacular item being a credence made from birch with intarsia, gilded bronze, leather and veneering. Upstairs are examples of 20th-century Lithuanian craftsmanship, including textiles, ceramics, glass, amber jewellery and enamels.

Paths to the rear of the cathedral and the Museum of Applied Arts both lead up the 48m-high Gediminas Hill to the **Higher Castle** on its summit. The original wooden fortress was replaced in the late 14th century and early 15th century with a brick and stone Gothic castle which featured three towers, a palace, a chapel and various other buildings. Badly damaged in the wars of 1655–61, it was thereafter abandoned, only to be revived as a fortress by the Russians following the 1831 uprising. A wooden superstructure containing an optical telegraph was built on top of the truncated western tower, the only one of the three which was retained. This was removed in 1930, and replaced by a reconstruction of one of the two octagonal storeys which had previously been lopped off.

Nowadays designated the **Castle Museum** (open Wednesday–Sunday 11.00–17.00/18.00/19.00), the tower contains displays of historic arms and armour, plus models showing the changing appearance of Vilnius' medieval fortification system. However, the main attraction is the wonderful view from the observation platform on top. As all the main landmarks of the Old Town are clearly visible (it is the only publicly accessible place from which this is so), it makes an ideal place to begin or end a tour of the city. The best light for photography is normally in the later part of the day. Other than the tower, little remains of the Higher Castle, save for the ruins of the palace and fragments of the outer walls.

Bernardine churches
At the extreme eastern edge of the Old Town, on the far side of Sereikiškės Park, which stretches south from Gediminas Hill, is the **Bernardine Friary**. An offshoot of the Franciscan Order, the Bernardines arrived in Vilnius in 1469. They initially built a wooden church on the site, which was granted to them by Grand Duke Kazimierz, but this was destroyed by fire.

Its replacement, the brickwork **Church of SS Francis and Bernardino**, was erected at the beginning of the 16th century under the patronage of the Radvila (Radziwiłł) family. Unusually large by the standards of medieval Lithuania, it is in the hall church style (with nave, aisles and chancel of equal height), and features some spectacular examples of late Gothic vaulting. Following repeated damage by fire and in war, the church was given a twin-turreted Renaissance façade, though the single tower on the southwest side was restored to its original Gothic form. The baroque Chapel of the Three Kings, which is used for weekday services, was added in 1632. Among several impressive funerary monuments in the nave is that to Stanislovas Radvila by Willem van den Block, the leading Renaissance sculptor of

Danzig (now Gdańsk). In the Soviet era, the church was allowed to fall into a dilapidated state. It is now back in Franciscan hands, and for some years past has been the subject of what will be a very long-term restoration programme.

The much smaller and better-preserved **Church of St Anne** in front is undoubtedly the most celebrated building in Lithuania. According to an oft-quoted tradition, Napoleon was so captivated by it that he declared his wish to carry it back to Paris in the palm of his hand, and it has long been an inexhaustible source of inspiration to local painters and photographers. No fewer than 33 different shapes of bricks were employed in the construction of its unforgettable flamboyant Gothic façade, which is symmetrical in appearance, being twice as high as it is broad. Its decoration is a bravura medley of extravagant ogee arches, narrow oriel windows, slender pinnacles, openwork octagonal towers and crocket-studded steeples. When lit by the setting sun, the upwardly sweeping lines take on a truly incandescent appearance.

For all its fame, the church is something of a mystery, there being no general agreement as to exactly what its function was in relation to the friary, nor exactly when and by whom it was built. Until recently it was thought to have been constructed by German masters at the very end of the 15th century, though new evidence suggests that the façade, at least, is not older than the mid-16th century and is the work of local craftsmen. In dramatic contrast to the exterior, the inside of the church is disarmingly modest, though it does preserve some fine original vaulting. The detached belfry, which was added in 1873, imitates the elaborate brickwork of the church, but fails to rise above the level of a pastiche.

Directly across the street is the former **Church of St Michael**, built between 1594 and 1625 by order of Leonas Sapieha, Chancellor of the Grand Duchy of Lithuania, to serve as a convent for Bernardine nuns, as well as a mausoleum for his own aristocratic family (also known as Sapiega or Sapiegos). The only important Renaissance building to survive in the city, the church has an elaborate façade with a massive central pediment, twin turrets, and pilasters with capitals bearing stylised depictions of leaves of the rue (*rūta*), the national flower of Lithuania. In the early 18th century, a wall was constructed round the church in order to create an enclosed courtyard for processions. Entry to the complex is now via a sturdy baroque tower which serves as both belfry and gateway.

Most of the furnishings of the hall-like interior, which boasts a richly stuccoed vault, were stripped away by the Soviets, but several Sapieha memorials remain. The most prominent is a 10m-high red marble monument commemorating the founder and his two wives; also of note is that to Stanislovas Sapieha, which has an eccentric location above the sacristy doorway.

Since 1971 the church has housed the **Museum of Lithuanian Architecture** (open daily, except Tuesday, 10.00–17.30). This is divided into two sections, the first featuring plans of the main architectural projects, notably public buildings in Kaunas, undertaken during the inter-war republic. Particularly intriguing are rejected designs for a visionary neo-Gothic appearance for the Church of the Resurrection. The post-war part of the display concentrates on housing projects and the re-creation of Trakai's Island Castle.

Rest of the northeastern quarter
Bernardinų, which follows a winding northwesterly course from the Church of
St Michael, is one of the best-preserved streets of the Old Town, lined with
many splendid urban mansions. The **Mickiewicz Museum** (open
Tuesday–Friday 10.00–17.00, Saturday and Sunday 10.00–14.00) at Bernardinų
11 has been set up in the courtyard building where the great Romantic poet
Adam Mickiewicz (known to Lithuanians as Adomas Mickevičius), who had
previously spent four years in Vilnius as a student at the university, lodged for
two months in 1822. It was during this stay that he wrote the Byronic verse
tale *Grażyna*. Old editions of Mickiewicz's main works are on display in the
museum, as well as paintings and engravings showing Vilnius as it was in the
poet's day. A memorial to Mickiewicz can be seen nearby, just a few paces to
the south of the Bernardine Friary. Designed in 1984 by Gediminas Jokubonis,
this shows the influence of the socialist realist style of which the sculptor had
long been a favoured practitioner. Just to the north is the gleaming white
Orthodox **Church of the Holy Mother of God.** There has been a church
on the site since the late 14th century, though the present building dates mainly
from the 1850s.

At number 8 on Šv Mykolo, an atmospheric old street running west from
the Church of St Michael, is the **Amber Gallery** (open daily 10.00–19.00).
Like its pioneering counterpart in Nida, which is owned by the same family,
this offers informative displays on the geology of 'Baltic gold', as well as
temporary exhibitions of amber jewellery. Being a modern museum, lighting is
good and all descriptions are given in English and German. There is also a shop
selling fully authenticated pieces of amber and amber artefacts.

Both Bernardinų and Šv Mykolo terminate at Pilies, the northern part of the
Old Town's central axis. Stalls selling handicrafts can be found all along the
street, and these increase greatly in number and quality whenever a festival is
taking place. Of particular note among a picturesque jumble of buildings of
various dates are the Renaissance mansion at Pilies 4 and the gabled Gothic
houses at numbers 12 and 14. Now part of the Hotel Narutis, Pilies 24 was the
setting for the signing of Lithuania's declaration of independence on February
16 1918. The downstairs section of the **Šlapelis Museum** (open
Wednesday–Sunday 11.00–16.00) at Pilies 40 is a recreation of the pioneering
Lithuanian bookshop established in 1906 by Jurgis Šlapelis and his wife Marija
Šlapelienė. Displayed in the couple's flat above, which is entered from the
courtyard, are books and other objects associated with the national cultural
revival they did so much to promote. Backing on to the western side of Pilies
is the sprawling university campus; this can usually be entered via the Žaltvykslė
café, though the main public entrance is from Universiteto, the next street to
the east.

University
It is fitting that the **university** is by far the largest and most prominent complex
of buildings in the Old Town, as it has played a key role in the life of Vilnius
since its foundation in 1569, despite suffering many vicissitudes at Russian
hands over the past two centuries – it was closed down altogether between
1832 and 1919, and for most of the Soviet period was forced to tailor its
activities to Marxist-Leninist dogma. It is grouped around no fewer than 12

courtyards in a picturesque huddle of structures of widely varying dates and aesthetic merit. In summer 2000 an admission charge of 4Lt was introduced for tourists wishing to look around.

The **University Library** (open Monday–Friday 08.00–18.00) is entered via the doorway labelled Vilniaus Universitetas on the south side of the courtyard opening directly on to Universiteto. Its oldest room (which is reached by taking two consecutive left turns then descending a short flight of stairs) is known as Smuglevičius Hall in honour of the neo-classical painter Franciszek Smuglewicz, who frescoed the vault. The central scene shows the Holy Trinity blessing the Madonna of Mercy, who shelters a group of Jesuits under her cloak. On the spandrels above the windows are monochrome *trompe l'oeil* busts of distinguished scholars of classical antiquity. A small selection of the library's most valuable books and manuscripts is displayed in the show-cases.

Immediately behind the library is the **Astronomical Observatory**, the fourth oldest surviving example of its type in the world. Built between 1753 and 1773 by Tomas Žebrauskas (Thomas Żebrowski), the Professor of Mathematics and Astronomy, it is actually two separate observatories, one of which occupies the entire length of the building, with a smaller one above. No longer in use, the interior is not generally accessible, but the peaceful courtyard to the rear offers a fine view of the building's façade, with its handsome portal, twin turrets and frieze of zodiacal symbols.

A gateway at the northeastern corner of the Library Courtyard leads into the Sarbievijus Courtyard, which is named in honour of Maciej Kazimierz Sarbiewski (1595–1640), who served as Professor of Rhetoric, Philosophy and Theology but is better known as a prolific writer of both sacred and secular Latin verse. At the far end is the **Littera Bookshop**, whose interior is covered with a colourful fresco scheme painted by Antanas Kmieliauskas in 1978–79. Inspired by the Vatican frescos of Michelangelo and Raphael, this pays symbolic tribute to the subjects which have loomed largest in the university's history.

A small hall on the first floor of the **Centre for Lithuanian Studies** next door is decorated by an even more ambitious fresco cycle entitled *The Seasons*, which Petras Repšys completed in 1985 after nine years' work. There are over a hundred different scenes, illustrating episodes from Lithuanian history and mythology as well as work, pastimes and popular customs. Also worth seeking out is the classically inspired coloured stucco frieze of *The Nine Muses* by Rimtautas Gibavičius which can be found on the first floor of the **Philology Department** in the Daukantas Courtyard immediately to the north.

A large archway on the southern side of the Sarbievijus Courtyard leads into the **Great Courtyard**, which is also known as the Skarga Courtyard in honour of Piotr Skarga, the Jesuit scholar who was the university's first rector. The academic buildings lining three of its sides were erected in the early 17th century in the Mannerist style which marks the transition from Renaissance to baroque. All along their lower storey are open arcades which impart a sunny Mediterranean flavour, even if the local climate is only occasionally warm enough for them to be enjoyed to best advantage. Between the pilasters are faded 18th century frescos portraying important figures in the history of the university.

The eastern side of the Great Courtyard is closed by the **Church of St John**, which was founded by Grand Duke Jogaila immediately after his conversion to Christianity, and completed in 1426. A presbytery and apse were added to the original hall church after it was allocated to the Jesuit college in 1571, and much of the Gothic fabric is clearly visible underneath the overlay added between 1738 and 1749 by Jan Krzysztof Glaubitz, the presiding genius of the final phase of Vilnius baroque.

The monumental façade, in which the plain horizontal rustication of the lowest storey forms a dramatic counterpoint to the sweeping vertical emphasis of the elaborately contoured tiers above, ranks among the greatest achievements of the style. Almost equally impressive is the assemblage of ten interconnected altars which together make up the high altar. There are memorials honouring, among others, Adam Mickiewicz, Tadeusz Kościuszko and Stanisław Moniuszko, the Polish composer who served as the church's organist in 1840–58. Of the six side chapels, the most elaborate is that dedicated to St Anne, which has both an ornate portal and a carved altar of *Christ as the Tree of Life*.

Nowadays, the building has a curious double life, serving as the university church once again, yet still retaining its Communist-era role as the **University Science Museum** (open daily 10.00–17.00) – hence the scattering of cases displaying old scientific tracts. The detached **belfry**, one of the Old Town's most prominent landmarks, was built in the first decade of the 17th century and raised to its present height as part of the programme of baroque renovations.

Northwestern quarter

Daukanto aikštė, the triangular space immediately west of the university, is dominated by the vast pile of the **Presidential Palace**. The Bishop's Palace which had stood on the site since the 14th century was remodelled to serve as the residence of the Russian Governor-General, and Tsar Alexander I and Napoleon both held court there in the fateful year of 1812. Between 1824 and 1832 this was expanded and rebuilt by a Russian architect, Vassily Stasov, in late neo-classical style. In Soviet times it served as the Artists' Palace and was the French Embassy in the first years of independence, before assuming its present role, following a costly refurbishment, in 1997.

In August 2000 the palace started opening on Fridays and Saturdays for pre-booked groups. A tour showing the main reception rooms, the president's office and the gardens takes about 45 minutes. The furnishings are entirely modern, but the designs are from the early 19th century. Oak and birch are the main woods used. One room has four large portraits of the previous Lithuanian presidents, three from the 1920–40 period and one of Algirdas Brazauskas, in office 1993–98. An even larger painting shows Vytautas the Great riding into the Black Sea, when the Polish-Lithuanian Empire stretched that far in the mid-15th century.

Opposite stands the modest little **Church of the Holy Cross**, a foundation of the Bonifratrian Order, who came to Vilnius in 1635. The original building was remodelled in the course of the first half of the 18th century, and the twin towers, pediment, porch and exterior fresco of *The Madonna and Child* all date from this period. The Soviets renamed it the Baroque Hall and used it for concerts, but it now functions as a place of worship once more. Beside the church is a monument to Laurynas Gucevičius, architect of the cathedral and Town Hall.

At Vilniaus 22, towards the far northwestern edge of the Old Town, is the **Radvila Palace** (open Tuesday–Sunday 12.00–18.00). Built in the 17th century for Jonušas Radvila, Grand Hetman of Lithuania, this splendid urban palace has been much altered subsequently, and now serves as a branch of the Lithuanian Art Museum. One room is devoted to a gallery of 165 portrait engravings of members of the dynasty commissioned by Mykolas Kazimieras Radvila from an amateur artist, Herszek Leybowicz (1700–70). Apart from an unexpected collection of Oceanic art, the rest of the display space is given over to old master paintings and graphics. Most of the former are by little-known artists; among the few works of special note are two striking Mannerist compositions: *St Ursula and the 10,000 Martyrs* by Bartholomeus Spranger, court artist to Emperor Rudolf II in Prague; and *An Allegory of the Old and New Testaments* by the Dutchman Cornelis van Haarlem. There are also a couple of fine examples of 17th century Dutch landscape painting in *The Old Mill* by Meindert Hobbema and *The Waterfall* by Jacob van Ruisdael.

A little further up the same street is the **Church of St Catherine**, which originally belonged to a Benedictine convent founded in 1618. Following a series of fires, it was rebuilt between 1741 and 1753 by Jan Krzysztof Glaubitz. In order to overcome the restricted nature of the site, he adopted an audacious design based on a nave which is as high as it is long. The exterior features an elaborate rear-facing gable as a counterbalance to the majestic twin-towered façade; the interior is richly furnished, but has not been accessible for some time because of ongoing restoration work. A statue of Stanisław Moniuszko stands in the garden in front of the church.

Diagonally opposite, at the corner with Klaipėdos, is a long, low-lying baroque palace which was formerly another of the Radvila properties. For the first 15 years of Tsarist rule, it housed the municipal theatre; nowadays it contains the **Lithuanian Theatre, Music and Cinema Museum** (open Tuesday–Friday 12.00–18.00, Saturday 12.00–16.00). This offers a mixture of temporary exhibitions and permanent displays on the history of the performing arts in Lithuania.

Šv Ignoto, a block to the east of Vilniaus, is named after the Church of St Ignatius, part of the former **Jesuit Noviciate**, a vast 17th- and 18th-century baroque complex with three large courtyards. Following the suppression of the Order in 1773, the buildings served successively as a seminary and a barracks; they are now home to, among others, a technical library and the St Christopher Chamber Orchestra.

Šv Ignoto leads to Dominikonų, which takes its name from the Dominican friary established there in 1501. Its **Church of the Holy Spirit**, one of the most extravagant manifestations of Vilnius baroque, was one of the few churches kept open during the Soviet years, and is nowadays the main place of worship for the Polish-speaking community. Although retaining some of the fabric of its fire-ravaged 17th century predecessor, its main features – the dome, the side gables and the sumptuous array of furnishings and decoration which give the interior an almost rococo appearance – date from the second half of the 18th century. A sculptor of German origin, Franz Ignatius Hoffer, designed the assemblage of 16 artificial marble altars and the curious pulpit, which is combined with the confessionals below in a single unit. Also of note is the elegant tribune gallery housing an organ whose richly carved case with statues of King David and angel musicians still shelters the original pipework.

Didžioji

The Old Town's central thoroughfare changes its name from Pilies to Didžioji at a little square which has become an open-air gallery. Forming a backdrop to this is the **Piatnickaya Orthodox Church**, the favoured place of worship of the younger members of the Russian community. Although the church's present appearance is the result of a remodelling carried out in the 19th century, it was originally built in 1345 for Marija, the wife of Grand Duke Algirdas, and was the place where the grandfather of the great Russian poet Alexander Pushkin was baptised.

Immediately to the rear is the baroque Chodkevičius Palace, which was adapted to house the **Vilnius Picture Gallery** (open Tuesday–Sunday 12.00–18.00), a branch of the Lithuanian Art Museum, when the latter was forced to vacate its previous premises in the cathedral. The early 19th century interiors on the first floor form a setting for period furniture, *objets d'art* and paintings, including portraits of Mickiewicz by Valentinas Vankavičius, and of the artistic patron Duke Mykolas Oginskis by François Xavier Fabre. There then follows a section on baroque religious art featuring several fine altarpieces by the Polish painter Szymon Czechowicz. One room on the floor above is devoted to portraits of leading lights of 18th-century Lithuania, including that of Chancellor Jonas Sapieha by Silvestre de Mirys, an artist born in France to Scottish Jacobite exiles. There then follows a large collection of paintings by Franciszek Smuglewicz and his successors at the Vilnius Academy of Arts, plus a display of architectural drawings by Laurynas Gucevičius. The participants in the celebrated exhibitions of Lithuanian art in the first decade of the 20th century dominate the final rooms of the circuit, with the little paintings entitled *Storm* and *Mountains* by Čiurlionis being among the very few works by him outside his memorial museum in Kaunas.

A few paces further on, just before the point where Didžioji broadens out to form Rotušės aikštė (Town Hall Square) is the **Orthodox Church of St Nicholas**, which was originally built in a hybrid Gothic–Byzantine style in 1514. In 1609, the church was granted to the Uniates, remaining in their hands until 1827. Extensive renovations were carried out in the 1860s, when a neo-Byzantine façade and belfry were erected, and a new iconostasis added to the interior.

Tucked away in a courtyard at Savičiaus 11, the next street to the south, is the **Čiurlionis House** (open Monday–Friday 10.00–16.00), the home of the composer-artist during his residency in Vilnius. It often hosts recitals of his music, but unfortunately contains no original paintings by him. A little further along the same street stands the **Church of St Mary the Soothing,** which was formerly part of an Augustinian friary. Built between 1746 and 1768, it was among the last of Vilnius' great series of baroque churches, and is dominated by its elegantly tapering single tower which displays clear classicising tendencies. Now in a totally decrepit state, it is awaiting a much-needed restoration.

Coincidentally, the nearby Jesuit **Church of St Casimir** at the southern end of Didžioji marked the debut of the baroque style in the city. It was begun in 1604, just two years after Casimir's canonisation, and completed in 1618. Although probably designed by the Italian Giovanni Maria Bernardoni, it was built by a local architect, Jan Prochowicz. Despite being modelled on the Jesuits' much-imitated mother church of Il Gesù in Rome, the addition of twin towers (which are now lower than when first built) give it a distinctive Lithuanian accent. The crown atop the lantern of the central dome was added as recently as 1942 in recognition of St Casimir's royal lineage. In 1966, in a humiliating affront to Lithuania's Catholics, the Soviet authorities installed a Museum of Atheism in the church's bare interior. However, it was returned to the Jesuits in 1988, and a strong musical tradition has since been established.

Immediately opposite, its grand Doric portico fronting the square named after it, is the former **Town Hall**. Designed by Laurynas Gucevičius, it was built between 1781 and 1799 on the site of its medieval predecessor. The municipal offices have long moved elsewhere, though the building is still used for receptions. It also functions as an 'Artists' Palace', and as such its foyer is regularly used to show-case contemporary Lithuanian arts and crafts.

Southwestern quarter

Vokiečių, which leads northwest from the Town Hall, was widened considerably as part of a 1950s' planning project, and now has a pedestrianised area down the middle. The new layout necessitated the demolition of part of the former **Ghetto** to the east, including the 17th century Great Synagogue on Žydų, which lost its roof during the Nazi occupation period but otherwise survived largely intact. In recent years, there has been talk of re-instating it. A monument on Žydų commemorates Eliyyahu ben Shelomoh Zalman (1720–97), otherwise known as the Gaon of Vilna, one of the greatest Talmudic scholars of all time, and a virulent opponent of the revivalist Hasidic movement.

At the head of Vokiečių, right alongside the Town Hall, is the concrete and glass **Contemporary Art Centre** (open daily 11.00–19.00). Although an ugly blot on the face of the Old Town, it provides much-needed display space for exhibitions which are predominantly, but not exclusively, of living artists. Upstairs is a permanent display on *Fluxus*, the experimental art movement founded in the United States by the Lithuanian-born George Maciunas.

Hidden away at the back of a courtyard at Vokiečių 20 is the **Evangelical Lutheran Church**. Vilnius' first Protestant church was established on the site in 1555. The present building, a plain baroque preaching hall which is whitewashed both inside and out, was built in the 1740s by Jan Krzysztof Glaubitz, with the neo-Romanesque belfry being added in 1872. The focal point of the interior is the high altar, which adapts traditional Catholic forms to the requirements of Lutheran doctrine, giving a prominent role to the carved depiction of The Last Supper.

Šv Mikalojaus, the little street immediately to the east, is named after the **Church of St Nicholas** at its far end. An unassuming example of the Gothic brickwork style, it is the oldest intact church in Lithuania, and the only one pre-dating the official adoption of Christianity in 1387, having been built earlier in the century to serve the German merchants and artisans who had made the city their home.

According to tradition, the **Church of the Virgin Mary**, situated a short distance to the northwest on Pranciškonų, was founded by Franciscan missionaries before the mass conversion of Lithuania. However, the present building, constructed between 1773 and 1785, is in a classicising baroque style, and while it incorporates a few fragments of its Gothic predecessor (notably the façade portal and the crystalline vaults of the south aisle), these appear to be 15th century in date. Having been closed since 1949, the church was handed back to the Franciscans in 1998, leaving them with the massive task of repairing the worn fabric and bringing the faded frescos back to life.

On Rūdninkų, close to the now-vanished western gate to the Old Town, is the **Church of All Saints**, formerly part of a Carmelite friary. The main body of the church was built in 1620–31 and is modelled on the Jesuits' Il Gesù. The single bell tower was not added until 1743 and is somewhat more elaborate in appearance, but nonetheless blends in well. What would otherwise be a rather plain interior is enormously enlivened by the kaleidoscopic colours of the somewhat folksy carvings and paintings adorning the altars.

Southeastern quarter

The southernmost section of the Old Town's central axis is known as **Aušros Vartų** (Gates of Dawn) after the gateway at which it terminates. On the western side of the street, the first major landmark is the **National Philharmonic Hall**, which was built in 1902. The massive street frontage, built in the turn-of-the-century eclectic style, seems rather out-of-scale in comparison with the concert hall itself, which is of very modest dimensions. Nonetheless, it is the most important venue in the country for classical music, and has also hosted some fateful political meetings, including the 1940 'application' for Lithuania to be admitted to the Soviet Union.

A bit further up the same side of the street is the **Basilian Monastery**, which takes its name from the Uniate monks who settled there in 1608. Access from the street is via the recently restored entrance gateway, a swaggering baroque masterpiece built in 1761 to designs by Jan Krzysztof Glaubitz. Its gable bears a carved depiction of the Holy Trinity, this being the dedication of the now very dilapidated church in the courtyard behind, which was originally built in 1514 but much altered down the centuries. A congregation of Ukrainian-speaking Uniates currently worships there. For six months in 1823–24, Adam Mickiewicz was imprisoned in a cell in the monastery for anti-governmental activities, and was shortly afterwards deported from Lithuania, never to return.

Across the street, again in a secluded courtyard, is the Orthodox **Church of the Holy Spirit**. It is the most important Orthodox church in the country, though its external appearance differs markedly from all the others, being very obviously a product of the Vilnius baroque style, with only the merest traces of Russian influence. Indeed, it is in large part the work of Jan Krzysztof Glaubitz, who was entrusted with rebuilding the original 17th century church following a fire in 1749. Glaubitz is also believed to have designed the colossal lurid green iconostasis, which incorporates baroque paintings of the life of Christ in addition to traditional icons. In front of the altar, a baldachin shelters the miraculously preserved bodies of SS Anthony, Ivan and Eustachius, whose feet can be seen peeking out from under their shrouds. The trio were servants at the court of Grand Duke Algirdas but were martyred for their faith in 1347, as a result of a militant pagan backlash against the previous policy of religious tolerance.

Back on the street a short distance beyond stands Vilnius' most Italianate building, the **Church of St Teresa**, which was designed for the Discalced Carmelites by Constante Tencalla, and built between 1633 and 1652. The façade, the only part erected under Tencalla's direct supervision, is a strikingly vertical composition culminating in a pediment adorned with the coat-of-arms of the aristocratic Pacas (or Pac) family, who provided funds for the construction. Following a fire in 1760, the interior was supplied with a new set of furnishings, and the walls were frescoed by Mateusz Sluszczański. The scenes he painted in the nave illustrate the life of the church's patron, the Carmelite mystic St Teresa of Avila.

A stairway to the rear of the church, up which pious penitents hobble on their knees, leads to the so-called **Gates of Dawn**, Lithuania's most famous place of pilgrimage. Disabled people and beggars can almost invariably be found outside the gateway, which once formed part of the city wall, and is the only one of the nine it formerly had which survives. When viewed from the south its original defensive function is still obvious, but the northern side looks completely different, having been revamped in neo-classical style in 1829 in order to provide a chapel to house the reputedly miraculous image of *The Madonna of Mercy*. Despite adopting the form of a traditional icon, this was probably painted in the early 17th century, and was later provided with a gold and silver setting which covers the entire picture except for the face and hands. Densely hung ex-votos left by grateful pilgrims are attached to the wall panels of the chapel.

The other significant surviving fragment of the municipal defences is the **Artillery Bastion** (open Wednesday–Sunday 10.00–17.00), which is reached by following Šv Dvasios in a northeasterly direction. This was built in the early 17th century in order to provide extra protection for the nearby Subačius Gate. It consists of three parts: a tower on a round base, a horseshoe-shaped gallery for firing cannon, and an underground tunnel. The bastion encloses a natural hillock, from which there is a good, albeit partial, view over the Old Town.

New Town

In the 19th century, the **New Town** (Naujamiestis) was built immediately to the west of the Old Town, in the process engulfing a few older buildings which had hitherto stood in isolation. In addition to serving as the commercial and administrative heart of the city, it is also a residential area, its streets lined with large tenements which were originally thrown up to house a rapidly growing population.

Pylimo

Pylimo is the street which marks the boundary between the Old and New Towns. Near its southern end, at the corner with Bazilijonų, is the rather cramped **Central Market**. Downhill, on the left-hand side of the street, is the **Synagogue**, the only survivor of the hundred or so Jewish temples Vilnius had prior to World War II. Built at the turn of the 20th century, it is modelled on Moorish architecture. Above the doorway is a depiction of the tablets of the Ten Commandments.

Somewhat further down, on the opposite side of the street, is the **Reformed Church**, which was built in 1830–35 by Karolis Podčašinskis, the leading local practitioner of the late neo-classical style. It is fronted by a giant Corinthian portico surmounted by a tympanum carved with a scene representing *Christ Preaching to the People*. The interior, which was converted into a cinema in 1958 but has now been returned to the local Calvinists, is a large hall covered with a coffered wooden vault. Normally it is only open for services (usually on Sundays at 18.00).

Housed in a tenement building at Pylimo 4, a short distance to the north, is the **Lithuanian State Jewish Museum** (open Monday–Thursday 09.00–17.00, Friday 09.00–16.00). On the first floor are displays of liturgical objects, dolls used for theatrical performances during the Feast of Purim, prints and drawings of Vilnius' Great Synagogue, and photographs, supplemented by a few tantalising fragments, of the wonderfully elaborate wooden synagogues, all now destroyed, which once graced several Lithuanian towns. Two rooms on the floor above are dedicated to a photographic record of memorial sites throughout Lithuania to victims of Nazism, and to a gallery honouring those who sheltered or otherwise saved Jews.

Round the corner, at Pamėnkalnio 12, the wooden **Green House** (open same times) serves as an annexe of the museum, with a documentary display focusing on Jewish culture and life in Vilnius and Lithuania immediately before World War II, and its destruction during the Holocaust. Outside stands a monument entitled *Moonlight*, which commemorates Chiune Sugihara, the Kaunas-based Japanese diplomat who is credited with rescuing up to 6,000 Jews. This he did by issuing transit visas against the instructions of his government. He even kept the consulate open after being instructed by the new Soviet authorities to close it. On his return to Japan, he was dismissed by the Japanese Foreign Ministry and his courage was only recognised after he died in 1985.

Gedimino

Gedimino, the New Town's central boulevard, stretches for 1.75km along a straight east–west line. Its name has changed many times since it was laid out in the early 1850s, with the appellations chosen almost invariably reflecting the nationality and ideology of the authorities of the time. Indeed, the present honouring of Grand Duke Gediminas, a historical figure with impeccable Lithuanian credentials, is as politically motivated as some of the names (which include those of Piłsudski, Hitler, Stalin and Lenin) bestowed on the street in the past.

The easternmost of the three large squares which open out from the northern side of Gedimino is Savivaldybės aikštė. On its northern side is the **Government building**, which was formerly the seat of the Central Committee of the Lithuanian Communist Party, while on the eastern side are the **Municipality** headquarters. Incorporated within the latter complex is a secluded courtyard, round which are the baroque buildings of a former convent of the Discalced Carmelites, centred on the **Church of St George**. Designed by Franz Ignatius Hoffer, this lacks a tower, but has a striking tiered façade; the interior is unfortunately not accessible at present.

The next square to the west, Lukiškių aikštė, was where the leaders of the 1863 rebellion were executed. On the far northern side is the baroque **Church of SS Philip and James**, which was begun in 1690 but not completed until 1748, when the twin towers were raised to their present height. A Dominican foundation, the church has a strikingly geometric appearance, with its single nave being exactly as high as it is long. Mass is celebrated in English every Sunday at 09.00.

A statue of Lenin once stood in the little park in the middle of the square, facing the KGB headquarters. The latter, originally built in 1899 by the Tsarist authorities to serve as a courthouse, is now designated the **Museum of Lithuanian Genocide Victims** (open Tuesday–Sunday 10.00–16.00). In due course, it is intended to present a full documentary record on Soviet repression against Lithuania (particularly the Siberian deportations), and on the resistance to it. In the meantime, the cells in the basement, which were used for the imprisonment and torture of political opponents until 1991, can be visited. These include an isolation cell which has neither heating nor windows, a special padded and soundproofed cell for suicide risks, and two cells where water torture was administered in order to keep prisoners constantly awake. There is documentary material on some of the most prominent victims, while sacks of incriminating documents shredded by the KGB in the final three years of Soviet rule are also on view.

Just off the eastern end of Gedimino, at Tortorių 2, is the **Bank of Lithuania Museum** which opened in late 1999. Currently it is only open Wednesday and Thursday 09.00–12.00 and 13.00–14.30. Two rooms of the bank are devoted to the museum. The coin collection dates back to the Polish-Lithuanian Empire of the 15th century. More modern exhibits date from each of the occupations that have plagued Vilnius in the last 200 years – Tsarist, German, Polish, and Soviet – and show the various designs for bank notes suggested when independence was again re-established in 1991.

Towards the western end of Gedimino is Nepriklausomybės aikštė. Despite its name ('Independence Square'), it is dominated by two of the most prominent buildings of the Communist era. The **National Library**, which is built in a debased modern version of neo-classicism, is a typical example of the cultural 'gifts' Moscow was wont to bestow on subsidiary republics and satellites. Ironically the **Seimas** (Parliament) alongside, which is no more distinguished from an architectural point of view, has gained an honoured place in the Lithuanian consciousness, being the place where the restoration of national independence was declared on March 11 1990.

Outside the city centre

Vilnius' location in the far southeast of Lithuania means that it is not ideally placed for day-trips into the countryside. However, its administrative county does have a few attractive destinations, notably the outstanding medieval town of Trakai, which probably preceded it as the nation's capital.

Vilnius' suburbs have a generous endowment of sights, and while most of these lie off the beaten tourist track, a few rank among the best-known landmarks of the city.

Rasos, Paupys and Markučiai

The **Rasos Cemetery**, which takes its name from the district in which it lies, is about 1km southeast of the Gates of Dawn, on the opposite side of the rail tracks. Its leafy, undulating site, which looks particularly wistful in autumn, contains the graves of some of Lithuania's most revered citizens. The tombstone of the composer–painter Čiurlionis is directly uphill from the main entrance, while that of Jonas Basanavičius, cultural guru and founder of the newspaper *Aušra*, is just across from the chapel. More controversially, the heart of Józef

Piłsudski, who bears the primary responsibility for Poland's annexation of Vilnius in 1920, is buried in the family plot to the left of the entrance; the rest of his body lies in the Polish national pantheon in Kraków's Wawel Cathedral.

Rasų leads from the western side of the cemetery to the district of Paupys and the former **Visitationists' Convent**, which directly overlooks the Old Town. At the heart of the complex is the domed Church of the Heart of Jesus, the only one of Vilnius' baroque churches built to a Greek cross design. Although a prominent feature of the city's skyline, the church can only be seen from afar, as the whole convent is currently a prison, enclosed within a high wall topped with barbed wire.

The former **Missionaries' Monastery** opposite is now a hospital and is likewise inaccessible, although at least good close-up views can be had of the exterior of its Church of the Assumption, which was begun in 1695 and remodelled by Jan Krzysztof Glaubitz in 1750–54. As with the Church of St Catherine in the Old Town, which he worked on at the same time, the architect concentrated attention on the monumental façade, so giving the building a sense of grandeur which belies its small size. The slender five-storey twin clock towers are unlike any others in Vilnius, being clearly influenced by those of the German-speaking lands.

Subačiaus leads eastwards from the Missionaries' Monastery to the residential district of Markučiai, at the far end of which is an extensive park in which stands the **Pushkin Memorial Museum** (open Wednesday–Sunday 10.00–17.00), a large wooden homestead which belonged to Alexander Pushkin's son Grigorij (1835–1905) and his wife Varvara (1855–1935). The ground floor is furnished according to Russian upper-class taste of the time, with a large ceramic stove being a feature of each of the main public rooms. Upstairs is a small exhibition on the works of Pushkin and their dissemination in Lithuania.

Užupis

North of the Missionaries' Monastery, just across the River Vilnia from the Old Town, is the district of **Užupis**, the city's bohemian quarter. Its tumbledown 19th-century tenements and courtyards are much favoured by artists and members of the 'alternative' set, and several collective galleries and craft workshops have been established there. In the southeastern part of Užupis, directly above the river, is the tranquil **Bernardine Cemetery**, the last resting place of, among others, many university luminaries.

The wooded **Hill Park** (Kalnų Parkas), which stretches northwards from Užupis to the Neris embankment, is one of the city's most popular recreation areas. Towards its northeastern end is the Song Valley, an open-air auditorium which is regularly used for a variety of folklore events. In medieval times, the Crooked Castle, one of the city's trio of fortresses, crowned the 91m hill above, one of the city's highest points. In its place are the **Three Crosses**, which first appeared there in the 17th century. According to tradition, they were erected to commemorate early missionaries of the Franciscan Order who were martyred for their faith. Substitute concrete crosses were erected in 1916, but these were destroyed by the Soviets in 1950. The present crosses were put in place on June 14 1989 to coincide with the inauguration of the annual festival of the Day of Mourning and Hope, which commemorates Lithuanians deported to Siberia after World War II.

Church of SS Peter and Paul

Situated in splendid tree-framed isolation at the edge of the Antakalnis district, immediately east of the Hill Park, is the **Church of SS Peter and Paul**, which was founded in 1668 by Mykolas Kazimieras Pacas (Michał Kazimierz Pac), Grand Hetman of Lithuania and Governor of Vilnius, and granted to a congregation of Lateran Canons. The design of the church, whose main external features are a squat, twin-towered façade and a large central dome, was entrusted to a Polish architect, Jan Zaor, who supervised the construction work for several years before being replaced by Giambatista Frediani, who worked simultaneously on the Pacas dynasty's other prestige project, the Pažaislis Monastery outside Kaunas.

When the fabric was completed in 1675, local sculptors were commissioned to make the façade statues. Pacas was dissatisfied with the results, and accordingly invited two masters from the Lake Como region of northern Italy, Pietro Peretti (or Perti) and Giovanni Maria Galli, to take charge of the decoration of the interior. Between 1677 and 1685 the Italian duo created a stuccowork scheme of stupendous richness and variety, in the process transforming the pleasant but unexceptional shell of the building into a High baroque masterpiece, one which has been regarded ever since as among the crowning glories of Lithuania's cultural heritage.

There are over 2,000 human figures, each of them differently characterised, though these form but a small part of the overall scheme, which also features carvings of plants (including accurately depicted local species), flowers, trees, mythological creatures, grotesques and purely decorative elements. The iconographic programme behind the decoration is highly complex and often symbolic. For example, the many battle scenes are a reference to Pacas' status as Lithuania's most senior soldier, while the recurrent fleur-de-lys was his family emblem, and several of the saints depicted in hagiographic fashion were those with whom his dynasty had a special affinity.

Instead of aisles, there are two chapels on either side of the nave. Those on the north are dedicated to the Holy Queens and to St Augustine, the patron of the Lateran Canons; those to the south to the Warrior Martyrs and to St Ursula and the Virgin Martyrs. The last-named chapel, with its coolly beautiful statue of St Mary Magdalene alongside a virtuoso relief of a palm tree, stands out even among the magnificence all around it. To appreciate the decoration to the full, it is necessary to come on a sunny day, when the shafts of light penetrating the clerestory and dome windows illuminate the stuccowork in a magical series of ever-changing reflections.

Among the church's most notable furnishings are the pulpit and the main chandelier, both of which adopt the form of a boat. At the entrance to the chancel is another curiosity, an impassioned *Ecce Homo* statue in the Spanish manner, which was carved in Rome in the late 17th century. A large painting of *The Parting of SS Peter and Paul* by Franciszek Smuglewicz has taken the place of the original unfinished high altar.

Antakalnis

Antakalnis itself was formerly the estate of another prominent dynasty, the Sapieha family. A short distance to the north along Antakalnio are the two main buildings, both dating from the 1690s: the **Sapieha Palace**, an Italianate *palazzo*, and the **Church of Our Lord Jesus**, which formed part of one of the city's two Trinitarian foundations. The latter is a domed octagon fronted by a porch flanked by two towers placed at strikingly oblique angles. It apparently still preserves stucco decoration by Pietro Peretti, but there is little prospect of seeing this, as the building is boarded up, with no sign of any much-needed restoration work.

The **Antakalnis Cemetery** to the east encapsulates Vilnius' complicated modern history. Close to the entrance are rows of identical tombstones of Polish soldiers killed in World War I. At the heart of the complex is a large circular memorial containing the graves of the nationalist martyrs of the 1991 standoffs with the Red Army at Vilnius' TV tower and the border post of Medininkai. Further on, colossal socialist realist statues guard an eternal flame which no longer burns, while a pantheon of the leading lights of Soviet Lithuania is laid out in tiers alongside.

Šnipiškės

From the New Town, the **Green Bridge** (Žaliasis tiltas) leads across the River Neris to the district of Šnipiškės. Adorning each of its four corners are socialist realist sculptures of happy workers and peasants. These now seem somewhat comical, but have been left in this prominent location as a deliberate reminder of the 'heritage' of the Communist era.

Just over the bridge is the **Church of St Raphael**, which was built by the Jesuits in the first decade of the 18th century. A typical example of the baroque architecture of the period, it has a monumental high altar with a large painting of the Archangel Raphael by Szymon Czechowitz. The church now stands at the edge of a pedestrian precinct which was something of a Soviet-era show-piece. Its facilities include the **Planetarium** (shows Monday–Friday 09.30–18.00, Saturday 12.00–16.00), the city's largest department store and two gargantuan hotels.

A short distance further west is the **National Gallery**, normally displaying the modern and folk art sections of the Lithuanian Art Museum, which has supplanted the Revolutionary Museum of the Lithuanian Soviet Socialist Republic from its custom-built premises. The gallery closed in 2000 for extensive renovations and was not expected to reopen until late 2001 or early 2002.

When it is open the highlights include the collection of folk sculpture which is dominated by numerous examples of the wooden crosses which are such a characteristic feature of rural Lithuania; around a score of those on view before the closure are by the acknowledged master of the genre, Vincas Svirskis (1835–1916). Also previously displayed was a set of four dozen coloured drawings of crosses in their original locations by Kazys Šimonis. There are also extensive collections of furniture, fabrics and pottery and a varied cross-section of the output of Vytautas Kašuba, donated by the sculptor himself. These include large wall reliefs, classically-inspired female portraits, erotic medallions of the Lithuanian Grand Dukes, and humorous hollowed-out carvings.

At the foot of Rinktinės, just over 0.5km east of the Green Bridge, the **Žalgiris Stadium** and the **Concert and Sports Palace** occupy the site of the city's main Jewish cemetery. This was levelled by the Soviets in 1950 in order to make way for the stadium, which hosts large-scale open-air events, including international football matches and the dance programme of the four-yearly Song Festival. Its indoor counterpart, which is two decades younger, stages everything from basketball tournaments to rock concerts.

A short distance further north, with entrances on Rinktinės and Kalvarija, the long street running northwards from the Green Bridge, is the **Calvary Market** (open Tuesday–Sunday 06.30–16.30). Like all the best Lithuanian markets, this has an almost bazaar-type atmosphere. Although dominated by stalls offering a huge choice of fresh fruit and vegetables, hardware items and clothing can also be bought, while a poignant touch is added by the people who stand in rows day after day, and somewhat desperately try to sell individual plastic bags or a few odd garments.

Northern suburbs

From Kalvarija, buses 26, 35, 36 and 50 run to the northern suburbs, which are primarily high-rise housing estates separated by large areas of greenery. In the district of Jeruzalė, some 5km north of the market, the **Calvary Church of the Rediscovery of the Holy Cross** can be seen on a hillock to the right of the road. One of Lithuania's most important pilgrimage sites, this one-time Dominican friary was among the few Vilnius churches kept open during the Soviet era. In its present form, it was built between 1755 and 1772, and features a characteristic twin-towered façade and a richly decorated interior. The most notable features of the latter are the combined pulpit and font and the illusionistic ceiling frescos on the theme of the Holy Cross and its rediscovery by St Helena, mother of the Emperor Constantine. Outside the church are four pilgrimage chapels, the only original ones remaining from the 19 which, together with a ceremonial archway which also still survives, formed a processional way similar to that in Žemaičių Kalvarija, one of Lithuania's best-known pilgrimage sites.

The others, which were razed by the Soviets but are gradually being reinstated, were scattered along a route which leads 1.5km southeast through the woods to the **Trinapolis Convent**, a Trinitarian foundation overlooking the River Neris. Designed by Pietro Putini, one of the architects of the Pažaislis Monastery, it was built between 1695 and 1709. It has recently been re-settled by a small community of nuns, and is now a popular retreat centre. Although the façade of its Church of the Holy Trinity is a characteristic example of Lithuanian baroque, the interior, an irregular octagon with highly complex spatial arrangements, is untypical, being modelled on the Trinitarian church of San Carlo alle Quattro Fontane in Rome by Francesco Borromini.

The landscaped **Verkiai Park**, a former estate which nowadays functions as Vilnius' Botanical Garden, can be reached from the Trinapolis Convent by the road alongside the Neris, or from the Calvary Church by continuing northwards along Kalvarija. At its heart is the **Verkiai Palace**, a late 17th century complex remodelled in neo-classical style by Laurynas Gucevičius as a summer residence for the Vilnius bishops. Unfortunately, the main building was demolished in the 1850s, but the two wings, which are themselves of palatial dimensions, both survive. One serves as the headquarters of the Botanical Institute, and is not accessible to the public. However, regular art exhibitions are held in the other, whose reception rooms were plushly decorated in the late 19th century with oak panelling, marble and stuccowork.

Bus 36 continues northwards from Verkiai to the **Green Lakes**, a hugely popular recreation area. On summer weekends especially, it swarms with day-trippers who come to go boating or swimming in the chain of lakes and to have a relaxing picnic or barbecue by one of the shores.

Western suburbs

The setting for many of the big nationalist rallies during the final years of Soviet rule, the **Vingis Park** is bounded on three sides by a loop of the River Neris, and to the east by the New Town, one of whose major thoroughfares, Čiurlionio, leads straight to the main entrance. In the middle of the park is the Song Dome, whose covered auditorium, which can seat 20,000 people, can serve two completely different functions. On the last day of the four-yearly Song Festival, it serves as the stage for the concert by the massed choirs, which the audience watches from the field alongside. However, the roles can be reversed, in order to have open-air performances watched by an audience seated under cover.

A footbridge at the northern end of the park leads to **Žvėrynas**, a residential suburb of wooden houses and grand villas, which can also be reached from the New Town via the bridges at the end of Gedimino and Jasinskio. Just west of the latter, on Liubarto, is the Kenesa, an early 20th-century temple whose vaguely oriental appearance reflects the exotic origins of the Karaites who worship there.

In 1957 a Jewish graveyard, the only one in Vilnius, was established within the **Šaltoniškių Cemetery** in Viršuliškės, the next suburb to the west, which can be reached by trolleybuses 11 (from the city centre), 16 (from the station) and 19 (from Žvėrynas). This contains tombs brought from razed Jewish cemeteries, notably the large burial chamber of the Gaon of Vilna, though many gravestones were pillaged in the Soviet era and re-cycled as masonry in the construction of new buildings.

Lithuania's tallest building, the 326m-high **Television Tower** (open daily 10.00–21.00), rises above the apartment blocks of Karoliniškės, the suburb immediately south of Viršuliškės, which is likewise on the routes of trolleybuses 11 and 16. Outside the entrance, crosses commemorate the 14 unarmed civilians who were mowed down by Soviet tanks on January 13 1991 in the single most tragic episode in the run-up towards independence. A lift goes up as far as the observation deck at 165m, which rotates slowly on its own axis, and offers sweeping views over the city.

The **Gariūnai Market**, which lies just off the Kaunas highway, 10km west of the centre, is by far the most notorious in the country. All manner of second-hand and imported goods are sold there, and it is best-known for its huge array of used motor vehicles (not all of which have an impeccable provenance). Trading takes place every morning except Monday.

Paneriai

The name of the southwestern suburb of **Paneriai** has become synonymous with the killing fields of the Nazis, who murdered around 100,000 people there, including almost all of Vilnius' large Jewish population, between 1941 and 1944. There are several memorials to the dead. The earlier of these adopt the Communist practice of paying tribute to 'Soviet citizens' massacred as a result of 'Fascist terror'; the more recent, which date from 1990, make proper acknowledgement of the fact that 70,000 of the casualties were local Jews. A path round the site leads to the pits where the dead bodies were burnt, and to another where the bones where crushed. There is also a branch of the Lithuanian State Jewish Museum, which contains a photographic record of the site, as well as some of the retrieved personal effects of the victims. Inexcusably, it has no set opening times, and is regularly shut.

By far the quickest and easiest way to reach the site is by rail. All trains to Trakai and Druskininkai, and most of those to Kaunas, stop at Paneriai station. From there, it is a straight ten-minute walk onwards along a dead-end road which runs parallel to the rail tracks.

EXCURSIONS FROM VILNIUS
Trakai Historical National Park

The one unmissable short excursion from Vilnius is to the **Trakai Historical National Park**. With an area of just 8,000 hectares, this is by far the smallest of the country's national parks and – as the additional word 'Historical' in its title implies – it differs markedly from its four counterparts. Whereas the conservation of the landscape is their primary purpose, this one is mainly concerned with preserving the monumental heritage of Trakai, Lithuania's best-known and most impressive small town. That said, the scenery is an integral part of Trakai's charm, and is archetypally Lithuanian, with forests accounting for 33% of the park's area, lakes for 18%.

Trakai

Although its current population is a modest 7,000, **Trakai** has played an important role in Lithuanian history and is one of the country's oldest towns, perhaps dating back as far as the 12th century. The original settlement was the capital of one of the duchies into which early medieval Lithuania was divided, and at one time it rivalled Vilnius in importance. Indeed it may have served as capital of the whole country for a couple of years during the reign of Grand Duke Gediminas. Now known as Senieji (Old) Trakai, it lies 4km southeast of the replacement town founded some time around the middle of the 14th century by one of Gediminas' sons, Duke (later Grand Duke) Kęstutis. This occupies a highly strategic site on a peninsula bordered to the west by Lake Totoriškiai, to the east by Lake Luka (or Bernardinai), and to the north by the islet-strewn Lake Galvė. These lakes, and others beyond, are interconnected by narrow channels.

Trakai fell briefly to the Teutonic Knights in the internecine wars which led to Kęstutis' death. Under his son, Grand Duke Vytautas the Great, it was transformed into one of the strongest fortresses in Europe. Vytautas also encouraged Karaites, with whom he had made contact during his eastern military campaigns, to come and settle in the town, and they have made a distinctive mark, retaining a presence there to this day.

Trakai's multi-ethnic character was boosted in the 16th century, when Jews arrived in numbers. However, the 17th century wars with Russia left the fortresses in ruins. As a result it lost its strategic importance and went into economic decline, becoming just another small provincial town. Only in the late 19th century, when the nationalist movement stimulated interest in Lithuania's medieval past, did it begin to make something of a come-back.

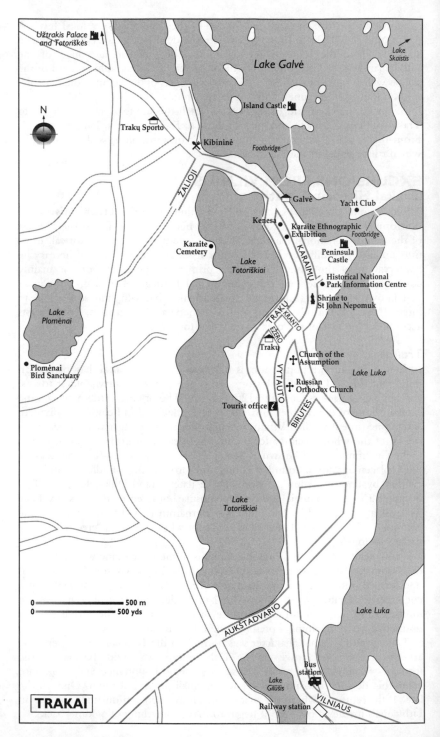

TRAKAI

Practical information
Telephone numbers
As for Vilnius, different dialling codes apply when calling from abroad or from within Lithuania. From abroad, Trakai numbers are reached by dialling (370) 238; from within Lithuania the code is 8238 and then the local number.

Information and maps
Historical National Park Information Centre Karaimų 5, tel: 51506 or 52759, fax: 51546. A 1:50,000 map of the Historical National Park, with a panorama of the town on the reverse, is available. Open Mon–Fri 08.00–17.00.
Tourist office Vytauto 69, tel/fax: 51934. Accommodation can be arranged; some English is spoken. Open Mon–Fri 09.00–17.00/18.00, also Sat in summer 10.00–15.00.

Public transport
Bus station Vytauto 33, tel: 51333. Located immediately south of the peninsula. There are over 30 services daily to Vilnius, two direct to Kaunas via Rumšiškes, and seven to Prienai via Aukštadvaris and Birštonas.
Train station Vilniaus 1, tel: 51055. Situated a short walk south of the bus station, this is the terminus of a branch line from Vilnius via Paneriai, on which seven trains run daily in each direction.

Restaurants
Kibininė Karaimų 65. The Karaite restaurant has a decent drinks list, including a freshly-made *gira*, but there are only two dishes to choose from (with only the former always being available): *kibinai*, which are meat pies resembling a Cornish pasty, and *troškinta mėsa*, meat and vegetable stew.
Prie Pilies Karaimų 53. This classy restaurant on the quayside directly opposite the Island Castle has a formal dining room and an outside terrace. The food is imaginatively prepared, and there is a particularly good choice of fish dishes.
Židinys Vytauto 91. This basic town centre café-restaurant, which serves standard Lithuanian fare, has a small terrace overlooking Lake Totoriškiai. This is a very pleasant venue for ending the day and watching the slow summer sunset. In good weather it is well worth paying the extra 10% charged to eat outside.

The town
Trakai's peninsula is bisected by a snaking main street. The southern part of this, known as Vytauto, leads past the 19th-century **Russian Orthodox Church** to the **Church of the Assumption**, which is set in splendid isolation on a hillock overlooking the street. One of Lithuania's oldest churches, it was founded by Grand Duke Vytautas around the turn of the 15th century. It was originally fortified, but was remodelled in the baroque style in 1718. Inside, the high altar has as its centre-piece a venerated image usually known as *The Madonna of Trakai*. This was painted in the 16th century, though the gilded silver surround was only added in the 18th century. From the church, Vytauto sweeps round to the east, terminating in what is effectively an open square, in the centre of which is another baroque monument, a pillar topped by a **shrine to St John Nepomuk**.

By the lakeside immediately to the east is the **Peninsula Castle**, the outer part of the elaborate defensive system begun by Kęstutis and completed by Vytautas.

Destroyed by the Russians in 1655, it has mainly been left as a ruin, though one of the towers, a gateway and the lower parts of the walls have all been restored.

Yachts, rowing boats and water bicycles can be hired at the various quaysides to the north of the castle or from the **Yacht Club**, which lies on the opposite side of the channel between Lake Luka and Lake Galvė. By road, it is several kilometres away, but it can be reached in a couple of minutes via two footbridges which command fine views over the town and its lakes.

The northern section of Trakai's main street is named Karaimų in honour of the Karaite settlers, and is lined with their colourful wooden houses. At Karaimų 22 is the **Karaite Ethnographic Exhibition** (open Wednesday–Sunday 10.00–13.00 and 13.45–19.00), a permanent display on the life of the community. The Karaites' military background is evoked in a collection of swords, knives, daggers, helmets, armour, shields and guns; other aspects of their culture are illuminated by displays of historic photographs, books, costumes, textiles, household goods and liturgical objects. A little further up the street is the **Karaite prayer house** or *kenesa*, a late 18th-century building with a distinctively oriental look. It was recently given a thorough restoration, but the chances of finding it open are slim.

Karaimų continues northwards across the bridge at the tip of the peninsula which spans the channel between Lake Galvė and Lake Totoriškiai. The wooden building at Karaimų 65 houses **Kibininė**, a Karaite restaurant which has gained cult status, in spite of its abbreviated menu. Just before it, Žalioji leads up to the **Karaite Cemetery**, which overlooks Lake Totoriškiai, with a fine view back towards the *kenesa*. The older tombs are scattered among the grass on the higher ground, while the more recent graves are clustered more closely together on a promontory by the lakeshore.

Island Castle

One of Lithuania's most famous sights, Trakai's **Island Castle** (open daily 10.00–19.00 in summer, reduced hours out of season) occupies almost the whole of one of the islets in Lake Galvė, and is linked by footbridge to the tiny Karaite Isle, from where another footbridge provides a connection to the eastern shore of the peninsula. The most secure and prestigious part of the town's medieval fortification system, it suffered the same fate as the Peninsula Castle in the mid-17th century wars with the Russians, and was left as a ruin, albeit a substantial one, whose relatively isolated setting meant that it survived in better shape than any of the country's other medieval castles. Plans to rebuild it were mooted in the late 19th century, and brought to fruition between 1951 and 1962, although it seems positively bizarre that the Soviet authorities were prepared to countenance the phoenix-like reappearance of a monument symbolising Lithuania's past as a great military power.

Although this type of conjectural restoration is now very unfashionable, it is hard to judge the result as anything other than a spectacular success. When seen from across the water – and there are marvellous views from all over Lake Galvė's shoreline – it looks an awesome sight, one which must have struck fear into the heart of any medieval attacker. Close up, it is not quite so impressive, mainly because of the very obvious difference between the original bricks and rough stonework of the lower parts of the walls, and the modern machine-made bricks used to reconstruct the missing sections.

There are two parts to the fortress, which has a highly irregular ground-plan. The **Outer Castle**, whose walls are up to 3.9m thick, is entered via a gateway with drawbridge. This is flanked by massive towers, with a third tower guarding the northwest corner. All round the trapezoid-shaped inner courtyard are casements, which were used as residential quarters and storage rooms. Those on the western side now contain a somewhat quirky collection of applied art, including furniture, amber, ceramics, snuff-boxes and pipes.

A short bridge connects the Outer Castle to the **Palace**, whose dominant feature is a 25m-high keep. From its inner courtyard, there are steps down to the basement, where the treasury was housed, and stairways to the upper chambers, including the Great Hall on the first floor. These contain displays on the Castle (including a series of archive photos showing how it looked prior to and during the reconstruction work), plus sundry historical artefacts.

Elsewhere in the Historical National Park

Outside Trakai itself, the main set-piece attraction in the Historical National Park is the 19th-century **Užtrakis Palace** on the eastern shore of Lake Galvė. Built in neo-Renaissance style for the Tiškevičius (Tyszkiewicz) dynasty, it is set in a formal park laid out by the French landscape gardener Édouard André, whose work for the same family can also be seen in Palanga. Unfortunately, the palace has been allowed to fall into dereliction, but restoration began in 2000. The quickest way to reach Užtrakis from Trakai by road involves circumnavigating the entire shoreline of Lake Galvė in a clockwise direction from the northern tip of the peninsula, approximately 7km in total.

Just to the west of Lake Totoriškiai is the **Plomėnai Bird Sanctuary**. This consists of the small, almost circular Lake Plomėnai, together with the much larger area of marshland to the west.

The Centre of Europe

The point which the French National Geographic Institute deemed in 1989 to be the **Centre of Europe** lies some 25km north of Vilnius, down a signposted dirt track from the main A101 road to Molėtai. There are plans to erect a suitably grandiose monument on the spot, consisting of a sundial and a giant map, but these have yet to come to fruition.

A rather more substantial attraction inspired by the Centre of Europe theme is the **Europe Park** (open daily 10.00–sunset), which lies much closer to the city, some 5km north of the Green Lakes. It can be reached by a 3km walk from the terminus of bus 36, but a better alternative is to take bus 92 from the Žalgirio terminal (one stop north of the Calvary Market). This service never runs more than four times a day, but it does stop at the side road leading to the park entrance. The Europe Park is an open-air museum of modern sculpture in a woodland and meadow setting, with exhibits specially created for the site by artists from all around the world. *Chair Pool* by the American Dennis Oppenheim is the most popular work – and also the most humorous, its subject being exactly what the title suggests, a giant chair with a small pool instead of a seat. Other sculptures which are guaranteed to catch the eye are Jon Barlow Hudson's *Cloud Hands*, which consists of four granite blocks seemingly suspended in the air; and the 6m-high *Woman Looking at the Moon* by the Mexican Javier Cruz.

Kernavė

Kernavė, which lies in the Neris valley, 40km northwest from Vilnius down a minor road, is nowadays an insignificant village of 200 souls. However, it was almost certainly Lithuania's original capital, a status it may have gained under King Mindaugas, and is securely documented as having held throughout the reign of Grand Duke Traidenis (1269–82). The **Historical and Archaeological Museum-Reserve** (open Wednesday–Sunday 10.00–15.00/17.00) is currently the most important site in Lithuania for archaeologists, who are slowly uncovering the foundations of the medieval town. Artefacts they have discovered are on view in the exhibition building. Additionally, there are five defensive mounds, the largest surviving example in the country of such a complex.

Kernavė is best visited by car. Although there are five buses daily from Vilnius, each immediately turns round and travels back to the capital, necessitating a wait of several hours for the next service.

Aukštadvaris Regional Park

West of Trakai Historical National Park lies another very pretty protected landscape, **Aukštadvaris Regional Park**. Within its boundaries are no fewer than 77 lakes, and it is seen at its best in September or October when cloaked in glorious autumnal colours. Buses from Vilnius to Alytus, or from Vilnius to Birštonas and Prienai, travel all the way through the middle of the park, enabling a good cross-section of its scenery to be seen. En route they pass through the village of **Aukštadvaris**, which lies on the northern shore of Lake Nava and has a fine twin-towered wooden parish church which has recently been repainted. In the woods some 4km to the north, and reachable by footpath, is the so-called **Devil's Cave**, a mysterious hole 40m deep and 200m in diameter which has been the inspiration for a host of legends.

The Island Castle, Trakai

Kaliningrad

Neil Taylor

For 46 years between 1945 and 1991 the Soviet Union occupied the Baltic states of Estonia, Latvia and Lithuania and also incorporated part of the former German province of East Prussia, renaming the town of Königsberg as Kaliningrad. Confusingly they used this name, too, for the surrounding region or *oblast*. A cultural and political uniformity was quickly imposed on all these territories and most former links with the outside world curtailed. Kaliningrad suffered most in this respect, with travel there even for Soviet citizens being difficult or impossible. Its history as a major German city was ignored; in the town centre British bombing in August 1944 and the final battle for the city in April 1945 left many buildings totally or largely destroyed. Much of what could have been restored was subsequently removed to make the break with the long German past even stronger. Tallinn, Rīga and Vilnius were still granted a history, albeit a distorted one as the Soviet Union was unhappy to publicise the period between 1920 and 1940 when these towns were not part of it. Many of their pre-war inhabitants, however, were unable to enjoy it, having been murdered in the Holocaust, or deported to Siberia in 1941, or having fled west ahead of the Soviet army in 1944.

From around 1960, the Soviet authorities allowed travel to Tallinn, Rīga and Vilnius but with a maximum stay of three nights. Travel between the cities was by air or on overnight trains. Longer stays were rarely granted to prevent serious contacts being established with the local populations. Tours always started and finished in Leningrad (now St Petersburg) or Moscow to stress the Soviet nature of the programme and to minimise the Baltic element. Travel outside the capitals only became possible in the 1980s toward the end of the Soviet period. Tourists first came to Kaliningrad from 1990 as the Soviet Union fell apart and the military were no longer able to prevent this. As Kaliningrad was a major naval base on the front line with NATO, admitting tourists was out of the question before then. The occasional visitor from Scandinavia came in the 1950s and 1960s but, in comparison, Tibet, North Korea or Albania seemed wide open in those days. Many former East Prussians were desperate to return and 60,000 Germans came to visit in 1992. Their largely hostile reports, and continued bitterness at what many regarded as an illegitimate occupation of their homeland, initially discouraged more general tourists. Now with many business, academic and voluntary organisations working towards reconciliation and with the successful rebuilding of several pre-war monuments, the image of Kaliningrad has greatly improved and visitor numbers are likely to increase again.

THE STATUS OF KALININGRAD

Independence in Estonia, Latvia and Lithuania brought an immediate influx of tourists to their capitals from all over the world, many taking tours that visited all three. Arrivals came to be counted in millions rather than in thousands. This added to the determination of the local town councils to eradicate the recent Soviet past. Cyrillic road signs were torn down, hard currencies introduced and visas abolished for most visitors. Active tourist boards were established, eager to work with the travel industry and with travel writers. In these capitals, the new private sector quickly adapted to tourism so that by 1994 visitors had no problem in finding a luxury hotel or a small two-star one, eating Chinese or Italian food, and reading a Western newspaper on the day of publication. Tourist visits are now similar to those in Stockholm, Lübeck or Kraków, with ample scope for specialist and general groups or individuals preferring to stay on their own.

World War II left savage human scars across the region but fortunately there was little fighting in the three Baltic state capitals so an architectural heritage stretching back for eight centuries welcomes all visitors. Many of the sites are within walking distance of each other and of the hotels which visitors are likely to use. Others are cheaply and easily reached by public transport.

The transformation in Kaliningrad would be, and remains, more ambivalent. British bombing and bitter fighting in April 1945 left the town centre a shell. By the end of the Soviet period most of the inhabitants were from Russia, a few from the other Soviet Republics. In 1991 they were suddenly cut off from home by three foreign countries – Lithuania, Poland and Belarus. Renewed contact from Germany with this former part of East Prussia was as much a threat as an opportunity. The year 1992 brought visions of Kaliningrad becoming the 'Hong Kong of the Baltics' but realism on the spot and hostility in Moscow soon put paid to this. A new role has still to be found.

The problems the rest of Russia faces are equally acute in Kaliningrad: nearly half the working population earns less than £20/US$30 a month, a sum which is regarded as a realistic minimum wage. The old age pension, if it is provided on time, is £10/US$15 a month. Tourists will appreciate the massive grants the Germans have provided in the last ten years as they admire the restored cathedral, the enlarged History Museum and the repainted seaside resort of Rauschen. They will enjoy the restaurants and the many 24-hour shops. Königsberg is methodically and aesthetically returning to many parts of Kaliningrad. Yet the abandoned fields in much of the countryside and the dismal blocks of flats in many of the suburbs show that little has changed for much of the local population. In some ways, Russia has left Kaliningrad behind. Those who never knew the Soviet Union can still take the chance to see Lenin looking down on most town hall squares. They can still do serious shopping in local markets as peasants prefer to bypass the official distribution structures. They can wonder why the name of the town has not been changed, since Kalinin, as a close associate of Stalin, hardly inspires reverence any more. Kant would be the obvious person to choose in renaming the town as he is respected by both the Germans and the Russians, but some local residents claim that the town is not yet worthy of his name. Tourists need not worry whether it is or whether it is not, but for the sake of the local residents let us hope for not too long a delay.

HISTORY

The history of the former German town of Königsberg began with bloodshed in 1255 and ended with bloodshed in 1945. The establishment of the first settlement by the Teutonic Knights was to lead by 1283 to the complete annihilation of the Prussian tribes. In 1945 the Germans would in turn be annihilated by Soviet troops at the end of World War II. In the intervening 700 years, war would generally pass the town by, its few temporary occupiers having established their authority in battles elsewhere. Membership of the Hanseatic League from 1340 ensured close relationships with all the other large ports along the Baltic coast and a common adherence to Lutheranism after the Reformation. It also ensured extensive trading links with Britain. During this long period of time, Germany and Russia would usually be friends, uniting just as easily against the French as against the Poles. Loyal former residents always refer to 700 years of German history, yet such rule can hardly be seen as continuous. For much of the 15th century, local rulers had to swear allegiance to the Polish crown. The Swedes followed in the 16th century and were only finally driven away in 1679. The first Russian occupation lasted four years, between 1758 and 1762. In 1807 Napoleon occupied the town for 39 days. Far worse than any occupation was the plague that killed a quarter of the population in 1709.

Learning and culture

Albertina University, founded in 1544, was a constant feature of the town's history. Foreign occupiers always respected it and eagerly encouraged its work. It was equally well-known throughout Germany. It pioneered in many fields, being one of the first to lecture in German instead of Latin, to introduce science degrees and to admit women students. Throughout its 400-year history, any prominent writer, historian or scientist living in Königsberg had a post at Albertina. Its academic standards were only to slip twice during this time. An honorary degree was awarded to Napoleon's General Pierre Daru who led the forces that occupied Königsberg. In the university's final 12 years between 1933 and 1945, the teaching was as dominated by Nazi ideology as it was in all other German universities.

The original 16th-century buildings of the university were beside those of the cathedral in the heart of the old town. These were all destroyed during the fighting at the end of World War II, including a library of over half a million books. As part of the 300th anniversary celebrations in 1844, further faculties were built on the northern side of the Pregel River and some of the buildings survived the war and are still in use. These followed other institutions that had been founded earlier in the century, such as the botanical garden and the observatory built by Germany's most famous astronomer, Friedrich Wilhelm Bessel (1784–1846).

The philosopher Immanuel Kant (1724–1804) was undoubtedly Königsberg's most famous resident and probably the only one ever to achieve fame outside Germany. He stayed loyal to the town throughout his life and never accepted posts elsewhere. In fact he went further than this and hardly left the town, indicating in many of his writings that travel would not have broadened *his* mind. Marxist philosophers see him as a precursor to Hegel and then to Marx himself. Because of the Russian occupation he was, like all other residents for that four-year period, a Russian citizen. One hundred and fifty years later these two factors would be crucial. During the Soviet period between 1945 and 1990, he was the one famous former resident who could officially be commemorated. His tomb outside the cathedral, erected in 1924 on the 200th anniversary of his birth, was not destroyed and his work continued to be published.

Kant was renowned for his rigid schedule and his regular companions. His butler always woke him at 4.45 each morning and he was always in bed by 22.00. He never married, to his regret, but he consoled himself with the thought that staying single kept his mind more alert. He held the Chair of Logic from 1770 until his death in 1804, the year of which he had actually predicted. He had a regular circle of friends whom he entertained each Sunday. Amongst the latter were two Englishmen, Joseph Green and Robert Motherby, whose shipping business, originally based in Hull, brought grain and herrings to Britain. They had lunch with him every Sunday for about 20 years. In the 19th century their successors started a regular steamer service between Hull and Königsberg, profiting in particular during the Crimean War when Königsberg was the only source of Russian goods.

The most famous visitor to Königsberg was Peter the Great, who came in 1697 en route to Western Europe. A Russian trading community had already been settled in the town for over a hundred years and was sufficiently large to hold regular church services. Officially he came incognito, but being some two metres tall (well over six feet) and bringing an entourage of 400, this pretence was impossible to maintain. He did enjoy disguising himself in a range of unlikely occupations but wildly drunken behaviour was on several occasions to let him down. On his visit to Königsberg the German court presented him with amber jewellery and horses from the famous breeding centre in Eastern Prussia, Trakehnen. Later they would present him with the Amber Chamber, which would adorn the summer palace at Tsarkoye Selo for two centuries, before being brought back to Königsberg by German troops in 1942. After his 1697 visit, Peter the Great continued his journey to Holland and England, settling in Deptford for several months to study shipbuilding. He would send students from St Petersburg to study at Albertina University but this link was broken in 1720 as too few Russian students had sufficient knowledge of German to follow the courses. It was restored during the Tsarist occupation (1758–62) when Russian students attended Kant's lectures.

Expansion and prosperity

The 19th century was one of fame in every commercial and intellectual field for Königsberg and the city enjoyed peace and prosperity throughout these hundred years. 'First' and 'largest' are adjectives that need to be used again and again. At the beginning of the century, in 1809, the famous Königsberg marzipan was first produced. At the end of the century, in 1895, Germany's first electric trams operated here and then, two years later, the first 11 women graduated from Albertina. Well before the end of the century, the port handled more grain and wood than any other in Germany whilst at the same time 'Gräfe und Unzer' had become the country's largest bookshop. Shipbuilding, printing, railway engineering and textiles were the industries that enjoyed particular success. The opening of the railway link with Russia in 1861 greatly expanded the scope of the port, as did the construction of the canal to Pillau (Baltiysk) on the coast. Uniquely it could guarantee ice-free access throughout the winter. The first British steamer had in fact arrived seven years earlier in 1854 and trade with Russia through the port would greatly increase following the completion of the railway link.

Culturally, Wagner, Schumann and Liszt paid several visits for performances of their works; Bizet's *Carmen* was successfully performed in 1879 after its initial failure in Paris. In architecture, the Luisenkirche and the Stock Exchange are the most famous of a wide range of impressive 19th-century buildings that are still in use.

Königsberg remained untouched by World War I, although it was sufficiently close to several battles for it to be used as a military relief station and for its hospitals to be greatly expanded. Under the Versailles Treaty of 1919, independence was restored to Poland after over a century of German and Russian occupation. This led to the division of East Prussia and its capital Königsberg from the rest of Germany. Although links with the 'mainland' were assured, Königsberg was forced to look for closer trading links with the new Baltic states of Lithuania, Latvia and Estonia and also with the Soviet Union. There are few realistic portrayals of the 26 years Königsberg was still to exist as a German city. The many memoirs that the exiles would produce after World War II present an idealised picture of a prosperous town with no crime, no tension and where the sun always shone. One writer does in fact admit that she cannot recall a rainy summer's day, so happy are her recollections of her childhood in Königsberg. There is no doubt that much was achieved there and evidence of this can still be seen in many parts of the town, despite the later bombing. One mayor, Hans Lohmeyer, was in office from 1919 to 1933 and he relentlessly drove the town forward. In Carl Gördeler, his deputy from 1922 to 1930, he had an equally active supporter. (Gördeler then become Mayor of Leipzig and, had the July 1944 plot to kill Hitler succeeded, he would have been nominated as German Chancellor. He and several other East Prussians were among the many executed for their role in the plot.)

Lohmeyer built a new main railway station, probably the first in Germany with non-smoking waiting rooms, and with a bowling alley. He foresaw the role air travel would play so gave his city a large airport. He realised the need for close links with the new Soviet government so helped to establish Deruluft, a joint venture with them which operated regular flights to Moscow. The two-storey road and rail bridge across the River Pregel, which is still in use, was built at his instigation. His most famous achievement was the annual *Ostmesse*, the export trade fair that dominated trade to and from the city throughout the inter-war period. First opened in 1920, by 1923 it was attracting 2,500 exhibitors and continued operating until the autumn of 1941.

Yet an honest portrayal of the city between 1919 and 1939 has to reflect the developments that hit the whole of Germany. The rampant inflation of 1923 destroyed many long-established businesses and then unemployment in the early 1930s provided the breeding ground for Nazism. The Nazis' main opponents both on the streets and in the ballot box were the Communists. None of the centre parties appeared to offer solutions to the ever-worsening crisis. At the *Ostmesse* in 1932, many stands were empty and an art exhibition had to fill up the empty space.

The Nazi era

In the last free election to be held in Königsberg the Nazis were elected on March 5 1933, with 54% of the vote. Democracy and racial tolerance died that night throughout Germany. Opposition to the Nazis was dealt with as ruthlessly in Königsberg as elsewhere. Mayor Lohmeyer was sacked on March 9. On May 10 a book burning was organised on the Trommelplatz, the main parade ground. Any books which could be stigmatized as 'Un-German, Jewish or Bolshevik' went up in flames. Sixteen staff at the university were immediately sacked on account of their political views or racial background.

The most famous Jew who left Königsberg in 1933 was the song-writer Max Colpet who wrote 'Where Have All the Flowers Gone' for Marlene Dietrich. In his American exile he went on to write for Charles Aznavour and to translate *West Side Story* into German. A five-year old Jewish girl who also left in 1933 later achieved prominence as Lea Rabin, wife of the Israeli Prime Minister. By the end of the year, the Hansaring had been renamed Adolf Hitler Strasse, to mark the supposed permanence of the Nazi regime.

On November 7 1938 a junior diplomat Ernst von Rath was shot in the Paris Embassy and died two days later. He had joined the Nazi Party in 1932 whilst a student in Königsberg. His assassin, Herschel Grynzpan, was a young impoverished Polish-Jewish refugee who had just been expelled from Germany with all his family. This murder gave the Nazis a pretext for launching a new wave of attacks on all Jewish businesses and synagogues in Germany, on what later became known as *Kristallnacht*. November 9 was already a symbolic date in German history since on that day the Kaiser had abdicated in 1918 and in 1923 Hitler had launched his unsuccessful 'Beer Hall Putsch'. Because of von Rath's links with East Prussia, these attacks were particularly brutal in Königsberg and the main synagogue was totally destroyed. Destroyed, too, were any hopes some maintained that Nazism could be tamed. For those happy to support the Nazi regime, Königsberg would survive for another six years. For anyone else, Königsberg as a cosmopolitan, racially diverse city, rightly proud of its past and present, died in November 1938.

Until 1944 one can almost say that Königsberg 'enjoyed' the fruits of World War II. The destruction of Poland reunited East Prussia with the *Reich* and the advance into Russia again brought the Baltic states under German influence. 'Bombing' was what relatives in Hamburg or Berlin suffered, but it did not initially touch Königsberg. Food supplies were ample and prisoners provided cheap labour on the farms and in the factories. With most opponents of Nazism having been exiled by 1939, there could be no focus for any opposition and little need for it given the high standard of living enjoyed by most of the population. 1944, however, was a turning point. The defeat at Stalingrad in early 1943 and continuing German losses on all fronts after that could no longer be concealed from the population at large.

August 1944 presented the local authorities with an acute dilemma – how should the 400th anniversary of the founding of Albertina University be celebrated? In the past such celebrations had been particularly flamboyant and had been well documented for posterity. To continue in a similar vein might be seen as tasteless in the middle of an increasingly desperate war, yet to ignore the occasion could be termed as defeatism. Gauleiter Erich Koch took the second option, even sanctioning new buildings for the university. He probably bore in mind Hitler's interest in Frederick the Great and the commitment the Emperor had shown to the 200th anniversary in 1744. At one of the formal ceremonies, Koch presented three statues, of Kant, Copernicus and Hitler. In the British air raids that followed two weeks later, most of the university was destroyed, but two of these statues survived intact. Hitler did not.

The Royal Air Force launched two major bombing attacks, on the night of August 26–27 1944 and again on August 29–30. The desolation these caused can still be seen all too clearly in the former Old Town by the river. All the streets were destroyed and only the shells of the cathedral and the castle remained. The cathedral is still being rebuilt, but the castle was torn down in the late 1960s; none of the university buildings survived. Refugees from Lithuania started to come into East Prussia. Wild cattle, abandoned by their owners, drifted across the countryside. The Russians slowly encircled the town, the last train to Berlin leaving Königsberg on January 22 1945. The next one would not leave until August 1991.

Even during the following two months, reality was evaded. Food and fuel supplies were adequate, the zoo sold annual season tickets valid until December 1945 and hairdressers required clients to make appointments two weeks in advance. Children, as normal for January, built snowmen at the side of the streets and passing soldiers handed out chocolate bars to them. Officially nobody could plan to escape, but 100,000 East Prussians did so via the port of Pillau which stayed in German hands until the end of the war.

The occupation of Königsberg came quickly and brutally; after a three-day siege the German commander, General Otto Lasch, formally surrendered to the Russians on April 10 1945. He spent the next ten years in prison and then wrote his memoirs, which still remain contentious amongst the *Vertriebene*, the exile community who fled to West Germany. With 35,000 troops and no air cover against the 250,000 Russian force, the result of the battle could not be in doubt. Some argue that, with an earlier surrender, there would have been less suffering in the town as the Russians would not have felt so vengeful. Others argue that Lasch could have disobeyed Berlin earlier and arranged for a more orderly civil evacuation, as happened in other East Prussian towns. Cynics claim that he fought until his own life was in danger and then surrendered. Hitler had ordered him to fight to the last man, but he was one of many German commanders not to carry these orders out, even though he pursued such a policy further than was necessary.

The defence of Königsberg did not prevent war crimes being carried out to the last minute. In early April 1945 resources were still found to force-march 5,000 Hungarian prisoners from Königsberg to Pillau. Some 2,000 perished en route and most of the remaining 3,000 drowned in the sea or were murdered on the beach. Only 13 were rescued by extremely brave local villagers.

Soviet rule

Although leaflets dropped by Russian aircraft before the final attack promised a quick and pleasant return to civilian life, the population of Königsberg was exposed to every possible form of human depravity as the Russian troops arrived. Women were 'lucky' if they were only raped by one soldier. Men forced into work brigades were similarly fortunate in that this ensured just enough rations to survive. Stalin is alleged to have encouraged his troops with the slogan, 'Take these blonde German women. They are all yours.' Soldiers could loot at will and understandably took the chance to do so. If there was one German word that they all learnt it was *Uhr* ('watch') but their interests could not be expected to stop there. Most had spent the last years seeing town after town destroyed by the German Army and few would not have had many relatives killed. Despite the siege and the earlier bombing, Königsberg still had a modern vibrant feel to it. Russian troops expecting an impoverished German proletariat found thousands of townhouses full of clothes, china, furniture and jewellery. One soldier wrote home, 'It is hard to know where to look first when you enter a German house. Do you realise that they all have pianos the size of tables?' Some items were unknown to them, particularly to soldiers from Central Asia. They had never seen bicycles or flushing toilets and were equally inept with both.

For about a week, Russian troops were allowed to rampage as the German Army had done on their territory for the previous four years. Under the circumstances their behaviour was perfectly comprehensible, even though it can in no way be condoned. Königsberg was the first major German town to surrender. The soldiers knew that it was going to be incorporated into the USSR. Like Berlin and Dresden, in 1945 the town was to pay a particularly high price for its Nazi past. It would soon pay an even higher one.

If law and order were quickly restored, food supplies were certainly not and mere survival became a total preoccupation for the German population of around 100,000 who remained in May 1945. Survival was only possible through ingenuity and barter. Elderly relatives were abandoned so that their clothes could be sold and then their corpses would be cannibalised. (Only those who died of typhus could expect a burial.) Pets had to be eaten, as did any non-poisonous plants. Everyone turned their hands to thieving as honesty could only lead to starvation. The three letters LSR daubed across makeshift air-raid shelters were a familiar sight in the town since this was the German abbreviation for such cellars (*Luftschutzräume*). Under the occupation it soon came to mean *Lernt Schnell Russisch* ('quickly learn Russian').

In the early days of the occupation, it was assumed that the remaining German population would be allowed to stay. In fact, some German refugees who had reached what was now western Poland were returned. By 1946, though, the German population in the city had dropped to around 25,000. Relations between the Russians and the Germans became remarkably cordial and reminiscences from both sides dating from that time testify to this. The Russians needed the Germans for their skills and for their local knowledge. They admired their resilience and cleanliness. No Russian would regularly clean the doorstep and pavement outside his house, let alone outside a bombsite. Only the Germans could find the sewers, operate the drainage systems and restore production in the amber mines. When the Königsberg trams started to operate again in the summer of 1946, there were 400 German staff and only 70 Russians. The Germans needed the Russians for regular supplies of food and money, so became the workers, tradesmen and nannies that could ensure this.

The early Russian settlers had mixed backgrounds. Some soldiers simply stayed on, attracted by a potential lifestyle unlikely to greet them elsewhere in the Soviet Union. Those who had been imprisoned by the Germans, and could therefore be judged as traitors by the Red Army, felt less threatened here as their past could be more easily falsified or ignored. New settlers were positively encouraged from summer 1946. Those from a country background admired the asphalt and cobbles which were as novel to them as bicycles and flush toilets had been to the troops a year earlier.

The Germans still went to church, although the Russians by and large did not. There were of course no orthodox churches and many Russians feared that expressions of religious belief might prejudice their future careers. A German club was founded in February 1946 and some Russians also attended. Genuine relationships between both communities started to be formed. There were again grounds for optimism. Such hopes were shattered in July 1946. Königsberg was renamed Kaliningrad (Калининград) in honour of Michael Kalinin who had just died (of natural causes). He had been a senior member of the Soviet Politburo, a man of little vision, but of great staying power. Confusingly, the same name was given to the new surrounding region (*oblast* in Russian). Although every other town and village in East Prussia, and all the streets, would now receive Russian names, many were better honoured. Insterburg, the second largest town in the former East Prussia, was renamed Chernyakhovsk after a noted commander, Ivan Chernyakhovsky, who fought heroically in many battles on the Eastern Front and died of his wounds in February 1945. Only the rivers and the town gates kept their German names after 1947 so the Pregel still ran through the town centre, overlooked by the Brandenburg Gate.

In the same month, the whole *oblast* of Kaliningrad was declared a military zone. A barbed-wire fence along the entire length of the new border with Poland went up in September 1946, dividing families and cutting the link with Germany. The following winter was, as elsewhere in Europe, a bitter one, and many were to suffer almost as badly as they had done in the summer of 1945. Many older people felt there was no alternative to suicide particularly as rations were often restricted to 'specialists'. ('Parasites' were expected to fend for themselves.) In the countryside, conditions were worse as the months of hard frost and deep snow prevented any cultivation. Yet some Russians started to learn German and in June 1947 a German newspaper, *Neue Zeit* ('New Times'), was founded with six Russian staff and four Germans. Its contents were largely translations from Russian papers, but its publication did suggest a long-term future for the German community.

The complete opposite was made clear on October 10 when Stalin suddenly ordered what would now be called ethnic cleansing. On October 22, the first special train left for Germany and many others were to follow. By March 1948, the policy had by and large been carried out, with only a few specialists allowed to stay a little longer because their expertise was still needed. Kaliningrad became a unique region of Europe in many ways. It had been ethnically cleansed with total success and with the full agreement of the wartime Allies. It became a community with no past and with minimal links to the outside world. Guidebooks and school textbooks would talk of Kant being born in Kaliningrad in 1724, but no other reference was made to the German era or even to the Seven Years War when the Russians previously occupied Königsberg. Lhasa, Pyongyang and Tirana suddenly appeared cosmopolitan in comparison as they did at least see regular delegations from abroad and occasional groups of tourists.

Public displays of religion ceased as the German churches closed in 1948 and were only restored 40 years later when the Russian orthodox church took over some of the churches whose fabric could still be saved.

We must hope that those settlers who came in their twenties and are now retired will write up their experiences. For the time being, our knowledge of the next 40 years is restricted to the few official documents that have entered the public domain since the downfall of the USSR. Because of the military sensitivity of the area, minimal information was published during the Soviet era and there was no way in which it could be checked. We now know the background to the dynamiting of the castle ruins in 1969 which aimed to remove a clear visual link to the German past, but with the re-opening of the university in 1967 skilful students would in due course track this history down. The Bunker Museum was also opened in 1969, at the site of the German surrender. It displayed large-scale models of the fighting in Königsberg. In 1974 came a museum dedicated to Immanuel Kant which could not conceal his German surroundings, although he was portrayed as a 'citizen of all Europe' because of his fame. In 1975 a second German was commemorated, the astronomer Friedrich Wilhelm Bessel (1784–1846) when a memorial plaque, was erected on the site of his former observatory written in both Russian and German. (In 1989 Kaliningrad again had a Bessel Street, as it had before the war. A crater on the moon also bears Bessel's name.)

The destruction of churches continued until 1976. The last one to be blown up was the Lutherkirche, a beautiful neo-Renaissance building dating from 1907 which had not been seriously damaged during the war. The stagnation and inertia that took over during the later Brezhnev years in the USSR did not particularly affect Kaliningrad, any more than the earlier Khruschev thaw had done in the 1960s. The military maintained such a tight grip that political changes in Moscow were largely irrelevant. For the same reason, Kaliningrad was hardly to enjoy the *perestroika* ('reform') and *glasnost* ('openness') that characterised the final years of the Soviet Union in the late 1980s. Had visitors been allowed then, they would have found some lighter reading in the bookshops and a few Russian orthodox services taking place in the former Lutheran churches. That tourists were still not allowed, under any circumstances, speaks volumes.

After the failed military coup in Moscow in 1991, Kaliningraders were polled by a local newspaper and asked for their views: 25% were saddened at its failure, 25% were glad and 50% did not care. An older generation had known political terror under Stalin and then years of political inertia following his death in 1953. Younger people had only known the inertia, being totally cut off from foreigners and the more radical outbursts that flowered from time to time elsewhere in the Soviet Union.

Modern problems

1991 should have forced a break with this tradition. With the formal demise of the USSR at the end of December and the establishment of the various independent republics, Kaliningrad was now cut off from the rest of the Russian Federation by three foreign countries, Lithuania, Belarus and Poland. It had to adapt to new circumstances in the same way that Königsberg/East Prussia had done in 1919. Yet no new Hans Lohmeyer was forthcoming who could successfully maintain links with Moscow whilst at the same time achieving the local economic autonomy needed to trade successfully with Western Europe. There was talk of the town becoming the 'Hong Kong' of the Baltics but Moscow did not grant the full range of tax-free privileges that such a project needed.

Initially the sudden influx of high-spending nostalgic German tourists saved the town from making serious economic decisions. Some 60,000 came in 1992 and similar figures lasted for several more years. Many German charities became active and some businesses from Germany started to invest as low labour costs compensated for all the bureaucratic hurdles that still needed to be overcome. There are other resources, too. Amber is a unique and valuable local product and the legal sales abroad guarantee a regular income. Other export products such as timber have to compete against those from Poland and the Baltic states where an efficient business ethos has quickly taken root. Income is clearly also derived from smuggling as local cigarettes are known to have worldwide distribution networks.

Ten years after the fall of communism, there is still no alternative to take its place in Kaliningrad. Official statistics can now generally be believed and they make grim reading. An average wage is £30/US$45 a month, compared with £40/US$60 elsewhere in Russia. £17/US$25 is the official minimum wage but half the working population earn less and the old age pension is just £10/US$15 a month.

The solution can only be a subtle distancing from Moscow and in 1999 this started to be felt in a number of sectors. To encourage tourists, visas became available on the border which is still possible elsewhere in Russia. Contacts are being established in the English-speaking world to prevent over-dependence on Germany. Relations with Poland and Lithuania are being improved as cooperation, rather than competition, could well be in the interests of Kaliningrad. The EU is being taken seriously, both as a threat and as a stimulus. The in-laws of the Russian President Vladimir Putin are from Kaliningrad so perhaps he can be persuaded to interfere less than has been the case in the recent past.

Yet 'Königsberg' will never take over Kaliningrad as so few people on any side would wish for this. 'Königsberg' has returned and is making its presence felt where it is most welcome: in the churches, on the farms and in the factories. History begins again in 1255 and not in 1945. 'Königsberg' remains sensibly absent from the civil administration, from education and above all from the military. Agnes Miegel (1879–1964), Königsberg's most famous poet, wrote during her final years in exile: 'Königsberg, you are NOT mortal,' and she has turned out to be right.

Königsberg and Kaliningrad began to cooperate in 1990. They now happily coexist, as Russians and Germans have so often done in the past, but it is safe to predict that they will never embark on cohabitation.

PRACTICAL INFORMATION
Communications
Telephones
Calls from Kaliningrad to foreign countries require an international access code of 810 and then the relevant country code and foreign number. Calls made to Kaliningrad from abroad require the country code for Russia which is 7 then the Kaliningrad area code 0112 and the local number. The '0' is still used when dialling from abroad.

KALININGRAD: ORIENTATION

Direct dial is available abroad from some hotels but charges vary widely and should be checked before using the phone. There is often a three-minute minimum charge, even if the line is engaged or not answered. At telephone centres around the town, charges are lower and English or German are usually spoken. There are telephone centres in the main railway station, the Central Post Office, and in the Kaliningrad Hotel. All have extensive opening hours.

Post

The postal service out of Kaliningrad has greatly improved in the last two to three years even though everything goes via Moscow. Allow two weeks for cards to reach Western Europe, slightly longer for elsewhere. Charges are very cheap, even for air mail. Stamps are not sold at kiosks or hotel reception desks though larger souvenir shops do sell them with postcards. The two main post offices in Kaliningrad are not in the town centre; the main one is near the Zoo at Leonova 22 and another is in the main railway station to the south of the town centre.

Internet cafés

No internet cafés had opened by summer 2000 but the communications centre at the Kaliningrad Hotel offers reasonable charges, is open seven days a week and can also send faxes and provide photocopying services.

Tourist information

There are no tourist information offices anywhere in Kaliningrad. It is therefore advisable to prebook a transfer on arrival and a guide for a day or two to get used to the town layout, public transport and to be up to date on concerts. Kiosks sell town plans in Russian, but these can be several years out of date so may not show new hotels. *Kaliningrad in Your Pocket* is published annually in Vilnius but is sold in Kaliningrad. Like its well-known Baltic companions, it provides a lively digest of things to see and pithy comments on all hotels and restaurants, together with maps and a public transport guide. It can be consulted on line at inyourpocket.com and then bought locally for around £0.65/US$1.

Public transport

An efficient and extensive network of buses, trams and trolleybuses cover the town with very low fares. A ticket will usually cost the equivalent of £0.10/US$0.15, however long the journey. Tickets are bought on board, not beforehand in kiosks. The main bus station, beside the railway station serves other towns and villages in the region. Timetables are clearly listed there, as they are in the railway station, but there is no written guide to these services. Do not expect English or German to be spoken either in the bus station or in the railway station.

Taxis

These are now metered and are cheap by Western standards. A short journey within the town centre, should not cost more than £0.75/US$1.20 or around £1.50/US$2 to the more distant hotels.

Airport

There is no public transport to the international terminal. which is about two kilometres from the domestic terminal. Whilst some taxis wait for the daily SAS flight from Copenhagen, it would be unwise to rely on them and a transfer should be prebooked through a travel agent abroad.

Banks and money

Roubles can easily be obtained in the Baltic states and in Poland but not in Western Europe, At the Lithuanian and Polish borders, these local currencies can be exchanged into roubles, otherwise it is difficult to change anything apart from American dollars and German marks. The few exchange bureaux will accept other currencies such as British pounds but give very poor rates. Travellers' cheques can only be exchanged at a few banks so are best avoided. ATM machines are few and far between so remain unreliable. Credit cards are accepted by the main hotels and restaurants. The rouble has been very stable since 1999, maintaining a rate of around US$1 = RUB27, so £1.00 is worth about RUB40.

Accommodation
Hotels (see also page 187)

Although visas are issued on the border, they have to be pre-arranged on the basis of accommodation booked by a local travel agent who then requests visa authority and faxes it to the tour operator abroad. It is therefore not practical to book hotels directly since they cannot offer this visa service. Prices given are those likely to be charged abroad by specialist travel agents who work with Kaliningrad. They usually include breakfast. There is little seasonal variation although hotels get very heavily booked from mid-June to mid-August, the German holiday season. Most hotels have a dual pricing system, with Russians paying much less than foreigners. This distinction is strictly enforced and it is, of course, the higher prices applicable to foreigners that are listed below.

Chaika Pugacheva 13, tel/fax: 212816. Singles US$55, twins US$70.
This was a hotel in German times and was renovated in 1995 to what must have been its former standards. The surrounding area was and is a quiet, affluent suburb, largely untouched by bombing or fighting during the war. The décor remains German in all the 25 rooms and German is the only foreign language spoken by the staff. Breakfast is adequate, but not generous, and the menu is limited. The main road into town is a walk of 500m or so away, but then there are plenty of bus routes and passing taxis. It also has several 24-hour shops. Nearer at hand are several bars and restaurants, all with a calm, elderly clientele. Visitors who want to turn the clock back to the Königsberg era will be very happy in this hotel.
Deima Tolstikova 15, tel: 410814, fax: 410700, email: baltserv@bds.ru. Singles US$55, twins US$65.
The location of this hotel could not be more dire – in the middle of a dreary housing estate about 3km from the town centre – but standards inside are more than adequate compensation. Furnishings are modern and the staff welcoming, although only in German as none seem to speak English. The hotel is on several bus routes, but as taxis rarely cost more than US$1 into town, this is hardly a major bonus.

Hansa Bagramyana 6, tel: 433737, fax: 433771. Singles US$45, twins US$60.
In the early '90s this former Rhine river cruiser was brought from Germany to house
tourists unwilling to stay in the minimalist accommodation then available on land.
Rooms are therefore quite small, but are adequately furnished and have satellite
television. In early 2000 it was the only hotel in Kaliningrad to receive British channels.
This 'boatel' has stayed moored in the harbour about ten ten minutes' walk from the
cathedral and the Kaliningrad Hotel. Meal service is slow and the choice of items poor as
the restaurant is dependent on a tiny lift bringing food up from a kitchen two floors
below.

Kaliningrad Leninsky 81, tel: 469440, fax: 536021, email: market@hotel.kaliningrad.ru,
web: www.hotel.kaliningrad.ru. Singles US$75, twins US$90.
This hotel sells on the basis of its location in the town centre. It also has on site a choice
of shops, bars and restaurants enabling business visitors in winter to spend their whole
stay within the building. These all, however, charge about double or treble the prices
available within a few hundred metres of the hotel so are best avoided. The one
exception is the newspaper kiosk which has a good range of maps and postcards. The
exchange bureau handles currencies other than US dollars and German marks but not at
competitive rates. For the time being, this is by far the largest hotel in the whole region,
with over 200 rooms. All are adequately furnished and many have good views towards
the cathedral. Phones in the rooms each have separate numbers not linked to the main
switchboard, so if calls are expected from abroad, these numbers should be passed to
relevant contacts on arrival. Hotel staff and those in the shops speak good English.

Komandor Schastlivaya 1, tel/fax: 341815 and 341820, email: comandor@baltnet.ru.
Singles US$90, twins US$110.
This is without doubt Kaliningrad's best hotel, situated 20 minutes drive north from the
town centre in a new smart suburb. It will suit those determined to have no contact
with contemporary Russia: a portrait of Peter the Great dominates the reception area
and all prices are quoted in US dollars. Anyone paid in roubles is unlikely to be able to
afford to enter. The hotel has an underground car park, several private dining rooms,
satellite television in all rooms and a large swimming pool.

Moskva Mira 19, tel: 272089. Singles US$20, twins US$30.
Few foreign tourists have so far used this hotel but this should change in 2001 when
renovation of several floors will be complete. Eventually all 200 rooms will be brought
up to three-star standard, which could finally lead to serious competition between hotels
in Kaliningrad. The location, opposite the zoo, is very convenient for many sites, for
public transport and for shops.

Patriot Ozernaya 25, tel: 255023. Singles US$20, twins US$25.
For visitors on a budget this hotel is ideal. It is clean, well-maintained and adequately
furnished. Most rooms have a fridge for families wishing to prepare picnics. It is a high-
rise surrounded by others, about 2km to the north of the town centre. Locals who can
afford it come for dental treatment here as the surgery is regarded as one of the best in
town. The café has an unexpectedly wide menu with most main dishes costing around
£0.75/US$1.20.

Food and drink

Francis Drake Sovietsky 19, tel: 218353.
Only the names of the dishes here and the pictures on the walls have any link with
Britain. A Sir Drake salad for £0.90/US$1.40 is a mixture of meats, tomatoes and
mayonnaise. A Manchester for a similar price is a fillet of pork, mushrooms, sour cream

and garlic. The ice-cream has fortunately no hint of Britain in it. Transportation problems have prevented the flow of British beer so far but hopefully this will be resolved during 2001.

Kulinaria in the Kaliningrad Hotel.

On the ground floor with a street entrance to the right hand side of the hotel, the colours of the ingredients and of the décor at this self-service establishment make a refreshing contrast to the drab exterior surroundings. Although a wide choice of cold meats is offered, vegetarians will not be made to feel a nuisance here. Lingering is not possible as no tables are provided, only stools and a counter. However, a quick filling meal here can be followed by a leisurely coffee in the hotel at one of the upstairs bars which overlook the cathedral.

Monopol Frunze 17-21, tel: 468311.

Don't be put off by the awesome décor that dominates the entrance just as much as the restaurant itself. Although the table-cloths are starched, as are the waiters' collars, and the builders were given free rein with the marble, a fairly standard range of international dishes is offered at normal Kaliningrad prices. It will be hard to pay more than £3/US$4.50 for a substantial lunch or £5/US$8 for dinner. Allow at least two hours for proper indulgence.

Solyanka Prospekt Mira 26, tel: 279203.

Self-service restaurants in Russia tend to be basic, but the Solyanka has definitely broken with this pattern. Cleanliness is taken to an obsession, in the toilets as much as in the restaurant itself. Menus are only in Russian, but with the clear displays, this hardly matters. A wide range of hot main courses is available for about £1/US$1.50 each and there are also even cheaper snacks, while beer is around £0.40/US$0.60 depending on the brand. Smokers are segregated into a glass-covered alcove. A board at the entrance invites job applications from potential waitresses and cooks. The salary offered of 3,000 roubles a month, about £75/US$110, clearly gives the management a good choice as service always seems to be friendly and efficient.

Titanic Chernyakhovskovo 74, tel: 536768.

The décor was meticulously planned before this restaurant opened in the summer of 2000. The designer clearly did more than see the film to have constructed the 'life-boat alcoves', to have reprinted the old menus, and to have varnished the wood on the stairs. If the food is not quite first-class, it is well above steerage. The veneer is almost April 1912 and certainly a complete contrast to the rugged surroundings of the nearby market where the elderly attempt to supplement their minimal pensions by selling knitwear and vegetables. On the opposite side of the road are exchange bureaux with long opening hours and usually the best rates for dollars and marks.

Twelve Chairs Prospekt Mira 67, tel: 2109031.

Named after one of the few satirical novels published in Soviet times, this small cellar-bar mixes the old and the young, locals and tourists. The menu is a mixture of German and Russian, the décor and music likewise, so perhaps this is a portent of future collaboration. Whilst vodka is the usual £0.50/US$0.75 for a large measure, it is worth spending a little more on one of the fifty cocktails in which the restaurant specialises. Salmon salad accompanies them well. A bucolic evening here can happily be concluded with ice-cream drenched in a liqueur.

Valencia Ploshad Pobedy 1, tel: 433820.

Most tourists visiting the Baltics want to forget previous holidays in Spain, but for those who cannot, southern warmth and a predictable menu of pancakes, *paella* and strong red wine are always on offer here. Their hours, too, are Spanish, as they only close at 02.00

and happily serve both late lunches and late dinners. Local people always recommend it to Western visitors, on the assumption that they are looking for the familiar rather than the unusual.

Entertainment
Clubs and casinos
As clubs and casinos are the centres for criminal activity, they are best avoided by visitors, except for those in hotels, which restrict entry to guests and carefully vetted local people.

Theatre
The Drama Theatre at Mira 4 performs only in Russian but its repertoire is international and with cheap tickets. An enjoyable evening can be spent there even without following all the dialogue.

Music
Most concerts take place at the Philharmonia, converted from the former Church of the Holy Family. Over the next few years, more will take place in the cathedral, now that the roof is complete and the interior largely restored.

Medical services
Klinicheskaya Hospital Lower Lake, near Amber Museum, tel: 434556.
Emergency telephone numbers Fire: 01; Police: 02; Ambulance: 03.

Pharmacy
Apteka Mira 98, tel: 217883

Consulates
The SAS office at Sovietsky 1 also serves as the consulate for all EU nationals. The phone number is 550105. Other nationals have to turn to their consulate in Moscow

Places of worship
There was no public worship in Kaliningrad until the end of the Soviet era in the late 1980s when some of the former German churches were taken over by the Russian orthodox community. Some services are now held in German in the cathedral.

WHAT TO SEE
A one-day walking tour is suggested, then other sites are described separately. A day excursion to the coast is also outlined. About four or five days are needed to do justice to the town and the surrounding area. Other places in the Kaliningrad region(*oblast* in Russian) are beyond the scope of this book but offer a worthwhile extension to visitors with the extra time.

One-day walking tour
A sightseeing tour of Kaliningrad has to start at the lobby of the Kaliningrad Hotel. Little has been done to remove its 30-year past. In the small shops there will be an incongruous array of goods, many of which have probably spent

almost this length of time pressed up against the glass windows. Prices are absurdly low or absurdly high, never sensible. The staff will be polite and will speak reasonable English, probably more than happy to be in work in comfortable surroundings and to be paid on time. Lighting and décor is adequate but hardly enticing.

Those who came in the early 1990s, when the town was first open to tourists, might really have wondered whether such a visit was worthwhile. The hotel lobby could perhaps be passed off as mediocre. When they went outside, what stood before them and beside them was the Soviet Union at its very worst. Concrete was the sole building material and it was abused in many forms. To the left, the view was of an abandoned sixteen-storey tower block, an unfinished bridge and an enormous parking lot for trucks. Ahead was a wide straight road across a small island leading towards anonymous suburbs. To the Germans who had lived here before the war, sacrilege had been committed. This was their beloved Kneiphof, the island that had been the heart of Königsberg with the cathedral, castle, university and a cluster of surrounding lanes. Only the shell of the cathedral then remained, surrounded by an unkempt garden; its sole use was as a playground for local children, who could enjoy many variants of hide and seek. To the right a slightly less nondescript road offered a few shops with the relief of stone and granite. Few would imagine that it had once been the location of Germany's largest bookshop, Gräfe und Unzer.

The mood of the exiled Germans on their return – 60,000 came in 1992 – is perhaps best summarised by their most famous representative Marion Gräfin Dönhoff who became well-known as the publisher of the weekly *Die Zeit*. After her visit in 1991, she wrote, 'If I had been parachuted into this town and asked where I was, I would have perhaps replied Irkutsk. Nothing, absolutely nothing, reminded me of old Königsberg.'

The contemporary visitor will be much happier, mainly thanks to the fund-raising and reconciliation initiated by Marion Dönhoff since that visit. Through her paper, and by lobbying the German government and private foundations, funds have been raised to rebuild the cathedral and many other former churches. The **cathedral** (Кафедральный, open daily 09.00–17.00) must be the first port of call on any tour as it has been largely rebuilt to its pre-war format thanks to this support. Königsberg has returned to the heart of Kaliningrad.

Construction of the cathedral started in 1333 and was completed in the comparatively short period of 50 years. The first organ was installed in 1535. The early site bore an uncanny resemblance to the vista that greeted tourists in the early 1990s – an austere stone building with little decoration surrounded by greenery. It had as much military as religious significance, proving the power of the Teutonic Knights over the Prussian heathens. The oak piles, topped with copper, which form the foundations, are a credit to the advance in civil engineering at that time. They continued to support the increasing weight of subsequent builds, although it has been calculated that the cathedral has sunk 1.7m over 700 years. Finance was soon a problem and had to be resolved by the sale of Papal indulgences. In 1410 there was the first service of remembrance, to those who had died at the Battle of Grunewald, which saw the end of the Teutonic Knights as a major force in the area. The Reformation was eagerly taken up in the 1520s with Christmas 1523 being celebrated in

KALININGRAD CENTRE

German, a very popular move according to surviving reports. A second 58m tower was added in 1540.

Much of the interior was destroyed by fire in 1544 but it was again quickly rebuilt within six years and then expanded over the next century, when a larger organ was added and the clock built on the South Tower. It became the aim of every famous resident to be buried behind the gold altar.

However Kant, as a non-believer, never entered the building and his funeral procession stayed outside. The last restoration of **Kant's tomb** was carried out in 1924 and it was little damaged during the war. It can be seen beside the cathedral wall. (The Nazis left it intact after exhuming his skull to check on Kant's Aryan origins.)

There was minor damage to the cathedral during the French occupation at the beginning of the 19th century, when it was variously used as a stable, a prison and a hospital. Whilst Königsberg expanded in every other field over the next 100 years, it was only between 1903 and 1907 that the cathedral received much needed maintenance and rebuilding. It was the first time it had been cleaned since 1695 and many frescos were discovered as a result. The devotion of the population to the cathedral is best summarised in the writings of the poet Agnes Miegel, born in Königsberg in 1879, who stayed until she was forced to flee in February 1945. 'You are always part of my life, like my father and my mother. Your bells wake me in the morning and send me to sleep in the evening.'

The RAF raids in August 1944 seriously damaged the cathedral but in no way destroyed it. The library, for instance, remained intact. There was no direct hit but fire spread from neighbouring buildings, which destroyed all the woodwork and led to the collapse of the roof. The site was abandoned after the war and some of the bricks were casually looted; others were specifically taken for use in various Soviet cities. The cobbles from the surrounding streets were relaid in Moscow's Red Square. The surrounding area was cleared in 1972, probably in preparation for the destruction of the site.

During the Soviet era, there was considerable dispute about the future of this ruin. Some felt it symbolised both the powerlessness and irrelevance of both Germany and religion. Others felt it was an inappropriate reminder of these former phenomena. In Kaliningrad en route to Britain in 1973, President Brezhnev certainly expressed his eagerness to destroy it, having just four years previously ordered the destruction of the castle ruins. Perhaps it was Kant's tomb that saved it, a complete and restored monument to the precursor to Marxist philosophy, beside a ruin to what he opposed.

Much of the vaulting collapsed in 1975 and some minimal restoration was done in 1976. Arguments went on as late as 1994, well after the demise of the Soviet Union, when views were still expressed that the whole area should become a sculpture park. However, that year saw the first service being held since the war and the burial of joint Russian and German capsules which included a memorial to the suffering of the German population. Four bells were restored during the following year and since then the roof has been completed and a museum has opened in the South Tower. An orthodox chapel has been built in the North Tower, a compromise from the original Russian demands that the whole cathedral should be orthodox. At the time of writing in mid-2000, work was concentrating on the interior windows and walls. The baptistry was completed early in 2000 with four stained-glass windows. The original designs were followed by local Russian glaziers and they depict John the Baptist, Konrad von Tierberg, the founder of Königsberg and Martin Luther. Services and concerts now take place regularly. With considerable local enthusiasm and ample German money, the cathedral should be completely restored by 2004.

The **Cathedral Museum** already occupies several rooms in the South Tower and is regularly being extended. It shows the 1903–07 rebuilding plans, as well as others proposed earlier which were not in fact carried out. It also outlines plans for the next few years, including archaeological excavations under the former castle and university. One room is devoted to Königsberg city life around the cathedral and shows an extensive china and postcard collection. Several rooms are devoted to Kant. It is fortunate how much material on these subjects survived during the Soviet period or was taken west by refugees in 1945. The whole collection is well lit and generously displayed. Labelling is, however, only in German and Russian.

German visitors always look east from Kneiphof island, to the former Lindenstrasse, now Oktyabraskaya. The remaining brick building facing the bridge dates from 1905 and was a Jewish orphanage for around 45 children. The Synagogue, which had been built a decade earlier, was destroyed by the Nazis on *Kristallnacht*, November 9 1938.

The street was also famous for the house of Käthe Kollwitz, an artist born there in 1867. Although she moved to Berlin in 1891, she kept close links with Königsberg until the rise of the Nazis. She never made a secret of her left-wing views, and her paintings – similar in many ways to those of the English artist L S Lowry – show the suffering of working-class people under various regimes. She was invited to Moscow in 1927 as part of a delegation to the celebrations of the tenth anniversary of the Russian Revolution. She courageously stayed in Germany during the Nazi era, feeling she would be more of an embarrassment by staying than by going into exile. Her work was banned from public exhibition during this time. Despite this political background, her house was not restored during the Soviet period and she was never mentioned in local publications of that era.

Looking south from the island, the former **Stock Exchange**, painted in a light-blue pastel, stands out on the riverbank. As a contrast to German Gothic and Soviet concrete, it is a welcome Florentine Renaissance façade and was built in the 1870s, when the town's prosperity was at its height. Like the cathedral, it is built on a foundation of deep piles, the exact number used was 2,202 and they are mostly 4.5m (15ft) deep. Statues were erected beside the four corners of the building, which depicted four continents, and hence the extent of Königsberg trade at the time, but these did not survive the war. The ground floor of the building is now a pretentious restaurant, Monetny Devor, one of the few places where the local rich like to flaunt themselves. Unlike their counterparts in other Russian cities, successful business people in Kaliningrad tend to enjoy their wealth discreetly.

Walking north, back across the river, an incomplete Soviet-era office block, the **'Monster'**, as it is usually now called, dominates the skyline. It is built over the foundations of the famous castle (*Schloss* in German) that has haunted contemporary Kaliningrad. The castle dated from 1257 and dominated the

German town throughout its history. All major ceremonies of state took place in its main reception room. Peter the Great stayed there and Frederick the Great accepted the surrender of the Russian Army there at the end of the Seven Years War. In 1904 Russian and German Social Democrats were tried there, accused of smuggling Lenin's fledging journal *Iskra* ('The Spark') into Tsarist Russia. The castle housed the Prussian Museum and then, during World War II, the Amber Chamber, which had been brought back from Tsarskoye Selo, outside Leningrad, by German troops. The museum curator, Dr Alfred Rohde, vowed he would not leave Königsberg in 1945 without his treasure but neither he nor the Chamber was ever seen again. One mosaic panel was finally rediscovered in Bremen in 1997 and was sent back to Russia in April 2000 in return for paintings taken by the former Soviet government which had belonged to the Bremen Art Gallery before the war. A small panel has been rebuilt for the Amber Museum in Königsberg but a full restoration is planned for Tsarskoye Selo by 2003.

The former Amber Museum, which was also housed in the castle, boasted about 100,000 items. 11,000 of these were fortunately taken to Göttingen University in late 1944 for safe keeping and therefore survived. The rest of the collection was either destroyed or disappeared.

Much of the correspondence between Moscow and courageous local architects about the proposed destruction of the castle and a suitable replacement has recently come to light. To the politicians, the building represented 'centuries of German militarism and plunder' which should be replaced by a large modern civic building to display Soviet power in what had been the heart of the German city. The political activities of the exiled East Prussians in West Germany clearly influenced the final decision to remove all traces of the castle in 1969. They used the castle tower as the logo on all their campaign literature that lobbied vocally and frequently for the then West German government to continue its policy of regarding East Prussia as being 'temporarily under Soviet administration' rather than as being lost for good. It therefore made political if not aesthetic sense for this symbol of former German power to be eliminated. Architects pointed out the many historical links the building had with Russia, as outlined above, and how a Soviet war memorial could be incorporated into a restored building. Their pleas were ignored and a budget agreed for a new town hall.

The 25-year saga that followed showed Soviet planning and political bigotry at its very worst. An initial budget of 1.6 million roubles (about £500,000 or US$1 million at the official rate of exchange in 1969) was agreed for a 16-storey building. Over the first two years, around 1,100 concrete pillars, each eight metres in length, were dug into the marshy ground beside the castle. Cynics were soon to point out that they did not have the firmness of those laid by the Germans 700 years before. Twenty workers were employed on the site between 1972 and 1976 and they completed six storeys. The next ten stories took a further five years so the basic structure was finished in 1981. By then costs had increased to 9 million roubles, a surprisingly capitalist problem in a country that had been cut off from a market economy for 30 years. There was no money for moving the local government and none for installing electricity and heating. In 1988 money was found to furnish half the building but this work was not completed by the time the Soviet Union collapsed in 1991.

RETURN TO KÖNIGSBERG

My family left East Prussia in 1938 when I was aged 7: refugees from Hitler's Germany. We were to settle in New Zealand, on the opposite side of the world. My father had a globe of the world, and I was worried about where we were going, because looking at New Zealand on the globe, it seemed people had to walk upside down. My father said that wouldn't be a problem, and it wasn't; not being able to speak the same language was a greater worry, for a while. But New Zealand turned out to be a great choice for our new home.

Exactly 60 years later I returned to the place of my birth for the first time. My wife and I flew to Vilnius, then were driven to Kaliningrad, the city where I had been to kindergarten and (for two years) to school. As we crossed the border and moved deeper into the former East Prussia a number of memories came back. The light blue of the sky, the shape of the clouds, captured by pictures my grandfather used to paint, some of which we still have. Farmers hay-making, stacking the hay in round haystacks and transporting it by horse-drawn carts. Storks nesting on telegraph poles, some with large chicks. Swallows. Cobbled streets. As it grew dark, the road sweeping through avenues of trees in the countryside, the headlights catching reflector paint; vague childhood recollections of trips with my grandparents from Königsberg to Insterburg (Chernyakhovsk) to visit my grandparents there. We reach our hotel in Kaliningrad late at night and, despite the excitement, sleep well.

The next day, with our guide, we set out to look at Kaliningrad. The guide assures us that the trams have been replaced, but they seem to have been modelled on the ones I knew. I have a book with me, *Königsberg in 144 Pictures*, and recognise many of the buildings, although others have been destroyed. Some of the streets are familiar to me, Steindamm where my father had his office. Here the buildings have all gone, but the former shape of the streets is clear and unchanged. We come to the Hufenallee with its distinctive winding stretch and instantly I know where we are. I say to our guide, we are close to the Zoo – around the next corner we come to the Zoo entrance through which I was often taken as a child; it seems unchanged. A few minutes later, an unforgettable indescribable moment, we are outside the apartment building where my family was living in 1938.

Thomas Eichelbaum

Nothing has been done to the building since and at the time of writing in summer 2000, there are still no plans for it, not even just to tear it down.

Turning right along Moskovsky for about 100m, leaving behind the Monster and the Kaliningrad Hotel, the first major building on the right hand side is the **Art Gallery**. Soviet money fortunately did not run out here and the gallery opened in 1989, so just in time to give a final overview of art throughout the USSR at that point. Every former Soviet republic is represented, both by paintings and by applied arts. Ceramics and glass are both well covered, but more surprising are the copies of imperial china and lacquer. This style of china with its gold leaf represents a style of life to which few in Kaliningrad can or could ever relate. The gallery holds many exhibitions of children's art. They are now encouraged to paint Königsberg as well as Kaliningrad. The exploits of the Teutonic Knights provide ample material for them to portray happily. One of the most famous local artists is Boris Bulkagov, born in 1944, whose pictures are marked by his almost total use of dark colours.

Cross Moskovsky and head towards the Lower Lake, called *Schlossteich* or 'Castle Lake' in German times. The surroundings of the lake had been made communal in 1900 and the path around it built in 1937. The History and Art Museum, on the eastern side of the lake, can easily be identified as a former German concert hall.

The nondescript five-storey building on the western side used to be the town's most famous hotel, the Park, where on different occasions both Hitler and Molotov regularly stayed. Because of the notoriety of its former guests, this is now an office building.

The **History and Art Museum** (Историкохудожественный музей) has been totally transformed since the Soviet period. Most labels are in English and German. It originally consisted of the remains of the Prussian Museum collection, which had previously been housed in the castle. This was largely an archaeological collection, so did not cause political problems. It in fact enabled Soviet historians to claim a Slavic rather than a German origin for many of the artefacts. The museum has recently undergone considerable expansion, showing not only extensive material from pre-war Königsberg, but also from the early Soviet period in the 1950s. One can only hope that what is portrayed as a typical apartment from the 1950s is no longer typical of homes in the town outside. Fabrics, furniture, paintings and crockery from both eras have been salvaged. Some 'bourgeois' exhibits such as refined table linen and advertisements are displayed, as well as examples of the inflation banknotes from 1923 when they had to be constantly recycled and overprinted. Programmes and layouts are displayed for the major annual trade fair, the *Ostmesse*, which took place every autumn between 1920 and 1941.

The Königsberg room in other respects still shows considerable political bias. Far more is shown of the rise of the Communist Party than that of the Nazi Party, but no attempt is made to assess the communists' failure to overcome the Nazis in the years prior to 1933. The banners, the photographs and the pamphlets all date from earlier. Some items would seem more appropriate for a car-boot sale than for a serious town museum. Beer mugs and ashtrays seem an odd choice of exhibit but anything gathered from former Königsberg has a magical significance for those who still remember it.

The Soviet room is now frank about issues that were formerly taboo. There are photographs of the destruction of the castle, and portraits of both Stalin and Khrushchev, leaders whose pictures were not shown elsewhere in the later Soviet times. Other exhibits have not been changed since the 1980s and are reminiscent of the Moscow 'Exhibition of Economic Achievements'. Several spacemen came from Kaliningrad so photographs of them with the Politburo abound and a display case is devoted to the presents given to them by visiting foreign statesmen, such as a cigar from Fidel Castro and a ring from Le Duan, the Vietnamese Prime Minister. The **shop and stalls** within the museum offer a variety and value impossible to find elsewhere in the town. They offer good selections of amber, lacquer, woodwork and paintings and some books likely to be of interest to foreigners.

Cross the lake on the footbridge and note the modest **war memorial** to the left. It commemorates Colonel Tulan and his French regiment that fought as part of the Soviet air force in 1942–44. In February 1944 the regiment was named Normandy Neman, the Neman (or Niemen) being the river that traditionally divided Russia from Germany (and which now divides Lithuania from Kaliningrad). The memorial notes that the regiment made 5,000 sorties, fought in 869 battles and destroyed 273 German aircraft.

Next cross Proletarskaya which leads into the **university**. The buildings here date from the 19th century and were designed by August Stüler, one of the pupils of Karl Friedrich Schinkel, Germany's most famous architect of the early 19th century. They were all completed within a year between 1858 and 1859. Although seriously damaged at the end of the war, they could have been restored to show the original Italian façade but this was not done. It is necessary to wander inside for any memories of the 19th century. In the square which the university buildings surround, old sculptures are being restored and new ones being built. The original statue of Kant disappeared at the end of the war, but Marion Dönhoff paid for a replacement to be provided in 1992.

In the centre of the square is the entrance to the **Bunker Museum**, (Блиндаж Ляша, open daily 10.00–17.00), sometimes called the Lasch Bunker after General Lasch, who had it built as his headquarters for the final defence of Königsberg in 1945. Several of the rooms are much as he would have left them on April 10 1945 after signing the capitulation and surrendering himself to what would turn out to be ten years imprisonment. The heating pipes, the telephone wires and the electric cables have all remained intact. When the museum opened in 1967, it provided the only picture of former Königsberg that local residents were allowed to have, with detailed models of the town layout and of the military formations. Even a German slogan (*Wir kapitulieren nie* – 'We will never surrender'), daubed on a wall, is included. The smallest exhibit is a ticket for the last train to Berlin that left on January 22 1945. The leaflets dropped by the Russians stressed the futility of continued fighting and promised food supplies and family reunions to all who surrendered. Recently the museum has been extended to show the burial sites of troops from both sides.

Leave the museum in a westerly direction towards Lenin Prospekt. On the far side of the road is the town's major supermarket, open daily until 21.00. Turning left takes one back to the Hotel Kaliningrad after 100 metres. Readers of Russian will find the **kiosks** along here a good source of books, maps and magazines.

Another site within walking distance of the hotel is the **Oceanography Museum** (Музей истории мирового океана, open daily except Monday, 11.00–17.00) based in and around the ship *Vityaz*. This is now permanently moored on the Pregel about 700 metres from the hotel. During 2000 and 2001 the exhibitions are being considerably extended and will include new buildings on the shore. *Vityaz* was built as a cargo boat in Bremerhaven in 1939 and launched with the name *Mars*, after a river in western Germany rather than the planet. It was never used as a cargo carrier, being taken over as a troop ship on the outbreak of war. In March and April 1945 it made several trips between Pillau, the port on the coast nearest to Königsberg, and Denmark, rescuing about 20,000 civilians from the oncoming Russians. When the British liberated Denmark from the Germans, they took over the boat and renamed it *Empire Forth* but it only stayed in British hands until February 1946 when it was 'returned' to the Russians, being seen as based in territory now belonging to them. This British name would have been most appropriate for the Russians in view of the territory they seized at the end of World War II, but they renamed it firstly *Equator* and then *Vityaz* ('Noble warrior').

It was moved to Vladivostok and between 1949 and 1979 made constant oceanographic expeditions to the Pacific Ocean. It also made pioneering visits to Osaka and to San Francisco in 1958, the first in each case since the start of the Cold War. Jacques Cousteau was invited on board in Mombasa in 1967, again a symbol of an easier political climate. Its last expedition finished in Kaliningrad harbour where it would rot for ten years, becoming known as the 'rusty tin' until a restoration programme began in 1990. This was completed in 1994, partially with the help of surviving members of the *Mars* crew. (Meanwhile another *Vityaz* was built in 1981 and is now part of the Russian Black Sea fleet based at Novorossisk.)

The exhibitions are not limited to the life of the ship. One room covers the history of oceanography, the laboratories ships included, and two earlier boats that carried the name *Vityaz*. Pictures show the startled reaction of the inhabitants of New Guinea in 1870 to a white man when the captain of an earlier *Vityaz* landed. They assumed he had come from the moon, as his skin was a similar colour. The researches beneath the Pacific, including the measurement of the Marianas Trench, are covered extensively. The new political climate means that life on board in any era can be shown honestly, and where appropriate, ridiculed. The whims and needs of all former commanders, Tsarist, Nazi or Soviet are not hidden, be they for an absurdly large piano, a shredding machine or a portrait of Lenin. Mess rooms, too, with appropriate memorabilia, have been rebuilt. The museum authorities hope to set up a British room, if enough material from the 1945–46 period can be provided.

The 60th anniversary in 1999 of the building of the ship was a suitable pretext for further enlargement of the collections. One theme is 'Maritime Königsberg' showing the expansion of the harbour, firstly in 1901 when the canal to the sea at Pillau was widened, and secondly in the 1920s when Königsberg became eastern Germany's major port, following the loss of Danzig and Memel (now Gdańsk in Poland and Klaipėda in Lithuania respectively) at the end of World War I. Many of the buildings dating from those times, such as the grain silos, can still be seen along the riverside. In 2000 a miniatures gallery was added with replicas of ships from Egypt, Greece, Japan and Fiji. More familiar to British visitors will be the models of the *Revenge* and of Elizabeth I knighting Francis Drake. Columbus and Queen Isabella have not been forgotten, nor has the *Santa Maria*. April 2000 also saw the conversion of several cabins into displays of coral reefs, sharks jaws and underwater geological discoveries.

In July 2000 the opening to the public of a B-413 submarine greatly increased the scope of the museum. Originally built in 1969, it then travelled almost as much as *Vityaz*, being a frequent visitor to Cuba. The B-413 was the Soviet answer to the NATO Foxtrot submarines, being able to carry 22 torpedoes and to launch them from a depth of 100 metres. Only the small and the agile will be able to enjoy the displays on board as the interior has been maintained as closely as possible to the original. It is hard to believe that it housed 80 men for three month journeys; only the captain and the KGB agent had single rooms. An exhibition honestly portrays the history of the Russian/Soviet navy from 1834 until the present day. Tragedy and triumph are covered in equal measure.

Planned additions in 2001 will see the display of the skeleton of a sperm-whale 16 metres long which was caught in 1974 and the rebuilding of a coastal lighthouse. Global warming is a theme also soon to be covered by an exhibition. A space centre will give a 21st century perspective to a site that until now has understandably looked backwards. This new centre will commemorate in part the many spacemen who have come from the Kaliningrad region. Soon a whole day will be needed to do justice to the site.

Further afield

Many other sites within the city are just too far to walk from the Kaliningrad Hotel but can be easily reached by bus or taxi. Tour operators abroad can pre-book English-speaking guides with their own cars and this is the most convenient way to visit other sites in the town and also for visits along the coast. The following itinerary can be done in a long day, or be divided into two days.

The first port of call must be at the **Amber Museum** (Музей янтарья, open daily, except Monday, 10.00–17.30) housed in the Dohna Tower, one of six similar 19th-century fortifications that still dominate the city skyline. General Dohna fought against Napoleon. It replaced an earlier museum, which had been beside the mines at Yantarny on the coast. A few items come from the pre-war museum, which had been housed in the former castle.

Amber has formed the one thread that binds together the history of the region. Since 90% of the world's amber production comes from this area, its value was an incentive for many generations of conquerors and would-be conquerors. The Prussian tribes traded it with the Romans, who saw magical and practical value in it. Tacitus and Pliny the Elder both refer to it and gladiators wore it. Amber would become an important ingredient in medicine, in agricultural fertilisers, and in varnish. It would strengthen fishing nets and be used in fumigation. The Museum therefore presents a two thousand year artistic and political history of the region through the 6,000 amber products displayed. The natural history goes back millions of years to the formation of fossilised resin, which is the basis of amber.

The most interesting exhibits are those from the Soviet period; models from Aesop's fables such as *The Fox and the Grapes* are a surprising legacy but more obvious ones are the model Kremlins, dams, pylons, nuclear icebreakers and power stations with smoking chimneys. Examples of gifts to foreign dignitaries include jewellery boxes with the hammer and sickle emblem and statues of Soviet leaders. None have been deposed from the museum so Lenin, Stalin and Khrushchev sit peacefully side by side. There are some replicas of famous pieces in the Hermitage and Kremlin collections. The largest of these weigh over a kilo. Clearly the lost Amber Room cannot be forgotten in these surroundings, so some of the original panelling has been copied and paintings show how the complete original looked when it was displayed at Tsarskoye Selo, outside St Petersburg.

Do not miss the **museum shop** before leaving. Its lack of taste rivals that of much of the collection and the use of amber dust enables 'pictures' to be sold very cheaply. Leonardo de Caprio and Diana, Princess of Wales both cost little more than £1/US$1.50 in early 2000.

The museum is on Vasilevsky Square, named after the commander responsible for the final victory over the Germans. The **memorial** at the centre of the square commemorates this victory, in particular 216 Heroes of the Soviet Union and 20 who received this award twice. On the opposite side of the road from the museum is a **distillery**; its shop sells vodka liqueurs at prices low even by Kaliningrad standards. Perhaps it is just as well nobody can really tell how dependent the local economy is on drink and cigarettes smuggled out to Poland and then on to the rest of Europe.

Proceeding west from the museum, along Chernyakhovskovo, the **Central Market** (Центральный рынок) is on the right hand side of the road after about 800m. Between the First and Second Wars, the halls housed the famous *Ostmesse*, an annual trade fair which brought together major traders from East Prussia with their opposite numbers in the Baltic states and the Soviet Union. Being the largest building in Königsberg, it was also the centre for all political rallies during both the Weimar Republic (1920–33) and the subsequent Nazi era. President Ebert opened the building and the first fair in 1920 and Hitler and Himmler spoke here on several occasions.

Now it has a largely local function and for tourists gives a clear indication of what is available and what is fashionable. The 2000 stands within the halls are clearly regulated with prices listed and satisfactory hygiene. Those outside bring together sellers and buyers both of whom look equally desperate. A guide is useful since, when prompted, an otherwise banal stand can suddenly produce caviar or silk at prices much lower than elsewhere. Good picnic ingredients available here include German sausage, Polish ham, Lithuanian fruit, local cheeses and the famous Russian black bread. Few tourists can take advantage of all the fresh fish that arrives here at least once a day.

Chernyakhovskovo continues to **Ploshchad Pobedy** (Площадь Победы; 'Victory Square') the former Hansaplatz, which Gauleiter Erich Koch renamed after himself in 1933. It had by then become the business and administration centre of the town. On the north side of the square, a dominating statue of Lenin makes it clear who are now the masters here but he will soon be overshadowed by the first Orthodox cathedral now being built in Kaliningrad. Boris Yeltsin laid the foundation stone. For the time being, there is a small wooden Orthodox chapel at the side of the building site. There are no chairs as believers stand through the service. In the garden to the southeast of the square stands a statue of Mother Russia; she replaced Stalin on this plinth in 1974.

The former **North Station/Nordbahnhof** built in 1930, still functions as such but it now also includes offices of several government departments and private businesses. Foreign businesses such as the SAS Scandinavian Airlines office and the Hamburg Chamber of Commerce are in a new building behind the station on Sovietsky Prospekt (Советский проспект). The town hall building on the south side of the square dates from 1923 and is one of very few to have served the same function both in German and in Soviet/Russian times.

Leaving Victory Square to the west, along Prospekt Mira (Проспект Мира; 'Peace Avenue') note first the bronze **statue** of the fighting bulls on the right-hand side of the road. They are the work of a sculptor August Gaul whose bronze animals became famous all over Germany before World War I. In early Soviet days the statue was moved to the zoo, but it was returned here to its original location in the late 1970s. Local people now read a contemporary theme into the statue, seeing it as a representation of Kaliningrad locked into battle with Moscow. Behind the statue note the baroque entrance of the former courthouse which dates from 1913. Beside the courthouse are the former postal headquarters constructed in 1924. This building now houses the senior staff of the Baltic Fleet so is one of the best maintained in the whole town centre.

The next major building on the right hand side is the Drama Theatre, built in 1927 but given its current bolshoi façade by the Soviet regime. In the six years prior to the Nazi regime every German actor of note played here and the Soviets continued the high standards, once it was finally reopened in 1980. On the other side of the road is a statue of the German writer Friedrich Schiller (1759–1805) which was allowed to stay during the Soviet period, probably because his work was regarded as very 'progressive'. A rather implausible story is told to explain its survival at the end of the war: the words 'don't shoot' were allegedly daubed across it in both German and Russian.

Prospekt Mira now widens and soon the entrance to the **zoo** (Зоопарк) comes up on the right hand side. It is open daily at 09.00, closing at 21.00 between May and September, at 17.00 during other months. It was founded in 1896 and is the only institution in Königsberg/Kaliningrad to have had a continuous history through German, Soviet and now Russian times. It might well be the world's first theme park; its early posters were decades ahead of their time, the funfair was always as crucial as the collection of animals and no secret was ever made of its commercial intent. Slot machines competed with donkey rides, cycle races and tennis tournaments. There were free family days when cooking facilities would be provided, thereby encouraging long stays and extensive patronage of the fairground attractions. Within two years of its opening, it sold 25,000 annual season tickets, a present for which every young Königsberger yearned at Christmas. Its flamboyant first director Hermann Claass stayed in charge until his death in 1914, never letting his commercial flair interfere with the expansion and maintenance of the collection. Within a year of the opening there were 983 animals and by 1910 this number increased to 2,126, including two Siberian tigers donated by Moscow Zoo.

It closed on the outbreak of war in August 1914 but popular demand and the elimination of any threat from Russia enabled it to reopen in July 1918, before the end of that conflict. It was completely rebuilt during the 1930s and these buildings largely remain despite the zoo being a battleground in April 1945. The zoo stayed open throughout the war this time and the Soviet government even presented two elephants in 1940, while the cynical Nazi–Soviet Pact was still in effect. Annual season tickets were printed for 1945 and were sold from Christmas 1944 until the following March. The director throughout the war was Dr Hans-Georg Thienemann whose father Johannes was founder of the bird sanctuary at Rossitten (see page 186).

Many stories circulate about the number of animals who survived through

May 1945 – most of course were killed by the starving residents. Four is the most quoted figure, representing a hippopotamus, a deer, a fox and a badger. Several Russian soldiers tried to feed the hippopotamus which had apparently lost its appetite. Conventional nourishment failed, but a fortnight of vodka, allegedly four litres a day, succeeded in reviving it. The hippopotamus is now therefore the zoo's logo. In the midst of the tragedy that engulfed Königsberg in the summer of 1945, it is good to find one amusing story.

The zoo reopened in 1947, it is claimed with a collection of 2,000 animals, though this figure is now doubted. For the local population, it is again a major attraction although they must feel frustrated at the rather run-down air it now presents. 300,000 come each year and a pet shop has been added to the traditional attractions. With a brochure printed in colloquial English, it is, however, well in advance of other Kaliningrad tourist sites in attracting foreign visitors. They are promised 'baboons with colourful bottoms' and 'apes who so closely resemble humans that they look like someone you have probably met before.' Hermann Claass would be proud of the marketing flair shown by his Russian successors.

Almost opposite the zoo south of Prospekt Mira is the **Cosmonaut Memorial**, its circular format with the space in between portraying the journeys around the globe that Kaliningrad's most famous sons accomplished in the 1970s. One, Alexci Leonov, was the first to leave a spaceship whilst it was in orbit. Another, Victor Patzayei was killed in a failed landing when his rocket returned to earth.

Leaving the zoo and continuing along Prospekt Mira out of town, Germany begins to take over the architecture from the Soviet Union. After 200m on the left, the **Luisenkirche** makes this point emphatically. It was built around 1900, paid for largely by one benefactor Louis Grosskopf. He founded a cigar factory in 1857 but expanded the business so successfully that by 1900 he was employing 400 people there and had opened 18 shops around the town. The consecration of the church in 1901 commemorated the 200th anniversary of the crowning of King Frederick I in 1701. The German community worshipped here until 1948 when it was turned into a storeroom for gardening tools used in the surrounding park. Its conversion into a puppet theatre in 1976 possibly saved it from destruction as that was the last year in which German churches were still being pulled down.

A further kilometre along the same road brings up on the left the first new church to be built since the war. It uses the German name **Auferstehungskirche** ('Church of the Resurrection') and was completed in 1999 on land that had earlier been a German cemetery. The large Lutheran exile community in Germany had wanted to re-establish a church in Kaliningrad, theirs having been the predominant religion in the former East Prussia since the 16th century – both Martin Luther's son and daughter had been active in the area and were buried in Königsberg. Every former church considered for this gave rise to considerable difficulties. The current Russian organisation was in some cases not willing to move, in others the bureaucratic and financial hurdles in rebuilding turned out to be too great.

The church now serves a local Russian community, the Volga Germans, who have settled in Kaliningrad with the hope of eventually being resettled in Germany, and the increasingly large number of Germans who now work in

Kaliningrad. Attending a service or a concert, or seeing all the voluntary activities that take place during the week shows how strongly German/Russian reconciliation can work. The altar is of great significance, being assembled from bricks taken out of eight different ruined churches.

The oldest church in East Prussia, the **Juditterkirche**, is another kilometre or so along Prospekt Pobedya, but on the right hand side. The Juditter suburb, (renamed Mendeleevo (Менделеева)) was as sought after by successful Germans as it now is by successful Russians. The area offers space, greenery, cleanliness and above all privacy. The public parks near to the church rivalled the zoo as an attraction for children. Reminiscences from former East Prussians tell of collecting anemones in spring and acorns in autumn, of climbing trees, of open-air concerts, and the climax of the afternoon, buying peppermint drops and lemonade at the sweet-shop. The church dates originally from the 13th century with the tower being added at the turn of the 14th/15th century. It was extensively restored in 1906 and this revealed wall paintings which had been hidden for centuries. Although the church was totally untouched by the war and fighting, much of the intricate woodwork was plundered in the immediate aftermath and then 35 years of complete neglect left little of the former interior. Germans were allowed to continue worshipping here until their expulsion in 1948.

The ruins were given over to the Orthodox Church in 1984 and a basic restoration was completed in 1988. Services started in 1986, the first to be held in the Kaliningrad region since 1948. Official atheism had therefore lasted 38 years. It would take another two or three years before any other churches reopened. Given the vigorous support that the local Orthodox community gives to the church, the building is unlikely ever to return into Lutheran hands. However, the German cemetery beside the church is being slowly restored and a memorial plaque is planned to all Germans killed in Königsberg at the end of the war.

Another visit should be made within the town and that is to the **Brandenburg Gate** (it has kept the same name in Russian) situated south of the river on Ulitsa Bagrationa (Улица Багратиона) near to the main railway station. Architecturally, it has nothing in common with its Berlin namesake although being as large, trams and cars also go through it. Like six other similar gates that date from the early 19th century, it is a redbrick structure built so well that it survived both the RAF bombs and the subsequent Soviet onslaught. It even retains two statues, of General von Boyen and General von Aster, two prominent 19th century commanders.

If Lenin dominates the square in front of the North Station, Kalinin has to have his glory here in front of the **South Station** (Южный Вокзал). As most visitors, whether local or international, will arrive here or at the neighbouring bus station, he can perhaps claim to be more prominent. There are now slow attempts to bring back some of the fame that the station rightly deserved in German times although a wooden roof still takes the place of the former glass one. A small **railway museum** was opened in summer 2000 with two restored steam engines and the promise of more.

The current home of the Kaliningrad Philharmonic Orchestra is in the former **Kirche zur Heiligen Familie** ('Church of the Holy Family') known as Philharmonia in Russian. It is on the same road as the Brandenburg Gate, Ulitsa Bagrationa, and it is a walk of about 700m from there or from the station.

Originally one of four Catholic churches in Königsberg built around 1900, it was saved from serious damage at the end of the war because it was surrounded by narrow streets. It therefore avoided the worst of the fighting and the bombardments. In the early 1970s, whilst other churches in Kaliningrad were still being pulled down, restoration started here and in 1980 it opened as a concert hall. An organ was added in 1982 and good standards of maintenance have been upheld ever since, together with equally good standards of catering in the crypt-café underneath.

OUTSIDE THE CITY

If time only allows for a one-day trip outside the town of Kaliningrad, this must be to the coast and along the Curonian Spit (Куршская коса) towards the Lithuanian border. It should be done by car and with a guide since it involves a number of stops and signing in many places is not good. Such a trip can start in **Yantarny** (Янтарный), which will very likely be the backbone of the Kaliningrad area's economy for the next 100 years, when the amber mine there is expected to run out. Known as Palmnicken in German times, the village is on the coast about 35 kilometres from Kaliningrad. Its wealth is well disguised since the village houses have a forlorn look and its roads are poorly maintained. Bomb damage was minimal so older German tourists can recognise the layout and again enjoy Sunday afternoons along the beach.

There is now just one large open-cast mine in use, producing about 450 tons of amber a year, about 90% of world production. Water has now seeped into the others, although Russian children follow their German predecessors in collecting amber pieces from the beach when they have been washed up after storms.

There is a somewhat precarious viewing point from which the whole mine can be seen; strong footwear is necessary to reach it and an equally strong constitution to tolerate the dire environmental pollution that it causes. The site was privatised in 1990 and then re-nationalised three years later with the hope of returning most of the profits into government hands. The Baltic Germans in the 13th century had similarly tried to control this trade and although they publicly hanged private traders, they were as unsuccessful at controlling it as their contemporary Russian successors. A small **shop** near the site is sometimes open for the purchase of amber; otherwise the Amber Museum in Kaliningrad is the best source.

If ever a reward could be made for the town in the Kaliningrad region least affected by the Soviet occupation it must go to **Rauschen** or as it is still officially called **Svetlogorsk** (Светлогорск). Its role as a seaside resort did not alter, and having official Soviet status as a spa town, money could always be found for maintenance. The Russian name translates as 'bright city', the German one as 'to rustle'. Both are equally appropriate for a well-designed spacious town full of trees and shrubs. A good regular train service operates from Kaliningrad and the town is small enough to be explored *in toto* on foot. It was the introduction of this train service in 1900 that brought day-trippers from Königsberg to Rauschen and so made it less exclusive than it had been in the 19th century. The Soviet Union, rather than Russia, intrudes with the street names. Marx, Lenin, Kalinin, Gagarin and the October Revolution are all remembered but, unique for the region, the statue of Lenin has been removed. Perhaps he may in due course be replaced by Prussia's King Friedrich

Wilhelm I who first made the town famous in the early 18th century. Otherwise one could be in any small German town on the Baltic coast. At weekends, the town is as lively in the winter as it is in the summer. Its year-round population is around 4,000 compared to 2,500 before the war, but this trebles in the summer season when Russians come from all over the federation for their holidays and for medical treatment. Svetlogorsk likes to think of itself as the Sotchi of the north, rivalling this Black Sea resort in its facilities and in its prestige.

The red-brick Gothic church was designed by August Stüler, famous for many grander buildings in Berlin. It was consecrated in 1907, converted into a sports centre after the war but was then given to the Orthodox Church in 1990. Chamber music concerts are held there throughout the year. A second church was built in 1994 as a memorial chapel to 25 children killed when a military aircraft crashed into their kindergarten in May 1972. Following normal Soviet practice, no official mention of the crash was made at the time. The photographs inside are of the children and their teachers, but there are none of the air crew who also all died.

The promenade by the sea, with its funfair, sundial and stairway decorated with mosaics has survived largely intact. Some villas and sanatoria are newly built but most of the grand wooden villas with their intricate window designs and elaborate roofs date from around 1900. They are all at a discreet distance from each other, allowing for extensive shrubbery and flower gardens between them. Some are now in private hands, some still belong to state organisations, but all can be proud of their paintwork and varnish.

Sculpture from Rauschen's most famous artist, Hermann Brachert, (1890–1972) has survived throughout the town. He fell out of favour with the Nazi regime on account of the pessimistic tone of many of his pieces. They did not allow him to teach or exhibit but fortunately they did not destroy his work and some of his most moving sculptures date from that era. He worked with equal effect in marble, limestone and bronze. His house in the neighbouring village of Otradnoye (Отрадное), formerly Georgenswalde, is now a museum.

Oktyabrskaya Ulitsa (Октябрьская Улица) is the main shopping street and it is very clear which shops are for the German tourists and which for the local population. Number 13 has the best bookshop in the whole region with excellent and cheap English–Russian dictionaries. The street also has a very Soviet cafeteria with tin trays and poor lighting. As a full meal from an extensive menu can, however, be had for about £0.25/US$0.40), it seems churlish to complain. Those who do can turn instead to a pretentious café with the surprising name of the Lame Horse (Хромая лошадь) where a mediocre German meal can be obtained for around £6/US$9.00. Cynics might claim that 'lame' refers to the level of service and cuisine.

A 20km drive from Svetlogorsk is needed to reach the start of the Curonian Spit at **Zelenogradsk** (Зеленоградск), formerly Cranz. Not being granted any special status during the Soviet period and having been the scene of serious fighting in April 1945, what was once a glamorous, vibrant resort is now a neglected village best driven through as quickly as possible. The young people drifting around the streets clearly do not represent the success stories of the new regime. The Russian name translates as 'Green City' which perhaps aptly sums up the weeds growing in the streets and the moss that has gripped the former villas. A grotesque concrete walkway along the coast offers no consolation after seeing the main street through the town.

The **Curonian Spit**, however, will without doubt be worth the drive from Königsberg. Visitors with more time may well consider continuing their tour to Nida, just over the Lithuanian border. It is also possible to start a tour in Nida as Kaliningrad tour operators can bring visas over the border and then drive back their passengers.

The spit is an 80km tongue of land which divides the Baltic Sea from the Curonian Lagoon. Half the territory belongs to Kaliningrad and half to Lithuania. The history of the Spit shows nature at its most brutal. Humans fought the elements rather than each other in this area. Most visitors travelling on a calm summer's day will see an alternation of dunes and forests, interspersed with the occasional village. It is hard to believe that a graveyard of whole villages lies beneath the sea and sand just a few hundred metres away.

That nature was finally controlled here is due to one man, Franz Epha (1828–1904) whose plans for forestation took 40 years to implement between 1860 and 1900, but which finally made the area secure. The Prussian regime encouraged the work initially to safeguard the road to the end of their empire and also to provide good communications with St Petersburg. If the rail network had developed sooner, this work might never have been carried out. Epha's work has been respected by all the governments that have ruled here since, by Nazis as much as by Communists, and now by the new independent regimes. A sand dune that was named after Epha shortly before he died has retained its name throughout the subsequent century, not being changed in the Soviet era. The isolation of the area at that time also spared it from development so animals roamed at will. Wild boar, beavers and elk now predominate in the pine forests, which take up 71% of the land on the Russian side. The Spit is designated by both Russia and Lithuania as a national park and a small tax is charged for entry by car. Cars were banned from the Spit between 1920 and 1940 so access was then by boat, bicycle or on horseback.

There are two main villages on the Russian side of the Spit between Zelonogradsk and the Lithuanian border, **Lesnoy** (Лесной) and **Rybachy** (Рыбачий), Sarkau and Rossitten in German. In Lesnoy new money flaunts itself behind formidable metal grilles. One of the villas belongs to the Moscow Central Bank. It shows reasonable taste in architecture though one must regret the passing of many of the former more modest houses in the village.

Halfway between Lesnoy and Rybachy is the **Spit Museum**, founded in 1987 in what had formerly been a Communist Party guesthouse. The first German guidebook to the area, produced in 1996, tells visitors not to be put off by the austere concrete exterior and that it really is worth entering. This is true. 1987 was sufficiently into the *glasnost* era for a detailed and honest history of the area to be given. An extensive collection of photographs, models and stuffed animals covers contemporary and past natural history.

More unexpected is the history of the gliding centre which was founded in Rossitten in 1920. This resulted from the ban on motorised aviation in Germany stipulated by the Versailles Treaty at the end of World War I. Although neither German nor Russian historians like to dwell on the matter, there was close cooperation between the USSR and Germany throughout the early interwar period here. Soviet pilots came for training and Germans were in return invited to the Soviet gliding school in the Crimea. There had been similar cooperation between Imperial Germany and Tsarist Russia for a time after 1895 when gliding first began in this area. A recently-erected plaque commemorates a world-record eight-hour flight undertaken in 1925 by a local pilot, Ferdinand Schulz. The inscription, carved in both German and Russian, proclaims that 'gliding should overcome frontiers and bring nations together.'

Seven kilometres further along the road towards Rybachy, the **bird sanctuary** founded by the German Ornithological Society in 1901 continues its work. It welcomes visitors and helpers. It broke an earlier culture amongst the fishing community of killing local birds, mainly crows, for food. Now they were ringed and then released. The first and most famous director, Johannes Thienemann ringed 103 himself in 1903. By 1936 this annual total had reached 140,000. The larger birds included seagulls, sparrow-hawks, kestrels and buzzards. Regular smaller ones were robins, thrushes and wagtails. Thienemann was soon able to work out the migratory routes of the white stork through Hungary, Egypt and Kenya to South Africa. He remained as director until 1929. The German staff all fled in 1945 and it was not until 1956 that the sanctuary was reopened by the Russians. They gave it the name Fringilla, from the Latin for chaffinch which is one of the most common birds to be found there. In 1991 the very precise statistic was provided that 1,672,071 birds had been ringed since the re-opening. Its traps are thought to be the largest in the world, one being 100m deep, 30m wide and 15m high. The birds fly in totally unaware that they are in a trap so around 60,000 can be ringed each year. The traps are relocated each season, facing north in the spring and south in the autumn to catch the birds on both their outward and return migrations. The large nets are renewed each year; song-birds in cages entice the migrants.

In Rybachy/Rossitten itself, several wooden houses have preserved their original 19th century carvings. The main building of interest is the red-brick village church, consecrated in 1873, and like the one in Svetlogorsk/ Rauschen, it was designed by August Stüler. None of the building was ever damaged and the vicarage beside it is still intact. Even the bell and the windows remain. It was not used between 1945 and 1963 when it was taken over by the 'Dawn of Communism' fishing collective as a storage depot for their nets. In 1990 it was given to the Orthodox Church.

The Lithuanian border is a further 16km from Rybachy so this village is an appropriate point to finish the tour. By the summer of 2001 it may well be possible to return from Rybachy to Zelenogradsk by boat along the sea-coast or along the lagoon. Another likely route is across the lagoon to Polessk. This second route would offer a semicircular journey starting to the west of Kaliningrad and then finishing in the east. In the summer of 2000 it was still necessary to retrace one's steps by road but the variety of tracks through the forest or along the dunes offer so many tempting stops that this is hardly an imposition.

Hotels in Svetlogorsk/Rauschen

It is quite possible to visit Kaliningrad on a daily basis from Svetlogorsk by local train or vice versa. Svetlogorsk is developing as a health centre and as a summer holiday resort, both for Russian and for German tourists. It is attractive in winter, too, particularly after a snowfall, as temperatures rarely drop much below freezing point and day-trippers from Kaliningrad keep it lively year-round. The dialling code for Svetlogorsk is 01153 and the '0' is still used when phoning from abroad.

Azur Coast Dynamo 1a, tel: 33108. Singles US$45, doubles US$60, luxury US$80.
This large villa was opened as an exclusive hotel in 1999. It only has six rooms, two singles, two twins and two suites, but offers the full range of hotel services. Its private grounds are sufficiently extensive to ensure privacy and tranquillity. With prices not being much higher than those in conventional hotels, the luxury is well worth the modest extra cost.

Baltic Pearl Baltiskaya 15a, tel: 33552. Singles US$45, twins US$75.
Without doubt, this is the most pleasant hotel in the whole Kaliningrad region. It is surrounded by woodland but is only ten minutes walk from the town centre. The family feel is unexpected and most welcome. There are only 20 rooms but the hotel offers ample grounds, a large indoor swimming pool, a sauna and a billiard room. Prices for meals and refreshments are very low, tea in spring 2000 costing 5p/8c a cup and coffee 12p/18c.

Rauschen One and **Rauschen Two** Kaliningradsky 70, tel: 36183;
and Lenina 48, tel: 33452. Singles US$45, twins US$75.
These two hotels are within a few hundred yards of each other and were formerly Soviet trade union hotels. They are now largely used by German tour groups spending a night en route to the Baltics. This is why they have only a German and not a Russian name. They have both been sufficiently modernised to make a longer stay possible but neither has any really appealing features.

Rus Verestschagin 10, tel/fax: 33705. Singles US$80, twins US$130.
This new hotel is *the* place to be seen for young successful Russians. Everything is built on a lavish scale and its private grounds stretch to the sea. A winter garden is the most novel feature. It of course has a casino, tennis courts and a restaurant with an extensive wine list. The hotel achieved notoriety in February 2000 when Anatoly Sobchak, the former mayor of St Petersburg, died there from a heart attack after an evening of over-indulgence. He had been helping with Vladimir Putin's presidential campaign.

Appendix 1

LANGUAGE

Of necessity these are only basic words and phrases. Consult a dictionary if you would like to learn more.

Useful expressions

English	Estonian	Latvian	Lithuanian
hello	*tere*	*sveiki*	*laba diena*
goodbye	*nagemiseni*	*ata*	*viso gero*
good morning	*tere hommikust*	*labdien*	*labas rytas*
good evening	*head õhtust*	*labvakar*	*labas vakaras*
goodnight	*head ööd*	*ar labu nakti*	*labanakt*
yes	*jah*	*jā*	*taip*
no	*ei*	*nē*	*ne*
please	*palun*	*lūdzu*	*prašau*
thank you	*tänan*	*paldies*	*ačiu*
How much?	*Kui palju*	*Cik?*	*Kiek tai kainuoja?*
When?	*Millal?*	*Kad?*	*Kada?*
Where?	*Kus?*	*Kur?*	*Kur?*
Excuse me please	*Vabandage palun*	*Atvainojiet, lūdzu*	*Atsiprasau*
I do not understand	*Ma ei saa aru*	*Nesaprotu*	*As nesuprantu*

Useful words

English	Estonian	Latvian	Lithuanian
airport	*lennujaam*	*lidosta*	*aerouostas*
bus station	*bussijaam*	*autoosta*	*autobusu stotis*
railway station	*raudteejaam*	*dzelzceļa stacija*	*geležinkelio stotis*
toilet	*WC*	*tualete*	
beer	*õlu*	*alus*	
coffee (with milk)	*kohv (piimaga)*	*kafija (ar pienu)*	*kava ( )*
drinking water	*joogivesi*	*ūdens*	*sultys*
juice	*mahl*	*sula*	
mineral water	*mineraalvesi*	*minerālūdens*	*mineralinis vanduo*
wine (red, white)	*wein (pumane, valge)*	*vīns (sarkans, balts)*	*vynas ( )*
sugar	*suhkur*	*cukurs*	

NUMBERS

English	Estonian	Latvian	Lithuanian	Russian
1	*üks*	*viens*	*vienas*	один [adeen]
2	*kaks*	*divi*	*du*	два [dva]
3	*kolm*	*trīs*	*trys*	три [tree]
4	*neli*	*četri*	*keturi*	четыре [chyetiyryeh]
5	*viis*	*pieci*	*penki*	пять [pyat]
6	*kuus*	*seši*	*šeši*	шесть [shest]
7	*seitse*	*septiņi*	*septyni*	семь [syem]
8	*kaheksa*	*astoņi*	*aštuoni*	восемь [vosyem]
9	*üheksa*	*deviņi*	*devyni*	девять [dyevyat]
10	*kümme*	*desmit*	*dešimt*	десять [dyesyat]

English	Russian
hello	Здравствуите [zdrahstvooytyeh]
goodbye	До свидания [dasvidanya]
good morning	Доброе утро [dobriy dyen]
good evening	Добрый вечер [dobriy vyechyer]
goodnight	Спокойной ночи [spahkoynigh nochee]
yes	да [da]
no	нет [nyet]
please	Пожалуйста [pazhalsta]
thank you	Спасибо [spahseebah]
How much?	Сколько? [Skol ka?]
When?	Когда? [Kagda?]
Where?	Где? [Gdyeh?]
Excuse me please	Извините, пожалуйста... [Izveeneetye, pazhalsta]
I do not understand	Я не понима [Ya nye panimayu]

English	Russian
airport	аэропорт [aeroport]
bus station	автовокзал [avtovokzal]
railway station	вокзал [vokzal]
toilet	туалет [tualyet]
beer	пиво [peeva]
coffee (with milk)	кофе (молоком) [coffee (molokom)]
drinking water	питьевая вода [peetyeva-ya vada]
juice	сок [sok]
mineral water	минеральная вода [meenyeralna-ya vada]
wine (red, white)	(красное, белое) вино [(krasna-yeh, byela-yeh) veeno]
sugar	сахар [sahar]

MEASUREMENTS AND CONVERSIONS

To convert	Multiply by
Inches to centimetres	2.54
Centimetres to inches	0.3937
Feet to metres	0.3048
Metres to feet	3.281
Yards to metres	0.9144
Metres to yards	1.094
Miles to kilometres	1.609
Kilometres to miles	0.6214
Acres to hectares	0.4047
Hectares to acres	2.471
Imperial gallons to litres	4.546
Litres to imperial gallons	0.22
US gallons to litres	3.785
Litres to US gallons	0.264
Ounces to grams	28.35
Grams to ounces	0.03527
Pounds to grams	453.6
Grams to pounds	0.002205
Pounds to kilograms	0.4536
Kilograms to pounds	2.205
British tons to kilograms	1016.0
Kilograms to British tons	0.0009812
US tons to kilograms	907.0
Kilograms to US tons	0.000907

5 imperial gallons are equal to 6 US gallons
A British ton is 2,240 lbs. A US ton is 2,000 lbs.

Temperature conversion table

The bold figures in the central columns can be read as either centigrade or fahrenheit.

°C		°F	°C		°F
−18	**0**	32	10	**50**	122
−15	**5**	41	13	**55**	131
−12	**10**	50	16	**60**	140
−9	**15**	59	18	**65**	149
−7	**20**	68	21	**70**	158
−4	**25**	77	24	**75**	167
−1	**30**	86	27	**80**	176
2	**35**	95	32	**90**	194
4	**40**	104	38	**100**	212
7	**45**	113	40	**104**	219

Appendix 2

FURTHER READING
General Books

Baltic Approaches by Peter Unwin is the result of many visits to the area and much research. Writing in 1995 he is able to put the sudden transition of 1990–1 into a longer-term perspective and the book has in no way dated. His chapter on Kaliningrad is one of the very few sources in English on this area. *The Baltic States, The National Self-Determination of Estonia, Latvia and Lithuania* by Graham Smith is an introductory political history covering the whole of the 20th century. For more detail on the 20 years of independence the Baltic states enjoyed between 1920 and 1940, *The Baltic States, Years of Independence* by George von Rauch is recommended. Earlier history is covered in *The Baltic World 1772–1993* by David Kirby.

Vytautas Landsbergis is the first Baltic independence leader to have written his memoirs. *Lithuania, Independent Again* was published in Britain in July 2000. Walking the calm streets of Vilnius now, it is all too easy to forget the struggles needed to remove the Soviet occupiers. Music and politics have always been linked in his life so it is not surprising that two chapters in this book are called 'Debussy and Despair' and 'The Power of Music'. A third has the title 'Čiurlionis' in recognition of Lithuania's most famous composer.

The literature on their former *Heimat* produced by East Prussians is voluminous. Much of it is tendentious and superficial. An exception, and fortunately one that has been translated into English, is *Before The Storm: Memories of my Youth in Old Prussia* by Marion Dönhoff. She has written many other books about both Königsberg and Kaliningrad but these are only in German. Those with knowledge of German are also recommended to read *Spaziergange einer Ostpreussin* by Agnes Miegel. She was a famous poet who lived in Königsberg before the war and these are her recollections of the 1920s there. The definitive book on German architecture appeared in early 2000. *Königsberg, Architectur aus Deutscher Zeit* by Baldur Koster was the result of four years work there and shows how much has remained. The best account of life and death in Königsberg at the end of the war is *Zeugnis vom Untergang Königsberg,* by Michael Wieck, a Jew who was under equal threat from both the Nazis and then from the Russians. *Königsberg* in the Merian Live series is the best German guidebook. The many still in circulation that date from the early 1990s should be treated with great caution. The writers are still embittered about the loss of the area and the whole Soviet period is described in totally hostile terms.

Travel guides

Individual guides to Estonia, Latvia and Lithuania have been published by Bradt, offering in-depth coverage of each country.

Estonia Neil Taylor. A practical guide to Estonia's complex history and many attractions: Tallinn; the unspoilt countryside and islands; German manor houses and elegant resorts.

Latvia Stephen Baister and Chris Patrick. All corners of Latvia, from the capital, Rīga, to the 13th-century town of Cesis, Sigulda National Park, the lakes of Latgale and the coast at Jurmala.

Lithuania Gordon McLachlan. Highlights of this rapidly changing country include medieval cities, national parks, pristine beaches and colourful local festivals.

Maps

Jāṇa Sēta in Rīga publish atlases of the Baltic states and individual town plans for each capital and for many smaller towns as well. Their maps are available at Stanfords in London and Bristol and all over the Baltic states. Their shop in Rīga is at 83–85 Elizabetes Iela. The Estonian map specialists are Regio whose main shop is at Narva Mnt, very close to the Central Hotel. They do not, however, sell abroad or cover the other Baltic states. There are no similar publishers to these two in Vilnius or in Kaliningrad, although a wide selection of locally produced maps is available. In Kaliningrad it is possible to buy bilingual maps produced in Germany giving both the former and the current names of all the streets in the town centre.

Local publications

Tallinn In Your Pocket and the parallel publications for the other three cities are essential purchases on arrival. They only cost about £0.60/US$1.00 and this cover charge enables them to comment freely on local restaurants, museums and shops without being beholden to advertisers. They are all on the **website** www.inyourpocket.com so this should be consulted for up-to-date information before departure.

Kaliningrad has still to realise the potential of providing tourists with nice books as souvenirs of their visit. A locally produced guidebook in Russian has still to appear, let alone one in German or English. Sets of postcards are easily available, both of pre-war Königsberg and of the contemporary Kaliningrad. The cathedral has produced, in German only, a few booklets on its history.

The other three capitals have suddenly produced a plethora of large photographic albums and manageable booklets. In Tallinn the little book *The Living Past of Tallinn* by Elena Rannu skilfully portrays the high life and the low life of the Upper Town throughout its history. Gustav German's *Estonia* published in 1996 in fact concentrates on photographs of Tallinn just before new building, rather than just restoration, took over in parts of the town. Sulev Maevali's *Architecture and Art Monuments in Tallinn* was first published in 1986 but it is regularly updated and has no equal in its detailed descriptions of church interiors. Tallinn deserves a lively book on its history but for the moment has to do with the rather ponderous *History of Old Tallinn* by Raimo Pullat published in 1998.

Most visitors to Rīga return with the two books written by Andris Kolbergs called *The Story of Rīga*. One covers the history of the Old Town, the other Rīga's expansion in the 19th century. Both are well illustrated with prints and contemporary photographs. A worthy extravagance is *Art Nouveau in Rīga* by Janis Krastins which covers every building in this genre. *Rīga, a City to Discover* by A Bruders, manages to include 300 original photographs in a book almost pocket-size. Many other books are likely to be published in early 2001 to coincide with the 800th anniversary celebrations. *The Jews in Rīga* published by the Jewish Museum in 1991, covers all buildings linked with their history, both those still in use and those destroyed during the war. It also has a very useful history of their community.

It would be impossible to leave Vilnius without buying a baroque book. The best is *Baroque in Lithuania* which concentrates on architecture. *Baroque Art in Lithuania* covers porcelain, tapestry and painting. *Lithuania, Past, Culture, Present* does manage to do justice to all three ambitious themes within the space of 270 pages, both in the text and in the illustrations. The title *Lithuania, Facts and Figures* hardly sounds inviting but, although it is an official publication, it is written in a lively manner and has far more photographs than statistics. *Vilnius*, an annual publication in English of the Lithuanian Writers Union, translates the best writing of the previous year and also has commentaries on art and film. *Vilnius 13.01.91* is a grim photographic reminder of the violence the capital had to endure in defending its independence from Soviet forces. (No individual authors are listed for these books as they all have several contributors.)

The various chapters earlier in this book include details of local bookshops with the best selection of recent English-language publications. The amazon.com and amazon.co.uk websites are always up to date on material in English on each of the Baltic countries and the parallel amazon.de site similarly covers books published in German.

Useful websites

Baltics Times	baltictimes.com
City Paper	balticsworldwide.com
Estonian Tourist Board	tourism.ee
Eurolines buses	online.ee/eurolines
In Your Pocket	inyourpocket.com
Latvian Tourist Board	latnet.lv
Lithuanian Tourist Board	tourism.lt
Rīga tourist office	riga800.lv
Tallinn tourist office	tallinn.ee
Vilnius tourist office	vilnius.lt/tourism

Index

Entries in **bold** indicate main entries; those in *italics* denote maps.